Study Guide

to accompany

Carson • Butcher • Mineka
Abnormal Psychology and Modern Life
Tenth Edition

Prepared by

Don C. Fowles
University of Iowa

 HarperCollins*CollegePublishers*

Study Guide to accompany Carson/Butcher/Mineka ABNORMAL PSYCHOLOGY AND MODERN LIFE, Tenth Edition

ISBN: 0-673-99458-9

96 97 98 99 9 8 7 6 5 4 3 2

TABLE OF CONTENTS

PREFACE

In many schools, abnormal psychology is one of the most popular courses offered. Commonly, there are students enrolled in this course whose major fields are quite diverse and who have taken only an introductory course in psychology. Similarly, some psychology majors will take this course before taking many other psychology courses. These students sometimes feel at a disadvantage in competing with upper-level psychology majors. In addition, the familiarity of the subject matter and its high relevance to real life may give some students the feeling that they "understand" the material when they do not. At examination time, they find out that they do not "know" the material in the way the instructor expected.

This study guide has been developed to assist you in learning the material presented in the textbook. It has been designed to help you overcome any lack of experience you may have in approaching psychological material and to make you familiar with the kind of information you should really know in order to do well on exams. It is written in a straightforward and serious style, minimizing games and other gimmicks. Most students find the textbook *Abnormal Psychology and Modern Life* so full of case histories, examples, and inherently interesting material, that they become interested in and motivated to learn the material without any outside props. What students often do need is help to decide what to learn and an organized place to write down the information that can be used as notes from which to study for examinations.

HOW TO STUDY

Many teachers recommend the following approach to studying course material:

1. Skim major headings and read chapter summaries.

2. Read and highlight (or underline) important sections of the text.

3. Outline the important points you have highlighted in your reading. (Psychological studies show that putting material into your own words helps you to learn and retain the information better.)

4. Study from your text notes and class notes for exams, as well as review the highlighted material in the text. The former is especially helpful for exam questions requiring recitation (e.g., essays, short answer, fill-in-the-blanks) of the most important points. The latter is especially helpful for multiple-choice questions requiring recognition of a wide range of more detailed points.

This *Study Guide* has been written as a check on the appropriateness of your Stage 2 reading. It indicates the terms and concepts many teachers feel are most important in the text. Do you seem to be underlining the same points? If not, the guide will help you pick up on points you have overlooked rather than have you wait until exam time for this feedback. The most important function of the *Study Guide*, however, is as a substitute for the difficult and time-consuming outlining recommended in Stage 3. In the *Study Guide*, you will find that a lot of the choosing and organizing of the material has been done for you. Also, in some places, charts have been constructed to help you consolidate and learn the material. You have been given the general outlines. Your job is to fill in the specific information so you can prepare a complete and efficient set of notes to use in studying for examinations.

HOW TO USE THIS STUDY GUIDE

The *Study Guide* follows the sequence of the textbook and uses the same chapter headings and section headings. Each *Study Guide* chapter consists of eight sections (with the exception that "Names You Should Know" is deleted from three chapters). It is recommended that you first read the "Overview," then read the chapter summary in the textbook. Next, skim the chapter by reading the major section headings so you get a mental picture of the overall organization of the chapter. Then read the next section in the *Study Guide* entitled "Learning Objectives."

After reading the Overview in the *Study Guide*, the major section headings in the text, and the Learning Objectives in the *Study Guide*, you should have a general orientation to the chapter and should be ready to begin reading and highlighting the text. As you do, in addition to highlighting material you see as important, you should consult the sections in the *Study Guide* entitled "Terms You Should Know," "Concepts to Master," and "Study Questions" and fill in the correct answers in each. These are the *core sections for mastering the material in the text*. The questions in each of these three sections are arranged in the order in which the material appears in the text and are page-referenced. Thus, you should have little difficulty in finding the correct answers. Finally, you should read the thought-provoking questions in the section entitled "Critical Thinking on Difficult Topics."

Once you have finished reading the text and have finished the relevant sections in the *Study Guide*, you should have all the information accumulated. Your remaining task is to memorize the material to prepare for examination. After doing this, you should take the "Chapter Quiz" at the end of the *Study Guide* chapter.

A more detailed description of each of the sections in the *Study Guide* follows.

1. Chapter Overview

This short section is designed to prepare you to begin the chapter. The overview attempts to orient you to the purpose and some of the implications of the material you are about to read. It is designed to alert you to the overall importance of the chapter so you will, hopefully, feel motivated to start reading it.

2. Learning Objectives

This section presents a more detailed overview of the material to be covered in the chapter and an indication of what you should have learned once you have completed the chapter. The listing of the learning objectives generally corresponds to the major headings and subheadings of the chapter but often will more specifically identify the goals of your studying. This section is intended to provide a general orientation to the chapter. You should *not* try to write out answers to these learning objectives.

3. Terms You Should Know

Here you will find listed all the major terms introduced in the chapter along with a page reference on which to find the definition (and often a discussion) of the term in the textbook. The focus of this section is to build your vocabulary--i.e., to ensure that you are familiar with the terms routinely used in the field of abnormal psychology. Many of the terms can also be found in the glossary at the back of the textbook. However, it is still a good idea to look up the definition of the term within the chapter to be certain you know the context in which the term appeared. In the space provided, write out a brief definition of each term.

4. Names You Should Know

This is a new section introduced with this edition of the text. Textbooks cite hundreds or even thousands of authors. Students often would like to know whose names they should learn. My own attitude is that, for the purposes of examinations, you should not have to try to memorize the names of all the authors cited in the text. Consequently, this section is not intended to identify names to be covered on an exam. It is, on the other hand, probably useful for you to begin to learn the names of prominent people in the field--especially if you intend to go to graduate school or in some other way pursue the field of abnormal psychology.

The task of deciding which names to list was difficult in part because *Abnormal Psychology and Modern Life* is not written to "feature" authors--with the result that I was often dependent on my own familiarity with the area to determine which of the authors cited should be listed. Consequently, in compiling these names, I adopted the conservative strategy of listing only names that I was sure almost anyone familiar with a given area would identify as major contributors. I decided to err on the side of identifying too few rather than too many names, in order to ensure that I did not overwhelm you with a long list. This section was omitted from three chapters (one, thirteen, and eighteen) where it did not fit the material presented. Overall, I hope that this section will help you to begin to learn the names of people who are generally familiar to psychologists who teach and do research in abnormal psychology. Unless your instructor indicates otherwise, these names are not likely to appear exams.

5. Concepts to Master

In this section, you are asked questions that require an essay type of answer. In general, these items focus on conceptual rather than factual material. As a result, they will require the most active learning on your part and will require the greatest amount of time. The rewards in learning will be commensurate with the investment of time. The questions have been worded in such a way as to clearly follow the presentation of the material in the text. By using the page numbers given, you should have little trouble identifying the material addressed by the question. In most cases, you should find that the answer to the question is obvious, though it will require judgment on your part as to how to extract the core information from the material in the text. I have attempted to provide sufficient space in the *Study Guide* after each question for you to write in the correct answer. Although it is impossible to precisely judge how much space a given student will require for each answer, in general more space is provided where answers are likely to be longer. In some cases, you may find that you have to continue your answers on a separate page, but I hope this will infrequently be the case unless your writing is very large.

6. Study Questions

The questions in this section focus on material that is more factual in nature than that covered in the previous section. A variety of formats are used--e.g., short answers, filling in blanks, completing a chart, matching two columns. The multiple formats are intended (a) to match the nature of the material and (b) to avoid the monotony associated with a single format. In general, the wording in the questions has precisely followed that in the text, with the result that by consulting the referenced page(s) you will have no difficulty identifying the correct answer. In order to help you see the organization of the material better, the major headings from the text have been used in this section (in italicized bold print) to divide the individual questions into groups dealing with specific topics. You may want to read the entire section in the text before attempting to answer the questions under a given heading

The Study Questions help you identify much of the factual knowledge you should learn about each topic. To complete the requested information, go to the referenced page, locate the appropriate section and read it over, then write a correct response in the *Study Guide*. In the case of fill-in-the-blanks questions, you should attend to the overall statement, not just to the information entered in the blanks. Your instructor may well ask the question in a different way, and important information is often provided in addition to what you are asked to provide in the blanks.

A word of warning is in order here. Although the coverage of factual material in this section of the *Study Guide* is extensive, it is simply impossible to ask about all possible factual material in a text as comprehensive as *Abnormal Psychology and Modern Life*. In order to maximize your learning, you should try to use the Study Questions as a guide to how you pick out important material and then highlight additional factual material in your text. Try to do this sparingly so that you do not end up with most of the text highlighted.

7. Critical Thinking about Difficult Topics

This is another new section introduced with this edition of the text. In sharp contrast with the other sections in the *Study Guide*, which focus on mastering material as presented in the text, this section asks you to think more deeply about many interesting and difficult issues in the field. In most--or, at least, many--cases, there is no right or wrong answer, but it is important that you understand the issues involved. The goal of this section is to challenge you to develop a more sophisticated conceptualization of these issues. These questions usually will spell out or emphasize points already made in the text, and the relevant pages are cited. In rare cases, these questions will offer an alternative to the perspective offered in the text. Often, I have attempted to provide guidance to at least a partial response to the question. Even when I have done so, I do not wish to imply that the answer I have suggested is necessarily the "correct" answer. Rather, it is a perspective you should understand, but with which you might disagree after weighing all the issues. To struggle with issues over which reasonable people can disagree is part of the pleasure and excitement of this section. Some of the issues might make excellent topics for class discussion.

8. Chapter Quiz

Each *Study Guide* chapter concludes with a short self-test of multiple-choice items. The self-test to some extent will allow you to assess your mastery of the chapter. Complete the self-test items after you have completed all the other *Study Guide* sections but while you still have time for additional study. Look up the correct answer to each item in the Answer Key at the end of the *Study Guide*. Go back to the referenced page for each item you missed and read over the correct answer. Then try to analyze why you made the mistake. Didn't you know the material? Did you misinterpret the item? (Try to read each item very carefully and make sure you know the definitions of all the terms introduced in the chapter.) It is unlikely that you will be able to answer all of them correctly, but if you find you incorrectly answer *a substantial portion*, you may well need to study more. You should be aware, however, that this short self-test can only serve as a rough guide to your knowledge of the text. It does not, of course, assess your response to exam items with other formats (e.g., essay, short answer, definitions) and it is too short to provide a *definitive* assessment of your knowledge of the material in the text.

HOW TO PREPARE FOR EXAMS

Many students become anxious about their performance on tests and this tension becomes greater as exam time grows nearer. Research suggests that the most effective preparation is accomplished under moderate levels of anxiety. Therefore, do *not* leave all your studying until the last minute when tension renders your behavior disorganized and less effective and when there is simply not time to master the material. Use your anxiety to motivate you to study well in advance of the exams. That is, read the text and complete the *Study Guide* on an ongoing basis during the term, and aim to complete these tasks several days before the exam.

Plan to study for a few hours each day on the several days before the scheduled exam. Study from your completed *Study Guide*, your class notes, and from the highlighted portions of your textbook. Re-reading the entire textbook is time-consuming and inefficient. If you've been conscientious in completing the *Study Guide*, it contains most of the material you need to learn. Start with the Terms You Should Know section. Cover the definition and try to recite it from memory. (If you have a private study area, it's even more effective to say the definition out loud.) Go back over the list and cover each term successively. Read the definition and try to recall the term to which it applies. This general approach is to be used with Concepts to Master and Study Questions, as well. Cover the answers you have written and try to generate them from memory. Continue to review the *Study Guide* until you can reproduce all the correct answers from memory.

Another important point is to take good lecture notes in class. For most students, it is not possible to write down all the important information during the lecture. As soon as you can find the opportunity (ideally, immediately after class but certainly on the day of the lecture), sit down and go over your notes and fill in as much additional material as you can remember from the lecture. Then read over your notes and be sure you understand the instructor's organization and major points. If you have missed material, ask your instructor or teaching assistant to help you fill it in. Almost all instructors will lecture on material they believe is most important and many will emphasize that material on the exams. Thus, your class notes may provide an invaluable guide as to what you should learn. In reading the text and using the *Study Guide*, give an even greater emphasis to any topics covered in lecture. Doing so may be doubly valuable, inasmuch as (a) it may help you answer questions on the exam that refer specifically to the lectures and (b) the instructor may be more likely to write exam questions on the text material that relates to the lectures.

Whether your teacher will be using multiple-choice or essay exams should not greatly affect how you will prepare--both types of testing require a command of the basic facts. Well-prepared students come out on top no matter what form of testing the instructor uses. Some students may argue that memorization is not necessary for multiple-choice tests which only require recognition of the right response. This is untrue. Instructors purposely write the wrong answers to look and sound plausible. If you don't know the facts, you'll be misled by these distracters.

It may be helpful for me to provide a context regarding how much time to allocate to studying for this course. The normative expectation for a three-semester-hour course is that students will spend six hours per week (every week) studying for the course. This estimate refers to *actual study time*--i.e., not time spent commuting to class, buying books, talking with the teaching assistant or instructor or fellow students about the course, etc. Assuming that all students spend this much time, it is important to understand that doing so will not guarantee an A in the course. Unless you are unusually gifted or well-prepared, you may find that you need to spend more than six hours per week to truly master the material in a demanding course such as Abnormal Psychology. Doing so can be very difficult. If you are registered for 15 semester hours, it means you may have to spend more than 30 hours per week studying. When you add in the time lost to commuting and everyday activities and that allocated to your social life, it is not easy to find extra hours for studying. This is doubly difficult if, as in the case of many of my advisees, you are working to earn money for 15 to 20 hours per week in addition to carrying a full-time academic load. My point here is that your time is scarce and valuable. You should give careful thought to how it is used and do all you can to allocate as much time as possible to studying. It is an important discipline to budget your time and use it for things that are most important.

CONCLUSION

I hope the *Study Guide* helps you master the material in this course and, of course, to do well on the exams. However, I also hope learning the material in this course serves you well in the future. The topics studied in abnormal psychology impact on everyone. Having a sophisticated understanding of these topics should help you understand events in your life better and may even help you provide information or help to a friend or relative suffering from some of the problems discussed in the course. For a sizable number of you, this course will provide a foundation for a future career in which knowledge of the material may be of value (e.g., in general medicine, nursing, teaching, etc.) or for a career as a mental health professional. Whether or not you pursue such a career, I hope the course and the *Study Guide* have been of value to you.

Don C. Fowles

Chapter 1
Abnormal Behavior in Our Times

◊ OVERVIEW

It has been said that psychology "has a long history but a short past." This is certainly true of abnormal psychology. Although examples of bizarre behavior are seen throughout history, and considerations of why people act as they do have appeared and reappeared in literature and philosophy, scientific study of abnormal behavior really only began around 1900. Chapter 1 begins with a discussion of the difficulty of understanding abnormal behavior and of the importance of developing explanations supported by scientific evidence rather than popular misconceptions. Then, the meaning of the term "abnormal" is discussed along with a description of contemporary procedures to classify the different ways psychological disturbance may be expressed. Finally, the value of scientific data is emphasized and research methods utilized to study behavior are described.

◊ LEARNING OBJECTIVES

After studying this chapter, you should be able to:

1. Adopt a skeptical attitude toward popular views of abnormal behavior and list the major popular myths and misconceptions. (pp. 3-6; Highlight 1.1, p. 7)

2. Explain why it is so difficult to define abnormal behavior, describe different approaches to such definitions, and examine the strengths and weaknesses of each. (pp. 6-10)

3. Identify the main personnel in the mental health arena and their distinctive characteristics. (p. 10-11)

4. Summarize the key concepts associated with the task of classification and describe the problems associated with labeling. (pp. 11-12, 16-17)

5. Describe the methodologies used to determine the rate of mental disorder in the United States and the results of the major recent epidemiological studies. (pp. 17-18)

6. Explicate the different methodologies and the methodological issues involved in research in abnormal psychology. (pp. 18-25)

7. List the concepts embraced by the authors as the basis of a sound and comprehensive study of abnormal behavior. (pp. 25-26)

8. Discuss the problems associated with use of the medical or disease metaphor in classifying abnormal behavior and describe the major alternative approaches. (pp. 26-28)

◊ TERMS YOU SHOULD KNOW

prognosis (p. 4)

abnormal (pp. 6-7)

syndrome (p. 9)

reliability (pp. 11-12)

validity (p. 12)

Diagnostic and Statistical Manual (DSM-IV) (pp. 12-13, see also pp. 8-9)

symptoms versus *signs* (p. 12)

operational criteria (p. 13)

comorbidity (p. 13)

axes (in DSM-IV) (pp. 13-14)

disorders secondary to gross destruction of brain tissue (p. 14)

substance use disorders (p. 14)

disorders of psychological or sociocultural origin (p. 14)

functional psychoses (p. 14)

disorders usually arising during childhood or adolescence (p. 14)

acute (p. 14, 16)

chronic (p. 16)

episodic or *recurrent* (p. 16)

epidemiology (p. 17)

prevalence (p. 17)

incidence (p. 17)

lifetime prevalence (p. 17)

hypotheses (p. 19)

representative sampling (p. 21)

control group (p. 21)

criterion group (p. 21)

correlation (p. 21)

path analysis (pp. 21-22)

epidemiological research (p. 22)

experimental method (p. 22)

analogue studies (p. 23)

learned helplessness (p. 23)

waiting list control group strategy (pp. 23-24)

statistical control (p. 24)

clinical case study or *N = 1 experiment* (p. 24)

retrospective research (p. 24)

prospective research (p. 24)

at risk (pp. 24-25)

categorical approach (to classification) (p. 27)

dimensional approach (to classification) (p. 27)

prototype (p. 27)

observable versus *hypothetical* (p. 28)

◊ **CONCEPTS TO MASTER**

_____

1. Describe two broad perspectives on the definition of abnormality or a mental disorder. (pp. 9-10)

2. List several reasons why a classification system is needed in abnormal psychology and explain the meaning of reliability and validity in reference to such a system. (pp. 11-13)

3. Why is it correct to assert that "validity presupposes reliability"? (p. 12)

4. Differentiate between the DSM and ICD classification systems and describe the five axes of DSM-IV. (pp. 12-14)

5. A distinct feature since DSM-III is "operational criteria." What does this mean? (p. 13)

6. The innovation of using "operational" criteria for defining different disorders began with the third edition of the DSM. Discuss the difficulties that arise when these precise definitions are applied to the real problems of real patients. (p. 13)

7. If operational criteria are achieved, reliability of diagnosis is greatly improved. On the other hand, the use of strict criteria causes much abnormal behavior to be assigned to "wastebasket" categories. What is meant by this term, and what problems does it create? (p. 13)

8. Compare and contrast the concepts of prevalence and incidence, including the associated concepts of point prevalence and lifetime prevalence. (p. 17)

9. Why are hypotheses critical supplements to observations of behavior? (pp. 19-20)

10. Explain why research on groups of people is usually preferred to single case studies and why those groups must be representative of larger populations. (pp. 20-21)

11. Explain why correlational research cannot establish cause and effect and yet has been extremely valuable in the form of epidemiological research. (pp. 21-22)

12. A mere correlation does not imply causation. A manic individual exhibits a euphoric mood, a high level of activity without regard for its consequences that may lead to financial bankruptcy, and a loosening of cultural inhibitions that may be associated with crude and inappropriate sexual advances. Mania is also associated with a high rate of divorce--a stressful life event. How might divorce precipitate mania and how might mania lead to divorce--i.e., consider how the direction of causation might go in either direction? (p. 21)

13. If one considers a large number of cities, the number of bars in a city is correlated with the number of churches in the city. What third variable probably accounts for this observation? (p. 21)

14. Explain why experimental studies are often inappropriate for abnormal psychology, and indicate how analogue studies have been used in their place. (pp. 22-24)

15. Describe the clinical case study and explain why it is easy to draw erroneous conclusions from this method of research. (p. 24)

16. Compare the advantages and disadvantages of retrospective and prospective research in abnormal psychology. (pp. 24-25)

17. List and explain three concepts about the study of abnormal psychology on which this text is based. (p. 25)

18. List and describe three basic approaches to the classification of abnormal behavior and some of the assumptions underlying each. (pp. 27-28)

◊ STUDY QUESTIONS

Popular views and misconceptions concerning abnormal behavior

1. List some popular plays, movies, and books that describe abnormal behavior, and explain why such sources are often inaccurate. (pp. 5-6)

2. Former mental patients are no more dangerous than people in general. True __ False __ (Highlight 1.1, p. 7)

3. Everyone shares a potential for becoming disordered. True __ False __ (Highlight 1.1, p. 7)

4. Mental disorders are natural adaptive processes. True __ False __ (Highlight 1.1, p. 7)

What do we mean by "abnormal behavior"?

5. What is the literal meaning of the word *abnormal*? (p. 6)

6. The authors of the text maintain that the best criterion for determining the normality of behavior is whether it fosters the well-being of the individual and, ultimately, of the group. This view is referred to as the abnormal behavior is _____ view. (p. 10)

7. How do the authors justify considering promotion of intergroup hostility, destructive assaults on the environment, irrational violence, and political corruption as forms of "abnormal behavior"? (p. 10)

8. What is the explicit value judgment in the "abnormal-behavior-is-maladaptive-behavior" framework? (p. 10)

9. What are the concerns of mental health personnel within an "abnormal-behavior-is-maladaptive-behavior" framework? (p. 10)

10. List three distinct but often overlapping concerns that must be considered by those who wish to study abnormal behavior. (p. 11)

Classifying abnormal behavior

11. What example was used to illustrate the concept of "cognitive prototype"? (p. 11)

12. What is involved in classification in abnormal psychology? (p. 11)

Diagnostic and Statistical Manual of Mental Disorders (DSM-IV)

13. Identify the five axes of DSM-IV (pp. 13-14):

    Axis I

    Axis II

    Axis III

    Axis IV

    Axis V

14. Why do some clinicians object to the use of Axes IV and V on insurance forms? (p. 14)

15. Axis I and II of DSM-IV list the mental disorders, but for purposes of clarity these disorders may be regarded as fitting into several broad groupings. Match the terms on the left with their appropriate headings on the right. (p. 14)

Term	**Category**
___ a. mental retardation	A. Disorders secondary to the destruction of brain tissue
___ b. alcohol abuse	B. Substance use disorders
___ c. psychophysiological disorders	
___ d. affective disorders	C. Disorders of psychological or sociocultural origin
___ e. Alzheimer's disease	D. Disorders arising during childhood or adolesence
___ f. schizophrenia	
___ g. autism	
___ h. anxiety disorders	

The problem of labeling

16. The authors of the text indicate that the process of labeling, no matter what classification system is used, has drawbacks. When a label has been assigned to a person, what impact may this have on the professionals who are treating the person? (p. 16)

17. How might labels affect the patients themselves? (p. 16)

18. How might labels affect the attitudes of others toward the patient (Note: There is disagreement on this point)? (pp. 16-17)

Assessing the extent of abnormal behavior

19. The NIMH catchment area epidemiological study estimated prevalence of major maladaptive behavior patterns in the United States. In the updated report by Regier et al. (1993), what was the one month prevalence for mental disorder and/or substance abuse? For nonsubstance-abusing mental disorder alone? When the 12.3 percent of the population determined to be new cases at wave 2 were added, what was the overall one-year prevalence of mental disorder and/or substance abuse? (p. 17)

Research in abnormal psychology: Observation of behavior

20. Verbal reports about inner processes are an important source of information that is both troublesome and interesting. Describe two factors that limit the value of self-observations as scientific data. (p. 19)

21. To make sense of observed behavior, psychologists generate more or less reasonable _____ to help explain the behavior. For example, a psychologist may observe some symptoms and guess that "schizophrenia" is the entity or hypothetical construct that caused the symptoms. This example demonstrates the process of inference in psychology. (p. 19)

Research in abnormal psychology: Sampling and generalization

22. The strategy of intensively studying a single case might yield important leads, but it suffers from a basic difficulty. What is this difficulty? (p. 20)

23. To overcome the limitations of studying the single case, psychologists usually rely on studies using groups of individuals. Explain why in such studies it is desirable to obtain a representative sample. (p. 21)

Research in abnormal psychology: Experimental strategies

24. Match definitions *a* through *f* below with the terms listed in the box.

   a. Therapist systematically monitors the precise relationships between treatment interventions and patient responses. (p. 24)
   b. Mathematical corrections are made for uncontrolled group differences. (p. 24)
   c. The study of behavior that is not actually pathological but is similar to it. (p. 23)
   d. Treatment is withheld for a period of time. (p. 24)
   e. All factors are controlled except for the one of interest, which is manipulated. (p. 22)
   f. A study that compares two or more treatments. (p. 24)

Term	Letter of Definition
I. Waiting list control	_____
II. N = 1 experiment	_____
III. Experimental method	_____
IV. Statistical control	_____
V. Analogue study	_____
VI. Comparative outcome research	_____

Research in abnormal psychology: Clinical case studies, retrospective/prospective strategies

25. After each of the following clinical research methods, write one strength and one limitation of the approach:

   a. Case study method (p. 24)
      Strength
      Limitation

   b. Prospective research (pp. 24-25)
      Strength
      Limitation

   c. Retrospective research (p. 24)
      Strength
      Limitation

A scientific approach to abnormal behavior and a critical attitude

26. What is involved in a "scientific approach" to abnormal behavior? (p. 25)

27. What does it mean to "take a critical and evaluative attitude toward research findings"? (p. 25)

28. What sources can help a student develop an awareness of "common human concerns" and what is the limitation of this information compared with that obtained through scientific observation? (p. 25)

29. How do the authors of the text view mentally disordered persons in order to respect their dignity? (pp. 25-26)

The categorical approach embraced in DSM-IV: Unresolved issues

30. DSM-IV is based on symptoms of illness. It is referred to as a categorical model which assumes that all human behavior can be divided into normal and abnormal, and within the abnormal there exist nonoverlapping types of behavior. As noted in the text, some observers argue that this is an inadequate model for organizing our observations of behavioral abnormalities. List as many problems with this model as you can. (pp. 26-27).

31. There are advantages to a prototype approach over a categorical approach. List the advantages of the prototype approach over a categorical approach and then explain why this approach is not used in the text even though the authors believe it is superior. (pp. 27-28)

32. The authors emphasize the importance of avoiding popular misconceptions and errors about abnormal psychology, and they urge you to adopt a scientific attitude and approach to the study of this topic. What three characteristics do they describe for such an approach? (p. 28)

◊ CRITICAL THINKING ABOUT DIFFICULT TOPICS

1. The authors of the text argue for a definition of abnormal behavior as maladaptive behavior and conclude that their definition would include "destructive assaults on the environment" (p. 10). Consider the case of an executive of a manufacturing company whose factory discharges pollutants into the air or water that are (a) perfectly legal, (b) within the range of common practice, (c) extremely costly to eliminate, but (d) harmful to the health of a significant number of individuals in the long run. Is his or her behavior indicative of a "mental disorder" (p. 10)? Try to think of other instances in which there is a conflict between "rational" reward-seeking behavior that is not in violation of cultural norms, yet which is "in serious degree contrary to the continued well-being . . . of the human community of which the individual is a member" (p. 10). Similarly, consider the case of the "subcultural delinquent" who acts entirely in keeping with the values, norms, and personal loyalties of his or her gang in committing various delinquent acts that are harmful to many members of the larger society. In what sense does such a person have a mental disorder?

2. The text describes a criterion group of depressed individuals and a control group of psychologically normal individuals (pp. 20-21). It also correctly states that the control group should be comparable to the criterion group in all respects except for the presence of the disorder. Assuming differences are found between these groups, can you think of variables other than depression per se that might account for the differences? It may help to think about using a control group of general medical patients (e.g., patients with diabetes) as a *general medical control* group or of patients with an anxiety disorder as a *psychiatric control* group.

3. The text refers to three basic approaches to classifying abnormal behavior (categorical, dimensional, and prototypal), and it seems to suggest that the prototypal combines the best features of the categorical and dimensional approaches while avoiding some of their problems (pp. 27-28). Earlier (p. 11), the text used "dog," "cat," "beaver," and "donkey" as examples of cognitive prototypes. In these examples, the distinctions are relatively clear--e.g., there is not a continuum of critical features along which a dog blends into a cat. In contrast, in abnormal behavior there often is such blending, as suggested by the text. For example, anxiety and depressive disorders often blend together, as do schizophrenia and affective disorders. Under such conditions, how effective is the prototypal approach? Is it still useful? What etiological models might account for such blending?

◊ CHAPTER 1 QUIZ

Circle the best of the four answers provided and check them according to answers provided at the back of this study guide. Be sure you understand why each answer is correct.

1. The word *abnormal* literally means behavior that: (p. 6)
   a. deviates from society's norms.
   b. interferes with the well-being of the individual.
   c. is "away from the normal."
   d. is undesirable.

2. Cultural relativists like Ullmann and Krasner maintain that abnormal behavior is that which is: (p. 9)
   a. deviant from social expectations.
   b. illegal according to the law of the land.
   c. immoral by religious standards.
   d. psychologically maladaptive.

3. The authors of the textbook maintain that the best criteria for determining the normality of behavior is: (p. 10)
   a. deviance from the norm.
   b. adaptivity of the behavior in furthering individual and group well-being.
   c. variance from societal expectations.
   d. the operational criteria listed in the DSM-IV.

4. When different observers agree on the classification of certain abnormal behaviors, the system is said to be: (p. 11-12)
   a. diagnostic.
   b. reliable.
   c. standardized.
   d. valid.

5. A distinctive innovation since the DSM-III of 1980 has been the use of "operational" criteria for defining disorders. This means that the DSM now: (p. 12-13)
   a. clearly specifies the causes or etiological factors.
   b. specifies the theoretical interpretation of the symptoms.
   c. identifies the adaptive function of the symptoms.
   d. specifies the exact behaviors that must be observed.

6. The first three axes of the DSM-IV assess: (p. 13)
   a. how well the individual is coping.
   b. stressors that may have contributed to the disorder.
   c. the person's present condition.
   d. the prognosis of the disorder.

7. Many clinicians object to the inclusion of an _____ diagnosis on insurance forms because it violates the client's confidentiality. (p. 14)
   a. Axis I
   b. Axis II
   c. Axis III
   d. Axis IV

8. In DSM-IV personality disorders are entered on: (pp. 13-14)
   a. Axis I
   b. Axis II
   c. Axis III
   d. Axis IV

9. DSM-IV's major categories or *broad groupings* of mental disorders include: (p. 14)
   a. disorders secondary to gross destruction and malfunctioning of brain tissue.
   b. schizophrenic disorders.
   c. adjustment disorders.
   d. psychosexual disorders.

10. Which of the following terms refers to a mental condition of relatively short duration? (pp. 14, 16)
    a. episodic
    b. acute
    c. chronic
    d. factitious

11. In order to make sense of observed behavior, psychologists generate more or less plausible ideas called: (p. 19)
    a. constructs.
    c. principles.
    b. hypotheses.
    d. theories.

12. Which of the following may be safely inferred when a sizable positive correlation is found between variables x and y? (p. 21)
    a. People high on x will usually be high on y.
    b. People low on x will usually be high on y.
    c. x causes y.
    d. y causes x.

13. Seligman induced learned helplessness in animals by subjecting them to repeated inescapable shock. This study is an example of _____ research. (p. 23)
    a. analogue.
    c. correlational.
    b. clinical.
    d. epidemiological.

14. A psychologist identifies 50 children who have schizophrenic mothers. At adolescence, the researcher compares those who break down with those who don't. This is an example of a _____ study. (p. 24)
    a. clinical case
    c. prospective
    b. comparative outcome
    d. retrospective

15. Widiger and Frances described three basic approaches currently possible for classifying abnormal behavior. Which of the following is *not* one of them? (p. 27-28)
    a. categorical
    c. prototypal
    b. dimensional
    d. configural

Chapter 2
Historical Views of Abnormal Behavior

◊ **OVERVIEW**

Abnormal behavior has fascinated humankind from its beginning, and various explanations of the causes of such behavior have developed over the course of history. It's important to know what a particular group of people think about the cause of bizarre behavior, because beliefs usually predict the way people treat mentally ill individuals. An understanding of the historical viewpoints presented in this chapter helps you to understand the background for and basis of many of the fundamental issues in our field.

◊ **LEARNING OBJECTIVES**

After studying this chapter, you should be able to:

1. Explain why in ancient times abnormal behavior was attributed to possession by a demon or god and why exorcism administered by shamans and priests was the primary type of treatment for demonic possession. (pp. 32-33)

2. Describe the important contributions from 460 B.C. to 200 A.D. of the Greeks Hippocrates, Plato, Aristotle, and Galen to the conceptualization of the nature and causes of abnormal behavior. (pp. 33-35)

3. Distinguish between medicine in Islamic countries in the Middle East and that in Europe during the Middle Ages. (pp. 35-36)

4. Give examples of mass madness or mass hysteria and summarize the explanations offered for this unusual phenomenon. (pp. 37-38)

5. Outline the contributions in the late Middle Ages and early Renaissance of Paracelsus, Teresa of Avila, Johan Weyer, Reginald Scot, and St. Vincent de Paul, all of whom argued that those showing abnormal behavior should be seen as mentally ill and treated with humane care. (pp. 40-41)

6. Describe the inhumane treatment that mental patients received in early "insane asylums" in Europe and the United States. (pp. 41-42)

7. Describe the humanitarian reforms in the treatment of mental patients that were instigated by Philippe Pinel, William Tuke, Benjamin Rush, and Dorothea Dix. (pp. 41-48)

8. Explain how the emergence of modern experimental science (largely biological), combined with the discovery of a biological basis for general paresis and a handful of other disorders (the senile mental disorders, toxic mental disorders, certain types of mental retardation), contributed in a major way to the development of a scientific approach to abnormal psychology. (pp. 50-51; Highlight 2.3, p. 51)

9. Distinguish between biological and non-biological versions of medical-model thinking about psychopathology. (p. 52)

10. Trace the important events in the development of psychoanalysis and the psychodynamic perspective. (pp. 52-55)

11. Contrast the biological and psychodynamic views of abnormal disorders. (pp. 49-55)

12. Identify the way in which the techniques of free association and dream analysis helped analysts and their patients? (p. 55)

13. List the major features of the behavioral perspective. (pp. 56-57)

14. Discriminate between classical and instrumental conditioning. (p. 57)

15. Explain the problems associated with interpreting historical events. (pp. 58-60)

Edwin Smith papyrus (p. 32)

exorcism (p. 32)

shamans (p. 32)

hysteria (p. 33, 53-55)

mass madness (p. 37)

tarantism (p. 37)

St. Vitus's dance (p. 37)

lycanthropy (p. 37)

humanism (p. 40)

bodily magnetism (p. 40)

Bedlam (p. 41)

La Bicêtre (p. 41)

moral management (p. 44)

alienist (Highlight 2.2, p. 47)

neurasthenia (Highlight 2.2, p. 47)

general paresis (p. 50; Highlight 2.3, p. 51)

Spirochaeta pallida (or "spirochete") (Highlight 2.3, p. 51)

psychoanalysis (p. 52)

psychodynamic perspective (p. 52)

mesmerism (p. 53)

Nancy School (p. 54)

catharsis (p. 55)

free association (p. 55)

dream analysis (p. 55)

Journal of Abnormal Psychology (p. 56)

behavioral perspective (p. 57)

classical conditioning (p. 57)

behaviorism (p. 57)

instrumental or *operant conditioning* (p. 57)

psychohistory (p. 60)

◊ NAMES YOU SHOULD KNOW

Hippocrates (p. 33; Highlight 2.4, p. 58)

Plato (p. 34; Highlight 2.4, p. 58)

Aristotle (p. 34; Highlight 2.4, p. 58)

Philippe Pinel (pp. 42-43; Highlight 2.4, p. 58)

Benjamin Rush (pp. 44, 45; Highlight 2.4, p. 58)

Dorothea Dix (pp. 46, 48; Highlight 2.4, p. 58)

Clifford Beers (pp. 49-50; Highlight 2.4, p. 58)

Emil Kraepelin (pp. 51-52)

Sigmund Freud (p. 55)

Josef Breuer (p. 55)

Wilhelm Wundt (pp. 55-56)

Ivan Pavlov (p. 57; Highlight 2.4, p. 58)

John B. Watson (pp. 57, 58; Highlight 2.4, p. 58)

E. L. Thorndike (pp. 57, 58)

B. F. Skinner (pp. 57, 58)

◊ CONCEPTS TO MASTER

---

1. Describe early beliefs in demonology and explain the reasons why exorcism was used as a cure. (pp. 32-33)

2. Hippocrates rejected demonology as a cause of mental disorders. What three aspects of his alternative approach were truly revolutionary? (p. 33)

3. What assumption did Plato make about mentally disturbed individuals who commit criminal acts and how is this assumption relevant to our current legal system? (p. 34)

4. What was Plato's contribution to understanding human motivation? How is this view relevant to current research with animals by psychologists? (p. 34)

5. From earliest times, Chinese understanding of mental disorders was based on natural causes, on the concept of Yin and Yang. Describe how this concept explained the development of mental disorders. (Highlight 2.1, p. 36)

6. In the concept of Yin and Yang in Chinese medicine, the human body is divided into positive and negative forces that must be balanced for physical and mental health. How does this theory influence the interpretation of treatments? (Highlight 2.1, p. 36)

7. The phenomenon seen as mass madness in the form of the tarantella and lycanthropy occasionally occurs today and is called mass hysteria. Describe two examples of mass hysteria, one in California in 1982 and one in the West Bank of Palestine in 1983. (p. 38)

8. Describe the treatment for mental disorders used by the clergy during the Middle Ages known as exorcism, or the "laying on of hands." (p. 38)

9. Explain the supposed connection between mental illness and witchcraft and comment on the accuracy of this assumption. (p. 39)

10. During the sixteenth century, Teresa of Avila, a Spanish nun who later became a saint, explained hysteria among a group of cloistered nuns as *comas enfermas,* which is translated "as if sick." Explain what she meant by this term. (p. 40)

11. What did Pinel do to provide more humane treatment for the inmates of La Bicêtre in Paris and what was the effect of these measures on the mental patients? Consider the implications of these results for the "demonic possession" versus the "psychological" theories of mental illness--were the results more compatible with one theory versus the other? (pp. 42-43)

12. How did general values and cultural attitudes in the Victorian era influence the interpretation and treatment of what we now call depression? (Highlight 2.2, p. 47)

13. Similarly, how did these Victorian values and attitudes influence the interpretation of anxiety and depression in women? (Highlight 2.2, p. 47)

14. It is generally acknowledged that the current system of classification of mental disorders (DSM-IV) has evolved directly from Kraepelin's system of classification. On what basis did he identify mental diseases and what did he think a diagnosis should tell us about the course of the disorder? (pp. 51-52).

15. The text notes that the medical-model orientation is not limited to biological viewpoints. In what sense did Freud's psychodynamic approach embrace the medical model? (p. 52)

16. Hypnosis played an important role in the early stages of psychoanalysis and in establishing psychological factors as important in abnormal behavior. What critical demonstration of the power of hypnosis by Liebeault persuaded Bernheim of its importance and ultimately led to the founding of the Nancy School? What was the nature of the dispute between Charcot and the Nancy School and why was the outcome of this debate important? (p. 54)

17. What technique employed by Josef Breuer resulted in the discovery of the unconscious, and on what result was this conclusion based? (p. 55)

18. Study of attitudes and treatment of mentally disordered persons in former eras is difficult. A primary difficulty is that we cannot rely on direct observation but have only historical documents from the period to study. List and explain several weaknesses of the kind of retrospective research that attempts to produce an accurate history of mental illness and its treatment. (pp. 58, 60)

19. The investigation of the explosion aboard the United States Navy ship the USS *Iowa* was discussed in the context of the method of "psychological autopsy." What major point was made about the use of psychological autopsies? (p. 60)

Demonology, gods, and magic

1. To what did the early writings of the Chinese, Egyptians, Hebrews, and Greeks attribute abnormal behavior? (p. 32)

2. What was the primary type of treatment used by these ancient peoples and which members of the community were charged with carrying out the treatment? (p. 32)

Early philosophical and medical concepts (400 B.C. to 200 A.D.)

3. Hippocrates stated, "For my own part, I do not believe that the human body is ever befouled by a God." He is considered the "father of modern medicine" and is credited in your text with five important new ideas that contributed to the development of abnormal psychology. Complete this listing of his important contributions. (pp. 33-34)
   a. He saw the _____ as the central organ of intellectual activity and viewed mental disorders as due to brain pathology. (p. 33)
   b. He emphasized the importance of heredity, predispositions, and head injuries as causes of abnormal behavior. (p. 33)
   c. He classified all mental disorders into three general categories: mania, _____, and phrentis--which means "brain fever." (p. 33)
   d. He considered _____ to be important in und ___ing the person. (p. 33)
   e. He advocated treatment methods that were far advanced over the exorcistic practices of his time. For the treatment of _____ he prescribed a regular and tranquil life, sobriety, abstinence from all excesses, a vegetable diet, celibacy, and exercise. (p. 33)

4. Hippocrates wrongly believed in the existence of four bodily _____, or "humors," which could cause mental disorder when disturbed. (p. 33)

5. Hippocrates wrongly believed that hysteria (the appearance of physical illness in the absence of organic pathology) was restricted to _____ and was caused by the _____ wandering to various parts of the body. (p. 33)

6. What did Aristotle conclude were two important motivational influences on thinking? (p. 34)

7. The Greek physician Galen used dissections of animals to make important original contributions concerning the _____. (p. 34)

8. The "Dark Ages" in the history of abnormal psychology began with the death of _____ in A.D. _____, after which the contributions of the Greek and Roman physicians were lost and replaced by a resurgence of belief in demonology as the cause of abnormal behavior. (p. 35)

Views during the Middle Ages (6th to 15th centuries)

9. The first mental hospital in the Middle East was established in the city of _____ in _____ A.D. The more scientific aspects of Greek and Roman medicine survived only in Islamic countries. (p. 35)

10. Describe the treatment of mental patients in Islamic countries around 792 A.D. and list the mental disorders described by Avicenna in *The Canon of Medicine*. (pp. 35-36)

11. The Middle Ages in Europe lasted from about 500-1500 A.D. The Middle Ages can be characterized as a relative _____ with respect to scientific thinking about the causes of abnormal behavior or enlightened treatment of mentally disordered persons. (p. 36)

12. How were the dancing manias, which were considered "abnormal behavior," related to ancient Greek religious practices? Why were these behaviors attributed to symptoms of a spider bite rather than being viewed as religious practices? (p. 37)

The occurrence of mass madness peaked in the 14th and 15th centuries. Why was mass madness so common during these years? (p. 37)

Early views of mental disorders in China

13. Around 200 A.D., Chung Ching, who has been called the Hippocrates of China, wrote two well-known medical works. Complete the following description of the views he expressed in these works. (Highlight 2.1, p. 36)

    a. The primary cause of mental disorders is . . .

    b. Organ pathology can also be caused by . . .

    c. Emotional balance can be regained through . . .

14. How did the "Dark Ages" for the mentally ill in China compare to the "Dark Ages" in Europe? (Highlight 2.1, p. 36)

Witchcraft and mental illness: fact or fiction? (15th and 16th centuries)

15. In fifteenth- and sixteenth-century Europe, how widespread were the beliefs in witches as having signed a pact with Satan in return for supernatural powers? (p. 39)

16. Most of the victims persecuted or killed for witchcraft were impoverished women "with a sharp tongue and a bad temper." Historians have suggested that women accused of being witches were not mentally ill. Explain how the belief in two types of demonic possession may have led historians to over-emphasize the "possessed" theory of witchcraft. (p. 39)

Growth toward humanitarian approaches (16th and 17th centuries)

17. Paracelsus, a Swiss physician in the early 16th century, adopted a more humane approach to those manifesting the dancing mania by arguing that it was not a possession, but a form of _____. Further, not unlike Freud's later writings, he postulated a conflict between the _____ and the spiritual nature of human beings. (p. 40).

Resurgence of scientific questioning in Europe

18. Give several examples of people who, during the latter part of the Middle Ages, began to question witchcraft and demon possession as reasons for abnormal behavior. (pp. 40-41)

19. The reappearance of humane treatment of the disturbed was facilitated by four persons. They were _____, a Swiss physician who spoke out against superstitious beliefs about possession; _____, who suggested that the mind can be sick just like the body; _____, who was scorned by his peers and whose step-by-step rebuttal of witchcraft was banned by the church; and, finally, _____, who wrote that witches were but victims of melancholy. (pp. 40-41)

20. King James I of England came to the rescue of demonology, but by that time many of the clergy also were beginning to question the practice. One of these clergy was St. _____, who said, "Mental disease is no different to bodily disease and Christianity demands of the humane and powerful to protect, and the skillful to relieve the one as well as the other." (p. 41)

Establishment of early asylums and shrines (16th and 17th centuries, England and the U. S.)

21. Henry VIII of England established a mental hospital in 1545 called St. Mary of Bethlehem, which soon became known as _____, adding a new word to our language. (p. 41)

22. Describe the atmosphere and treatment methods of these early "hospitals" as illustrated by La Bicêtre in Paris (note: before Pinel's reform in 1792). (pp. 41-42)

23. The first hospital in the United States devoted exclusively to the mentally ill was _____ _____, which was constructed in Williamsburg, Virginia, in 1773. (p. 42)

24. The _____ shrine was one of the few enlightened settings where humane care of disturbed persons was practiced during this period. This colony has continued their work to the present day. Describe their current activities. (p. 42)

Humanitarian reform (19th century)

25. Humanitarian reform of mental hospitals received its first great impetus from the work of _____ of France in 1792. Why is his work referred to as an "experiment"? (pp. 42-43)

26. Pinel's work was begun at _____ hospital and later at _____ hospital, which have become known as the first "modern" hospitals for the care of the insane. (pp. 42-43)

27. _____ was a famous American physician who wrote the first textbook on psychiatry in the United States. He encouraged more human treatment of the mentally ill. (p. 44)

28. During the years between 1833 and 1853, moral management resulted in a discharge rate at Worcester State Hospital of _____ percent among patients who had been ill one year or less and _____ percent among patients who had been ill longer than one year. (p. 45)

29. Moral management, despite its high degree of success, was abandoned by the late 1800s. Your text presents five reasons for this loss of influence. Complete the list. (pp. 45-46)

a. Ethnic and racial prejudice that came with the increased size of the immigrant population.

b.

c.

d.

e. Advances in biology and medicine fostered the hope that all mental disorders would ultimately yield to biologically based treatment.

30. The tireless work of Dorothea Dix was honored by the United States Congress with a resolution in 1901 labeling her as "among the noblest examples of humanity in all history." What type of conditions did she find in state institutions at the beginning of her career and how did she attempt to change them? (p. 46, 48)

Nineteenth century views of causation and treatment of mental disorders

31. On what basis did control of mental hospitals and the care of mental disorders shift from lay persons at the beginning of the 19th century to alienists or psychiatrists later in the century? (Highlight 2.2, pp. 47-48)

Changing attitudes toward mental health (20th century)

32. What was the subject of Clifford Beers' book, *A Mind That Found Itself?* (p. 49)

33. What was Clifford Beers' contribution to changing the general public's attitudes toward the treatment of mental patients? (pp. 49-50)

Events leading to the discovery of organic factors in general paresis

34. In 1825 Bayle gave a complete and accurate description of the symptom pattern of general paresis and convincingly argued that paresis should be differentiated as a _____ _____. (Highlight 2.3, p. 51)

35. In 1857 Esmarch and Jessen produced correlational evidence that _____ caused paresis. (Highlight 2.3, p. 51)

36. What was the crucial experiment reported by Krafft-Ebing in 1897 concerning paresis? (Highlight 2.3, p. 51)

37. In 1905 Schaudinn discovered that _____ is the cause of syphilis. (Highlight 2.3, p. 51)

Establishment of brain pathology as a causal factor

38. How did the emergence of modern experimental science ultimately help to establish brain pathology as a causal factor in mental disorders? (p. 50)

39. What specific examples of mental disorders were determined to reflect brain pathology? (p. 50)

Kraepelin and the beginnings of a classification system

40. In addition to an emphasis on the importance of brain pathology in mental disorders, the most important contribution of Kraepelin's 1883 textbook was his system of _____, which became the forerunner of today's DSM-IV. (p. 51)

41. Kraepelin noted that certain _____ occurred regularly enough to be regarded as specific types of mental disease. (p. 51)

42. Kraepelin saw each type of mental disorder as distinct from the others and thought that the _____ of each was as predetermined and predictable as the course of measles. (p. 52)

Advances achieved as a result of early biological views

43. How did the discovery of the cause of general paresis lead to the development of false expectations among researchers? (p. 52)

The psychodynamic viewpoint and psychoanalysis

44. Although Mesmer appears largely to have been a charlatan and held incorrect theories about his technique known as mesmerism, an important historical event was that he was reportedly

able to remove _____ and _____. In this respect, he predated the successful work of the Nancy School. (pp. 53-54)

45. In disagreement with the Nancy School, Charcot insisted that _____
_____ led to hysteria. (p. 54)

46. The Nancy School finally triumphed in their dispute with Charcot, representing the first recognition of a _____ caused mental disorder. (p. 54)

47. In an important development, Josef Breuer directed his patients to _____
_____ while under hypnosis, during which they usually displayed considerable emotion. This method was called _____. The patients, upon awakening, saw no relationship between their problems and their hysterical symptoms, leading to the discovery of the unconscious and the conclusion that processes _____ can play an important role in the determination of behavior. (p. 55)

48. Freud soon discovered that he could dispense with hypnosis by substituting two methods. What were they? (p. 55)

49. What event in 1909 made Clark University and G. Stanley Hall famous in the history of abnormal psychology? (p. 55)

Advances in Psychological Research

50. The first clinic to treat behavior disorders from a psychological perspective was founded by _____ at the University of Pennsylvania in 1896. (p. 56)

51. The psychodynamic approach views abnormal behavior as the result of inner psychological problems. In contrast, William Healy was the first to describe juvenile delinquency as a symptom of _____. (p. 56)

52. In so doing, Healy was among the first to argue in favor of _____ or _____ factors as the cause of abnormal behavior. (p. 56)

53. Behavioral psychologists believed that the study of _____ through the techniques of free association and dream analysis do not provide acceptable scientific data, because such observations were not open to _____ by other investigators. (p. 56)

54. Only the study of _____ behavior and the stimuli and reinforcing conditions that control it would do for formulating scientific principles of human behavior. (p. 56)

55. The behavioral perspective is organized around a central theme: the role of _____ in human behavior. (p. 56)

◊ **CRITICAL THINKING ABOUT DIFFICULT TOPICS**

1. In Concepts to Master Question 1 you were asked to describe early beliefs in demonology and explain the reasons why exorcism was used as a cure. Think about these beliefs as an example of the general point that a broad theoretical context (about the causes of lightning, thunder, etc.) influences our interpretation of abnormal behavior (attributed to possession) and leads to a theoretically driven method of treatment (exorcism). A similar point is made clearly in Highlight 2.2 in terms of the influence of Victorian attitudes and values on the interpretation of the symptoms of anxiety and depression and of the causes of these symptoms in women. Later in the text you will see the same phenomenon for psychodynamic, behavioral, and biological approaches to abnormal behavior. That is, each theoretical approach will influence the interpretation of abnormal behavior and the type of treatment offered. All of these examples illustrate the powerful influence of theories on our interpretation of abnormal behavior.

2. The text states that there has been a resurgence of superstition in contemporary society in which some still believe that supernatural forces cause psychological problems and should be treated with exorcism (pp. 38-39). Consider the following questions. With what types of religious beliefs might this interpretation of abnormal behavior be most compatible--e.g., a belief in devils as an active evil force as illustrated in the quotation from Martin Luther on page 39? Should exorcism be viewed as a form of treatment and evaluated with respect to its effectiveness like any other psychological or medical treatment? If so, how would you design

such a study? What excuses might be offered by clergy for failures of the treatment that would protect this practice from critical evaluation? Assuming that you agree with the text that possession by the devil is not an acceptable explanation for the behavior in question, exactly what arguments would you make to justify rejecting this theory of psychopathology?

3. Item 5 under Learning Objectives asked you to outline the contributions in the late Middle Ages and early Renaissance of many individuals who argued that abnormal behavior should be seen as mental illness and treated with humane care. Read the statement on page 39 that possessed people had "made a pact with the devil" in return for supernatural powers and the quotation from Martin Luther (on the same page) that those who were possessed were wicked and were being punished by God. To what degree do these differing views contrast "free will" versus "determinism"? That is, in one case the person showing abnormal behavior is said to have acted wickedly (presumably by choice) and/or *willingly* signed a pact with the devil and, therefore, deserves to be punished. In the other case, an illness is something that happens to a person through natural forces over which the person has no control (determinism) and for which, therefore, the person is not responsible. This contrast is seen throughout this chapter (e.g., in Pinel's argument on pages 42-43 that "mental patients should be treated with kindness and consideration--as sick people and not as vicious beasts or criminals"), and it can been seen in many discussions of mental illness today. At present, the issue is, perhaps, most clearly observed in the current debate over alcoholism. Think through the arguments and issues surrounding the opposing views that alcoholism reflects a free choice for which the individual is responsible versus the deterministic view that alcoholism is an illness that happens to the person and for which he or she bears no moral responsibility. This example shows a considerable continuity between the issue in the Middle Ages concerning free choice/blame/punishment versus determinism/humane care and current debates concerning the nature of abnormal behavior.

4. Along the lines of the preceding question, but with a somewhat different emphasis, the sociological perspective points out that abnormal behavior is a form of deviance and that deviant individuals are ostracized and stigmatized. An element of this perspective can be seen in the statements on page 41 that the "early asylums were begun as a way of *removing from society* troublesome individuals who could not care for themselves" (italics added) and on page 44 that prior to Pinel's reform there had been "the indiscriminate mixture of paupers and criminals, the physically sick, and the mentally deranged"--i.e., several deviant and stigmatized groups. Whereas only a small subset of abnormal behavior could be viewed as a manifestation of witchcraft (discussed in the preceding question), a large percentage represents deviant behavior. That is, deviance is a much broader concept than witchcraft. Think about the degree to which the stigma associated with abnormal behavior even today reflects the societal response to deviance--again reflecting a continuity between the historical issues presented in this chapter and views of abnormal behavior today.

5. In Highlight 2.2 the text comments that the vague symptoms of low mood, lack of energy, and physical symptoms, "viewed by the alienists [psychiatrists] as a definable medical condition, were then *considered treatable by medical men* of the times" (pp. 47-48, italics added). This statement clearly indicates that labeling a set of behaviors as a disease (a definable medical condition) serves the function of defining physicians as the appropriate group for dealing with the problem and, in this case, controlling hospitals. Consider the possibility that using the concept of "disease" primarily serves this social function rather than a scientific function of telling us about the nature and causes of the problem. Stating this in other terms, the use of the term "disease" carries little specific scientific meaning in the study of abnormal behavior, but it clearly asserts that the topic is of relevance for physicians. This issue applies generally to the phenomena of abnormal behavior today, and it is centrally involved in arguments between psychologists and psychiatrists as to the nature of abnormal behavior and in professional rivalry regarding the delivery of services.

6. The text describes the beneficial effects of Pinel's reforms (pp. 42-43), of the implementation of moral management (pp. 44-45), and the contrast for Clifford Beers between institutional care and his recovery in the home of a friendly attendant (pp. 49-50). These examples all show the beneficial effects of humane treatment compared with inhumane treatment. Can they be interpreted as evidence that humane treatment is effective in treating mental disorders, or are they more accurately interpreted as evidence that some types of treatment (in this case, inhumane treatment) can make mental illness worse? This question arises in the current literature on psychotherapy, where it is asked whether some treatments may actually be harmful. (Note that in either interpretation, the evidence points to the responsiveness of the abnormal behavior to the environment.)

7. Kraepelin, like most psychiatrists today, "noted that certain symptom patterns occurred regularly enough to be regarded as specific types of mental disease" (p. 51) and the medical model sees these "symptoms" as reflecting an underlying, internal pathology (p. 52). Thus, the ability to describe a "symptom syndrome" or a group of symptoms is often taken as evidence in favor of a disease model. Consider whether this is a false argument, in the sense that there are many examples of clusters or groups of co-varying features that in no way imply a disease process. For example, consider that differences in family income affect many aspects of the family's life: where the family lives, how large their house is, what types of furniture and appliances they own, what types of vacations they take, what type of medical care they receive, how they dress, etc. The point here is that a cluster or group of co-varying features does not, per se, indicate a disease process. The disease model also tends to assume a categorical approach, as embodied in DSM-IV and most medical approaches to diagnosis-- i.e., the disease is either present or absent and is not viewed as falling along a continuous dimension of illness. The example of differences in income shows that a cluster of co-varying features can be associated with a dimensional phenomenon, since income is a continuous

rather than categorical variable (e.g., one is not either rich or poor but rather has a specific income that falls somewhere on the continuous distribution of income in the population). Keep this issue in mind throughout your reading of the text as the medical model is employed in talking about "mental disease" and "mental illness." Do not allow this language usage to make you assume that abnormal behavior does, in fact, fit a disease model.

8. The text correctly states that the vast majority of abnormal behavior is not clearly associated with physical damage to brain tissue (p. 52). After Freud's emphasis on psychogenic causes of mental disorders, a clear distinction was made between organic disorders, such as general paresis, in which there is clear damage to brain tissue, and the "functional psychoses" such as schizophrenia and manic-depressive disorder, which at the time were presumed to result primarily from psychological causes. However, in the second half of the present century accumulating evidence strongly implicated genetic contributions to the development of schizophrenia and manic-depressive disorder. These genetic contributions, although biological, have not yet been shown to be associated with physical damage to brain tissue. Recalling that in the nature (genetic) versus nurture (environmental) distinction both factors are assumed to contribute to normal behavior, would you say that the important genetic contribution to major psychoses makes them organic disorders? As you read more about this issue later in the text, you probably will decide that the distinction between organic and functional disorders has become blurred with awareness of the genetic contributions.

◊ CHAPTER 2 QUIZ

Circle the best of the four answers provided and check them according to answers provided at the back of this study guide. Be sure you understand why each answer is correct.

1. Which of the following was from the sixteenth century B. C. and recognized the brain as the site of mental functions? (p. 32)
   a. the Ebers papyrus   c. the Old Testament
   b. the Edwin Smith papyrus   d. the Rosetta Stone

2. Hippocrates erroneously held which of the following beliefs? (p. 33)
   a. The brain is the central organ of intellectual activity
   b. Head injuries may cause sensory and motor disorders
   c. The environment is important in mental disorders
   d. There are basically four types of body fluids

3. Plato and Aristotle anticipated Freud in their emphasis on: (p. 34)
   a. humane treatment.
   b. the influence on thinking and/or behavior of "natural appetites" and the desire to eliminate pain and attain pleasure.
   c. the use of insanity as an excuse for crime.
   d. psychological factors, such as frustration and conflict, as causes of disturbed behavior.

4. The Greek physician Galen's most important contribution to abnormal psychology was his description of: (p. 34)
   a. the anatomy of the nervous system.
   b. medicinal herbs that could soothe mental patients.
   c. new treatments for the mentally disturbed.
   d. symptoms of common mental disorders.

5. The "Dark Ages" in the history of abnormal psychology began with the: (p. 35)
   a. "Black Death" of the fifteenth century A.D.
   b. death of Galen in 200 A.D.
   c. fall of Rome in the fifth century A.D.
   d. Roman monarchs around 100 A.D.

6. The physician who kept Greek and Roman medical concepts alive in Islamic countries after the fall of Rome was: (p. 35)
   a. Agrippa.   c. Asclepiades.
   b. Aristotle.   d. Avicenna.

7. The key concept emphasizing the balance of positive and negative forces in Chinese medicine is: (Highlight 2.1, p. 36)
   a. equilibrium.   c. Sun and Earth principle.
   b. homeostasis.   d. Yin and Yang.

8. Which of the following did not argue that those showing abnormal behavior should be seen as mentally ill and treated with humane care? (pp. 40-41)
   a. Paracelsus   c. King James I of England
   b. Teresa of Avila   d. Johan Weyer

9. The manual that was a complete guide to the detection and punishment of witches was called the: (p. 40)
   a. *Summes Deciderantes Affectibus.*   c. *Deception of Demons.*
   b. *Malleus Maleficarum.*   d. *Discovery of Witchcraft.*

10. In 1584, Oxford-educated Reginald Scot wrote *Discovery of Witchcraft* in which he stated that: (p. 41)
    a. demons, devils and evil spirits did not cause mental disorders.
    b. mental disorders were caused by witches.
    c. the clergy invented witchcraft.
    d. witchcraft was discovered by Galen.

11. The word *bedlam* originated from a(an): (p. 41)
    a. ancient Greek term for "disturbance of biles."
    b. contraction for St. Mary of Bethlehem mental hospital.
    c. description of mass madness in the Middle Ages.
    d. practice of burning witches in their beds.

12. Treatment of mental patients at the Public Hospital of Williamsburg, Virginia, was designed to: (p. 42)
    a. force patients to leave.   c. save inmates' souls from hell.
    b. intimidate patients.   d. surround inmates with love.

13. An institution noted for kindness and humanity in the care of the mentally ill was: (p. 42)
    a. The Geel Shrine, Belgium.   c. St. Mary of Bethlehem, London.
    b. La Maison de Charenton, Paris.   d. San Hipolito, Mexico.

14. In 1805, Pierre was sent to La Bicêtre mental hospital because of his bizarre delusions. Because this hospital was then administered by Philippe Pinel, he was probably treated: (pp. 42-43)
    a. as a beast or prisoner.   c. by letting out his red bile.
    b. by clerical exorcists.   d. in a humanitarian fashion.

15. The founder of American psychiatry is: (p. 44)
    a. William Tuke.   c. Benjamin Rush.
    b. Lightner Witmer.   d. Dorothea Dix.

16. Pinel and Tuke's moral management in mental hospitals was based on the idea that abnormal behavior is: (p. 44)
    a. a result of sinful living.
    b. due to possession of the devil.
    c. related to an immoral balance of the humors.
    d. the result of severe psychological stress.

17. All of the following are reasons that have been offered as explanations for the abandonment of moral therapy in the latter part of the nineteenth century *except:* (pp. 45-46)
    a. a rising tide of racial and ethnic prejudice.
    b. overextension of hospital facilities.
    c. general loss of faith among the general population.
    d. belief that mental disorders would yield to physical solutions.

18. In the Victorian era a person manifesting symptoms of depression would most likely be diagnosed as suffering from: (Highlight 2.2, p. 47)
    a. oligophrenia.
    b. dysthymia.
    c. neurasthenia.
    d. demoralization.

19. Dorothea Dix is noted for her highly successful campaign to do something about the: (p. 48)
    a. inhuman treatment accorded the mentally ill.
    b. problem of heroin abuse during the Civil War.
    c. view that women were biologically inferior.
    d. overcrowded conditions in large mental hospitals in rural areas.

20. One of the early treatments for general paresis involved: (p. 50; Highlight 2.3, p. 51)
    a. prescribing laudanum.
    b. prescribing specific wild herbs.
    c. prescribing lithium.
    d. infecting the sufferer with malaria.

21. The Nancy School centered around the use of hypnosis to treat: (p. 54)
    a. tarantism.
    b. hysteria.
    c. neurasthenia.
    d. depression.

22. Josef Breuer directed his patients to talk freely about their problems while under hypnosis--a method that was called: (p. 55)
    a. mesmerism.
    b. free association.
    c. catharsis.
    d. emotional desensitization.

23. One of the main features of behaviorism was the rejection of: (p. 56)
    a. subjective experience.
    b. associationism.
    c. the law of effect.
    d. theoretical constructs.

24. Classical and instrumental conditioning differ primarily with respect to: (p. 57)
    a. the types of reinforcers involved.
    b. an emphasis on animal versus human subjects.
    c. the number of trials to reach criterion performance.
    d. whether the outcome (reinforcer) is dependent on the animal's behavior.

Chapter 3
Biological, Psychosocial, and Sociocultural Viewpoints

◊ OVERVIEW

The models of abnormal behavior are discussed in this chapter. The biological viewpoint focuses on irregularities in the biochemical functioning of the brain to explain mental disorders. Beginning with the work of two men, Pavlov and Freud, the psychosocial model has grown to include the psychoanalytic, behavioristic, humanistic, and interpersonal viewpoints. The sociocultural viewpoint reminds us that humans are social beings and our behavior cannot be fully understood without reference to the values and practices of the group in which we live. Previously, clinicians believed that they had to declare allegiance to one viewpoint or another, but it is now widely recognized that no one model can adequately explain every aspect of every form of abnormal behavior. Consequently, one needs to assess and deal with the interaction of biological, psychosocial, and sociocultural factors to develop the total clinical picture.

◊ LEARNING OBJECTIVES

After studying this chapter, you should be able to:

1. Discuss the different conceptual approaches to understanding the causes of abnormal behavior. These approaches will include (a) necessary, sufficient, and contributory causes; (b) Feedback and circularity models; and (c) the diathesis-stress model. (pp. 63-67)

2. Summarize the biological theories of abnormal behavior, including neurotransmitter/hormonal imbalances, genetic and constitutional influences, and physical damage to brain structures. (pp. 67-78)

3. Outline the major psychosocial theoretical approaches to abnormal behavior, including the psychodynamic, behavioral/cognitive-behavioral, humanistic, and interpersonal perspectives. (pp. 78-95)

4. Discuss the substantive contributions of the psychosocial factors of deviant cognitions (schemas and self-schemas), early deprivation or trauma (e.g., parental deprivation, institutionalization, abuse, etc.), inadequate parenting and pathogenic family structures, and problems with peer relationships. (pp. 95-106)

5. Describe the sociocultural perspective and its contributions to understanding abnormal behavior. (pp. 106-113)

6. Explain why the field needs a unified viewpoint and how the biopsychosocial viewpoint may fulfill that need. (pp. 113-115)

◊ TERMS YOU SHOULD KNOW

etiology (p. 64)

necessary cause (p. 64)

sufficient cause (p. 64)

contributory cause (p. 64)

distal causal factors (p. 64)

proximal causal factors (p. 64)

reinforcing cause (p. 64)

diathesis (p. 65)

diathesis-stress models (p. 65)

stress (p. 66)

protective factors (p. 66)

resilience (p. 66)

paradigm shifts (p. 67)

eclectic (p. 67)

medical model (p. 68)

categorical approach (p. 68)

biopsychological model (p. 68)

synapse and *synaptic cleft* (p. 69; Highlight 3.1, p. 70)

presynaptic and *postsynaptic neurons* (p. 69; Highlight 3.1, p. 70)

biochemical imbalance (p. 69)

re-uptake (p. 69; Highlight 3.1, p. 70)

excitatory and *inhibitory neural transmission* (Highlight 3.1, p. 70)

receptor sites (Highlight 3.1, p. 70)

hormones (p. 69)

hypothalamus-pituitary-adrenal-cortical axis (p. 69)

chromosomes (p. 71)

autosomes (p. 71)

sex chromosomes (p. 71)

genotype (p. 71)

phenotype (pp. 71-72)

pedigree or *family history method* (p. 72)

proband or *index case* (p. 72)

monozygotic vs. *dizygotic twins* (p. 72)

concordance rate (p. 72)

shared and *nonshared environmental influences* (p. 73)

constitutional liability (pp. 73-74)

fetal alcohol syndrome (p. 75)

primary reaction tendencies (p. 75)

homeostasis (p. 76)

psychoanalysis (p. 79)

id, ego, and *superego* (p. 79)

primary and *secondary process thinking* (p. 79)

classical conditioning (p. 84)

operant conditioning (p. 84)

unconditioned stimulus (p. 84)

unconditioned response (p. 84)

conditioned stimulus (p. 84)

conditioned response (p. 84)

extinction (p. 84)

reinforcement (p. 84)

personal constructs (pp. 87-88)

internal reinforcement (p. 88)

◊ NAMES YOU SHOULD KNOW

Aaron Beck (pp. 88, 89)

Carl Rogers (p. 91)

Abraham Maslow (pp. 91, 92)

Alfred Adler (pp. 91, 92)

Erich Fromm (p. 92)

Karen Horney (pp. 92-93)

Erik Erikson (p. 93)

Harry Stack Sullivan (pp. 93-94)

◊ **CONCEPTS TO MASTER**

---

1. Contrast the essential features of necessary, sufficient, and contributory causes and distinguish among proximal, distal, and reinforcing causal factors. Which of these types of causes would apply to the statement that smoking cigarettes is a risk factor for lung cancer? (p. 64)

2. When should one use the term "causal pattern"? (p. 65)

3. Simple cause-and-effect sequences are rare in the behavioral sciences. How do the concepts of feedback and mutual, two-way influences differ from simple cause-and-effect sequences? (p. 65).

4. How do the terms proximal, distal, necessary, sufficient, and contributory causes apply to the diathesis-stress model? (pp. 65-66)

5. When does an environmental demand become stressful? (p. 66)

6. What is a "steeling" or "inoculation" effect? (p. 66)

7. What are the three distinct phenomena to which the term resilience applies? (p. 66)

8. How does the biopsychological model differ from the medical model? (p. 68)

9. A patient has the delusion that he is Napoleon. The delusion is the impairment. The specific idea that he is Napoleon is the content of the impairment. How does this delusion reveal that biological causes must interact with experience? (p. 68)

10. List the five categories of biological factors that are especially relevant to the development of abnormal behavior. (pp. 68-69)

11. The concept of biochemical imbalances is one of the basic tenets of the biological perspective today. Outline the sequence of events involved in neurotransmission, identify those mechanisms by which a biochemical imbalance might be produced, and explain how this imbalance might produce abnormal behavior. How do these processes relate to the mechanisms by which medications used to treat various disorders exert their effects? (p. 69; Highlight 3.1, p. 70)

12. Discuss the genetic approaches to abnormal behavior, including basic genetic concepts (e.g., chromosome, gene, genotype, phenotype, and zygote) and the process of sexual reproduction by which genetic influences are passed from parents to child. (pp. 69, 71-72)

13. Summarize the various methods (pedigree/family history, twin, and adoption) used in genetic research with humans. (pp. 72-73)

14. What major comparison is involved regarding concordance rates in twin studies and how are the results interpreted? (pp. 72-73)

15. Define the concept of constitutional liability and compare and contrast the forms of constitutional liability indicated by the terms physical handicaps, primary reaction tendencies, and temperament. (pp. 73-75)

16. Name the five dimensions of temperament seen at about 2-3 months of age and the three dimensions of adult personality to which they are related. (p. 75)

17. The text states that the temperament of an infant or young child can have profound effects on a variety of important developmental processes. Using the example of a fearful temperament, describe these different effects with respect to classical conditioning of fear, avoidance learning, reaction to environmental stimulation, and forming attachment relationships. (p. 75)

18. Distinguish between gross brain pathology and more subtle deficiencies of brain function and indicate which applies to only a small percentage of people with abnormal behavior. (p. 76)

19. The text documents the conclusion that dietary deficiencies can have long-term effects on cognitive functioning (well beyond the period of malnutrition) with several examples. Describe the results reported for former World War II and Korean War POWs and for 129 children in Barbados who were severely undernourished during infancy. (pp. 76-77)

20. Describe the interaction of the id, ego, and superego in Freud's conception of personality. (p. 79)

21. An important psychoanalytic concept is the unconscious. What types of memories, desires, and experiences exist in the unconscious? (p. 81)

22. Describe three types of anxiety described by Freud, and explain the function of the ego-defense mechanisms. (pp. 79, 81)

23. List and describe Freud's five stages of psychosexual development and their effects on personality. (p. 81)

24. Describe two of Freud's most outstanding contributions to our understanding of normal and abnormal behavior, and list several criticisms of his approach. (p. 83)

25. Contrast the newer psychodynamic approaches with the earlier Freudian perspective, including the greater emphasis on ego functions and object relations. Summarize some of the newer psychodynamic perspectives developed by Anna Freud, Melanie Klein, Margaret Mahler, and Otto Kernberg. (pp. 82-83)

26. Discuss both the major positive contributions of psychodynamic perspectives and the numerous criticisms of this tradition. (p. 83)

27. Define each of the following and explain its importance for abnormal psychology: classical conditioning, operant conditioning, reinforcement, response-outcome expectancy, conditioned avoidance response, generalization, discrimination, and differential reinforcement. (pp. 84-85)

28. List the major triumphs and criticisms of the behavioral tradition. (p. 85)

29. Contrast the focus of cognitive-behavior clinicians with that of the behavioristic therapists. (pp. 87-89)

30. State the distinctive contributions and limitations of the humanistic perspective. (pp. 89-92)

31. Explain how the work of Alfred Adler, Eric Fromm, Karen Horney, and Erik Erikson became the roots of the interpersonal perspective on psychopathology. (pp. 92-93)

32. Describe the major features of Harry Stack Sullivan's interpersonal theory of personality. (pp. 93-94)

33. What are the four categories of psychosocial causal factors that exemplify the psychosocial approach? (p. 95)

34. How are assimilation and accommodation involved in the processing of new experiences, and which is the basic goal of psychosocial therapies? (p. 96)

35. Explain how the psychosocial factors of early deprivation and trauma, inadequate parenting, pathogenic family structures, and maladaptive peer relationships contribute to the development of abnormal behavior. (pp. 98-106)

36. How are the variables of parental warmth and parental control related to the authoritative, authoritarian, indulgent, and neglecting parenting styles? (pp. 101-103)

37. There are types of serious disorders found among all peoples of the world. What features lead behavior to be considered abnormal in any society? (p. 107)

38. Two recent cross-national studies comparing the U.S. and Thailand found no differences in the prevalence of undercontrolled problems but a higher prevalence of overcontrolled problems. However, there were different forms of undercontrolled behavior. What cultural factors account for the differences in prevalence and/or types of problematic behavior? (p. 109)

39. Outline the major sociocultural factors that contribute to abnormal behavior and summarize the evidence in favor of their importance. (pp. 110-113)

40. What are the advantages and disadvantages of adherence to a single, systematic viewpoint? (pp. 113-114)

41. What is the one attempt at developing a single, comprehensive, internally consistent viewpoint that accurately reflects what we know empirically about abnormal behavior? (p. 114)

◊ STUDY QUESTIONS

Necessary, sufficient, and contributory causes

1. A _____ cause is one that *must* exist for a disorder to occur, but it is not always a sufficient cause. (p. 64)

2. A _____ cause guarantees the occurrence of a disorder, but it may not be necessary for the disorder to occur. (p. 64)

3. A _____ cause increases the probability of a disorder but is neither necessary nor sufficient. (p. 64)

4. Causal factors occurring relatively early in life that do not show their effects for many years are considered _____ causal factors that may contribute to a _____ to develop a disorder. (p. 64)

5. Causal factors that operate shortly before the occurrence of symptom onset would be considered _____ causal factors that in some cases may be no more than the straw that breaks the camel's back. (p. 64)

6. A condition that tends to maintain maladaptive behavior that is already present is a _____ cause--e.g., the extra attention, sympathy, and removal from unwanted responsibility that may be secondary to becoming ill. (p. 64)

Models for understanding abnormal behavior

7. Thomas Kuhn, an historian who focuses on scientific progress, has noted that theoretical orientations in science typically remain strong even in the face of evidence or alternate explanations. A theory typically lasts until a fundamental insight is achieved that appears to resolve problems left unsolved by existing theories. The new insights, also called _____ shifts, are complete reorganizations of the way people think about a particular issue or field of science. (p. 67)

8. In the study of abnormal psychology, we are still awaiting a new fundamental insight. In the meanwhile, competing viewpoints exist. Therefore, many researchers and practitioners choose to be _____, which means to select what appears to be best from various viewpoints. It is up to each student to select a particular preference, if any, after he or she becomes more knowledgeable about the field. (p. 67)

Biological viewpoints

9. The extreme biological viewpoint, held by many medical practitioners, states that abnormal behavior is the product of _____ of the central nervous system, the autonomic nervous system, or the endocrine system. In such a viewpoint, neither psychological factors nor the psychosocial environment of the individual are believed to contribute to the causes of mental disorder. (p. 68)

10. The electrical nerve impulse travels from the cell body of a neuron to the terminal buttons via the _____. (Highlight 3.1, p. 70)

11. The terminal buttons or synaptic _____ are the sites where neurotransmitter substances are stored until needed. When the nerve impulse reaches the axon endings, the transmitter is released into the _____, a tiny fluid-filled gap between the axon endings of the _____ neuron and the _____ or the cell body of the postsynaptic neuron. (Highlight 3.1, p. 70)

12. The neurotransmitter substances act on the dendrite of the postsynaptic neuron at specialized places called _____ sites. (Highlight 3.1, p. 70)

13. The effect of the neurotransmitter on the postsynaptic neuron can be either _____, which means it increases the probability that the neuron will fire, or _____, which means that it decreases the probability that the neuron will fire. (p. 69; Highlight 3.1, p. 70)

14. The action of the neurotransmitter substance is time-limited either by deactivation by an _____, such as monoamine oxidase, in the synaptic cleft or by a process called _____, which takes it back into the presynaptic neuron and stores it in the synaptic storage vesicles. (p. 69; Highlight 3.1, p. 70)

15. What is phenylketonuria (PKU), what causes it, and what dietary ingredient is involved? (p. 71)

16. Explain why Down syndrome is also known as Trisomy 21. (p. 71)

17. Highly intelligent parents provide an intellectually stimulating environment. This is an example of what has been termed a _____ effect of the child's genotype on the environment, resulting from the genetic similarity of parents and children. (pp. 71-72)

18. Happy babies evoke more positive responses from others than do passive, unresponsive infants. This is an example in which the child's genotype _____ _____ from the social and physical environment. (p. 72)

19. Extraverted children may seek the company of others, thereby enhancing their own tendencies to be sociable. This is an example in which the child's genotype plays a more _____ _____ in shaping the environment. (p. 72)

20. Why is the term "primary reaction tendencies" a broader concept than genetic influences and a narrower concept than temperament? (p. 75)

21. What are the two general types of physical deprivation or disruption that may contribute to abnormal behavior. (pp. 76-78)

Misconceptions regarding nature, nurture, and psychopathology

22. Between 1900 and 1960 the average height of boys reared in London increased about 10 cm due to improvements in diet. This example illustrates that the following is a misconception: strong genetic effects mean that environmental influences must be _____. (Highlight 3.2, p. 74)

23. One's potential can change if one's environment changes. This conclusion is supported by the example that children born to _____ biological parents who are adopted and reared with _____ parents have a mean IQ about 12 points higher than those reared in the environment of the biological parents. (Highlight 3.2, p. 74)

24. Concordance rates of less than 100% in monozygotic twins illustrate the importance of environmental influences. This example illustrates that the following is a misconception: genetic strategies are _____ for studying environmental influences. (Highlight 3.2, p. 74)

25. Babies born with the genetic defect causing phenylketonuria only develop the disease if they are exposed to diets with phenylalanine. This example illustrates that the following is a misconception: nature and nurture are _____. (Highlight 3.2, p. 74)

26. Dizygotic twins are more alike than monozygotic twins at birth for height, weight, and IQ, but over time dizygotic twins show greater differences than monozygotic twins. This example illustrates that the following is a misconception: genetic effects _____ with age. (Highlight 3.2, p. 74)

27. Juvenile delinquency and conduct disorder tend to run in families, yet do not seem to be due primarily to genetic factors. This example illustrates that the following is a misconception: disorders that run in families must be _____ and ones that do not run in families must not be _____. (Highlight 3.2, p. 74)

59

Basics of the Psychodynamic perspective

28. The id operates according to the _____ principle. (p. 79)

29. The id generates mental images and fantasies referred to as _____ thinking. (p. 79)

30. The id is the source of two instinctual drives: a) _____ and b) _____. (p. 79)

31. _____ anxiety is caused by the id's impulses, which, if expressed, would be punished in some way. (p. 79)

32. The ego operates according to the _____ principle. (p. 79)

33. The ego uses reason and intellectual resources to deal with the external world, which is referred to as _____ thinking. (p. 79)

34. The ego mediates between the demands of the _____ and _____ in such a way as to insure that needs are met and survival assured. (p. 79)

35. The superego is the outgrowth of internalizing the _____ and _____ of society. (p. 79)

36. The superego operates through the _____ to inhibit desires that are considered wrong or immoral. (p. 79)

37. The superego generates _____ anxiety, which arises from action in conflict with the superego and arouses feelings of guilt. (p. 79)

38. Anxiety is a warning of impending danger as well as a painful experience, so it motivates people to do something about it. The ego can cope with anxiety in basically two ways. First, the ego can cope with anxiety by rational measures. If these are not effective or sufficient, the ego resorts to _____. These alleviate the painful anxiety, but they do so by pushing painful ideas out of consciousness, which leads to a distorted view of reality. (pp. 79, 81)

39. Freud viewed personality development as a succession of stages, each characterized by a dominant mode of achieving sexual pleasure. Fill in the empty spaces on the following chart regarding psychosexual stages. (p. 81)

Stage	Age	Source of Gratification
Oral	_____ years	_____
Anal	_2-3_ years	_____
Phallic	_____ years	Self-manipulation of the genitals
Latency	_____ years	_____
Genital	_____ years	_____

40. Each stage of development places demands on the individual and arouses conflicts that must be resolved. One of the most important conflicts that occurs during the phallic stage is the Oedipus complex. Give the following information about it: (p. 81)

a. What is the role of castration anxiety in the Oedipus complex?

b. What is considered to be its proper resolution if development proceeds normally?

c. Describe the Electra complex which is the female form of the Oedipus complex.

Newer psychodynamic perspectives

41. Contemporary theorists have further developed psychoanalytic thought. In contemporary psychodynamic approaches the focus is not on the ego or on the id. Rather it is on the _____. (p. 82)

42. Object-relations theory is based on the concept of _____ which refers to the incorporation into memory of symbols that represent images and memories of persons the child viewed with strong emotions. (p. 82)

43. Describe the general notions of object-relations theory as developed by Melanie Klein and others in England. (p. 82)

44. The work of Margaret Mahler in the United States added insights to object-relations theory. Describe her concept of separation-individuation that is said to be essential for the achievement of a mature personality. (p. 82)

45. Otto Kernberg describes the result of poor early relationships, which he labels the "borderline personality." The chief characteristic of the borderline personality is _____, an inability to achieve a full and _____ personal identity because of an inability to integrate and reconcile _____. (pp. 82-83)

Impact of the psychodynamic perspective

46. _____ can be seen as the first systematic approach showing how human psychological processes can result in mental disorders. (p. 83)

47. Freud's views replaced brain pathology with intrapsychic conflict and exaggerated ego defenses against anxiety as the cause of at least some mental disorders. One of his most noteworthy contributions was to emphasize the extent to which _____ motives and _____ mechanisms affect behavior, the importance of _____ experiences in later personality adjustment and maladjustment, and the importance of _____ factors in human behavior and mental disorders. The second particularly noteworthy contribution was the realization that the same psychological principles apply to both _____ and _____ behavior. (p. 83)

48. Two important criticisms of psychoanalytic theory have been offered. First, it fails to recognize the scientific limits of _____ as the primary mode of obtaining information. Second, there is a lack of _____ _____ to support many of its explanatory assumptions or the effectiveness of its therapy. (p. 83)

The behavioral perspective

49. Behavioral psychologists believe that the data used by psychoanalysts, including material obtained by free association and dream analysis, is unacceptable scientifically. What data do behaviorists prefer? (p. 83)

50. The roots of the behavioristic approach can be traced to the study of _____
_____ by a Russian physiologist named Ivan Pavlov and to the study of
_____ by Edward Thorndike. Nevertheless, promotion of
the behavioral approach is credited to a young American psychologist named _____.
(p. 83)

51. The behaviorists focused on the effects of _____ on the
acquisition, modification, and possible elimination of various types of response patterns. (p.
83)

Basics of the behavioral perspective

52. Identify the following statements as referring to classical conditioning (C) or operant
(instrumental) conditioning (O)--i.e., place a "C" or "O" after each as appropriate. (pp. 84-85)
a. As we mature, this type of learning becomes more important. _____
b. Many responses, particularly those related to fear or anxiety, are learned through this type
of learning. _____
c. In this type of learning, the response typically precedes the stimulus. _____
d. The UCS follows the CS regardless of the person's response. _____
e. As we grow up, this type of learning becomes an important mechanism for discriminating
the desirable from the undesirable. _____
f. Consists of simple strengthening of a stimulus-response connection. _____
g. The person learns a response-outcome expectancy. _____

53. In operant or instrumental conditioning, initially a high rate of reinforcement may be
necessary, but thereafter it is especially persistent when reinforcement is _____. (p. 84)

54. Avoidance learning allows an individual to anticipate an adverse event and respond in such a
way as to avoid it. A boy who has been bitten by a vicious dog may develop a conditioned
avoidance response in which he consistently avoids all dogs. How does developing a phobia
of dogs lessen anxiety? (p. 84)

55. Match the following terms and examples: (pp. 84-85)

Terms	Example
a. Discrimination	_____ A person, previously bitten, avoids dogs.
b. Generalization	_____ An occasional win at gambling keeps the behavior going.

c. Intermittent   ____ A person, beaten as a child by an authority figure, has an involuntary fear of anyone in authority.

d. Reinforcement   ____ A child performs a response that in the past produced candy.

e. Avoidance conditioning ____ A child learns that although red and green strawberries look somewhat similar, only red ones taste good.

56. In contrast to simple extinction, in desensitization the stimuli eliciting avoidance behavior are repeatedly paired with _____. (Highlight 3.4, p. 86)

Impact of the behavioral approach on our views of psychopathology

57. Behaviorists believe that maladaptive behavior develops in two general ways. What are they? (p. 85)
   a.
   b.

58. Behaviorism has been praised for its precision and objectivity, its _____, and its demonstrated effectiveness in changing specific behaviors. (p. 85)

59. Behaviorism has been criticized for being concerned only with _____, and for ignoring the problems of _____, _____, and self-direction. (p. 85)

The cognitive-behavioral approach

60. What does the cognitive-behavioral approach consider that behaviorism does not? (p. 87)

61. In contrast to pure behaviorism, cognitive-behavioral theoreticians and clinicians have simply shifted their focus from overt behavior to the underlying _____ assumed to be producing the behavior. Then, the clinical goal becomes one of altering maladaptive _____ rather than maladaptive behavior. (p. 89)

The humanistic perspective

62. What is the focus of the humanistic perspective? (p. 89)

63. The humanistic approach recognizes the importance of learning and other psychological processes but it focuses, usually optimistically, on the future rather than on the past. How is the humanistic perspective in disagreement with: (pp. 89-91)

a. the behavioristic approach?

b. psychoanalytic theory?

64. There are the two "underlying themes and principles" that characterize the humanistic approach. These are the concept of _____ as a unifying theme and a focus on _____ and personal growth. (pp. 91-92)

Impact of the humanistic view on our views of psychopathology

65. The major impact of the humanistic approach has been its emphasis on our capacity for _____ as human beings. (p. 92)

66. Humanists generally believe that psychopathology is caused by the blocking or distortion of natural tendencies toward _____ rather than as abnormality or deviance. (p. 92)

67. The humanistic approach has been criticized for its _____, for its lack of _____, and for its high expectations and grandiose goals. (p. 92)

The interpersonal perspective

68. Theorists who share an interpersonal perspective believe that abnormal behavior is best understood by analyzing a person's _____ both past and present. (p. 92)

69. The roots of the interpersonal perspective lie in the psychodynamic movement, but the views have been most fully developed by four theorists who rebelled from the Freudian mold including: (pp. 92-93)

a. Erik Fromm, who focused on dispositions that people adopt in their interactions.

b. Karen Horney, who vigorously rejected Freud's demeaning female psychology.

c.

d. Harry Stack Sullivan, who maintained that the term *personality* was best defined in terms of an individual's characteristic way of relating to others.

70. Harry Stack Sullivan believed that development proceeds through various stages, involving different patterns of _____. (p. 93)

71. Sullivan believed that mental prototypes, or personifications, determine how we perceive our current relationships. Personifications are developed in childhood. Describe how a child comes to label some of his or her personal tendencies as: (pp. 93-94)
   a. "Good me"
   b. "Bad me"
   c. "Not me"

72. Respond to the following questions regarding several other interpersonal theories: (p. 94)

   a. The social exchange view (Thibault and Kelly, 1959) suggests that we form relationships with each other for what purpose?

   b. In relationships we each have social roles and role expectations. What are these?

   c. When two persons evolve patterns of communication and interaction that enable them to attain common goals and meet mutual needs, the process is called _____
   _____.

Impact of the interpersonal perspective on our views of psychopathology

73. The interpersonal perspective views unsatisfactory _____ as the primary causes of many forms of maladaptive behavior. (p. 94)

74. Supporters of the interpersonal perspective believe that it could be used to increase the _____ and _____ of psychological diagnosis. (p. 94)

75. What is the focus of therapy from the interpersonal perspective? (pp. 94-95)

Psychosocial causal factors: Schemas and self-schemas

76. Mischel identified five learning-based differences that emerge in early childhood: (p. 97)

   a. different levels of competency in different areas

   b.

c. different expectations concerning which things follow from certain others

d. different ways of coping with impulses and regulating their behavior

77. All psychosocial viewpoints of abnormal behavior emphasize the importance of _____ _____ in shaping a person's coping style. (p. 97)

78. Barlow and Mineka both emphasize that the key factor in developing anxiety is exposure to negative outcomes that are perceived to be _____ and _____. (p. 97)

Psychosocial causal factors: Early deprivation or trauma

79. In the much-referenced study by Provence and Lipton, at one year of age infants living in institutions show general impairments in their _____ and a marked retardation of _____ development, emotional apathy, and impoverished and repetitive play. (p. 98)

80. Two protective factors for children institutionalized at an early age are entering a _____ home and having _____ at school. (p. 98)

81. Abused children suffer from many deficits and are at heightened risk for later aggressive behavior, including abuse of their own children. List four protective factors that decrease the probability of intergenerational transmission of abuse. (p. 99)

a. A good relationship with some adult during childhood
b.
c.
d. Physical attractiveness

82. Bowlby found that, when children age 2 to 5 years are separated from their parents during prolonged periods of hospitalization, the acute effects include significant _____ during the separation and _____ upon reunion. (p. 100)

Psychosocial causal factors: Inadequate parenting

83. Many studies have indicated that parental psychopathology can have profound adverse effects on children, but many children do fine because of protective factors. These include a

_____ with the other parent or another adult, having good _____ skills, and being _____ to adults. (p. 101)

84. Match the following parenting styles with child outcomes: (pp. 102-103)

Style	Child Outcome
a. authoritative	____ impulsive and aggressive; spoiled, selfish, inconsiderate, and demanding; exploit people for their own purposes.
b. authoritarian	____ disruptions in attachment in childhood; moodiness, low self-esteem, and conduct problems later in childhood; problems with peer relations and academic performance.
c. permissive-indulgent	____ energetic and friendly, competent in dealing with others and the environment.
d. neglecting-uninvolved	____ conflicted, irritable, moody; poor social and cognitive skills.

Psychosocial causal factors: Pathogenic family structures

85. In their comprehensive review of the effects of divorce on adults, Bloom, Asher, & White concluded that it is a major source of _____, as well as physical illness, _____, _____, and homicide. (p. 104)

86. In their quantitative review of 92 studies of the effects of divorce Amato & Keith found that children in intact but _____ families were worse off than children in divorced families. They also found that children living with a stepparent were _____ than children living with a single parent. (p. 104)

Psychosocial causal factors: Maladaptive peer relationships

87. With respect to peer relations, the most consistent correlate of popularity is being seen as _____ and _____. This relationship is probably complexly involved with other variables, such as _____ and physical attractiveness. (p. 105)

88. One large factor associated with being persistently rejected by peers is an excessively _____ or _____ approach to ongoing peer activities. A smaller group of children is apparently rejected because of their own _____. (p. 105)

89. Kupersmidt and Coie found that _____ toward peers was the best predictor in the fifth grade of juvenile delinquency and school dropout seven years later. One causal pathway suggested by Patterson et al. is that peer rejection often leads a child to associated with _____ several years later, which in turn is associated with a tendency toward juvenile delinquency. (p. 105)

The sociocultural viewpoint

90. To demonstrate a convincing link between sociocultural factors and personality development, children with similar genetic or biological traits would have to be randomly assigned to be reared in diverse social or economic environments. This type of controlled study is impossible, because investigators cannot _____ rear children in this manner in order to find out which variables affect development and adjustment? (p. 106)

91. Malinowski, in his book *Sex and Repression in Savage Society,* found little evidence among the Trobriand Islanders of Oedipal conflict. He therefore concluded that the sexually-based behavior postulated by psychoanalytic theory was not universal, but rather was a product of the _____ in Western Society. (p. 107)

92. Malinowski's study and others led to the formulation of "cultural relativism." Explain this doctrine. Is cultural relativism a widely accepted doctrine today? (p. 107)

93. There is evidence that culture does influence the particular form a mental illness takes. For example: (p. 109)

   a. How do Italians differ from Swiss, American, and Irish patients in response to illness?

   b. How does the acute sense of guilt sometimes associated with depression vary across cultures?

Sociocultural influences

94. Factors in the social environment that may increase vulnerability include _____, disorder-engendering social roles,

_____, economic and employment problems, and social change and uncertainty. (p. 110)

95. How does Margaret Mead's comparison of the Arapesh and Mundugumor tribes in New Zealand demonstrate social influences on an important behavior? (p. 110)

96. In a longitudinal study of inner-city children in Boston, resilience was best indicated by childhood _____ and having adequate functioning as a child in _____, _____, and _____ relationships. (p. 111)

97. Many more women than men seek treatment for emotional disorders, especially anxiety and depression. Mental health professionals believe this is a consequence both of the vulnerabilities intrinsic to the _____ assigned to women and of the _____ with which many modern women must cope as their traditional roles rapidly change. (pp. 112-113)

98. Periods of extensive unemployment are typically accompanied by adverse effects on mental and physical health. In particular, rates of _____, _____, and _____ complaints increase during periods of unemployment, but usually normalize following reemployment. (p. 113)

99. In one prospective study, all the children born on Kauai, Hawaii, in 1955 were followed until age 18. One of the best predictors distinguishing children (especially boys) who experienced significant problems with mental health or delinquency was whether _____. (p. 113)

◊ SUMMARY CHART OF EGO DEFENSE MECHANISMS

Place the ego defense mechanisms in the appropriate blanks in the following chart: (Highlight 3.3, p. 80)

sublimation	**reaction formation**
acting out	**displacement**
denial of reality	**intellectualization**
fantasy	**undoing**
repression	**regression**
rationalization	**identification**
projection	**splitting**

Ego Defense Mechanism	Example
_____	a. A student explains to the teacher why he or she has neglected studies for cultural pursuits.
_____	b. An office worker goes home and is unreasonably angry with his or her family after being criticized.
_____	c. A prisoner scheduled to be executed says, "So they'll kill me, and that's that."
_____	d. "Conquering hero" and "suffering hero" are two common patterns.
_____	e. A child reverts to bedwetting when the new baby comes home.
_____	f. A student fails an examination and believes the teacher is to blame.
_____	g. College grads are terribly upset if their college doesn't have a winning team
_____	h. Terminally ill persons go through a stage where they refuse to believe they are dying.
_____	i. A soldier develops amnesia after seeing a friend killed.
_____	j. People become zealous crusaders, often referred to as the "reformed sinner syndrome."
_____	k. A woman in love spends all of her time creating a sculpture for the man she loves, but she never expresses this to him.
_____	l. Wilma Rudolph, crippled and unable to walk until she is eight years old, becomes an Olympic track winner.
_____	m. A man does not recognize the individual qualities of women. Instead, he views them as angels or whores.
_____	n. Unhappy at work, a person cheats on his or her spouse.

◊ CRITICAL THINKING ABOUT DIFFICULT TOPICS

1. Your text states that the belief that biochemical imbalances in the brain can result in abnormal behavior is one of the basic tenets of the biological perspective today (p. 69). It also describes the medical model, which relies heavily on the biological perspective, as in its extreme form using a strictly categorical approach to psychopathology (p. 68). At the same time, it is highly likely that there are naturally-occurring individual differences in each of the many aspects of neuronal functioning. For example, some individuals may naturally produce a larger quantity of a given neurotransmitter that is secreted into the synaptic cleft, others may deactivate this transmitter less well in the synaptic cleft, and still others may show greater receptor reactivity to a given amount of neurotransmitter. Given that such differences in neurotransmitter activity will have significant effects on behavior, temperament theorists will see individual differences of this type as the basis of the genetic influences on temperament (see pp.71, 75). Consider for yourself the difference between a disease model approach that emphasizes present-versus-absent categories and the temperament approach that views these differences as continuously distributed normal variations in brain functioning. In coming to an answer, you should see that there are two ways to invoke biological processes in understanding psychopathology. One, the medical model, expects a complete dysfunction (disease) that is either present or absent and makes no distinctions within normal functioning (i.e., when the disease is absent). The other, the temperament model, expects normal variation in brain functioning to affect the development of normal temperament and personality, but also sees these differences as risk factors for psychopathology. For example, individuals with a fearful or behaviorally inhibited temperament are at greater risk of developing anxiety disorders (p. 75), but the initial individual differences in brain functioning do not constitute a disease (see Gorenstein's criticism of the "biology equals disease" view, p. 78).

2. Referring to family history, twin, and adoption methods for studying genetic influences, the text says that "although each of these methods alone has its pitfalls of interpretation, if the results from using all three strategies converge, one can draw reasonably strong conclusions about the genetic influence on a disorder" (p. 73). List the weaknesses of each method taken alone and explain why convergence across these methods eliminates alternative interpretations.

3. Some behavior geneticists argue that one's genotype defines a *reaction range* of phenotypic outcomes. For example, in the case of IQ one genotype might restrict phenotypic IQ to the range from IQ = 70 to IQ = 105, whereas another genotype might restrict potential IQs to a range from 90 to 130. An intellectually stimulating environment will facilitate the development of a phenotypic IQ in the upper portion of the range for that person, whereas an unstimulating environment will tend to produce a phenotypic IQ in the lower portion of the individual's range. Highlight 3.2 (p. 74) reported that children born to socially disadvantaged parents who were adopted and reared with socially advantaged parents showed a mean IQ about 12 points higher than those children reared in the socially disadvantaged environment. How is this reaction range model consistent with such an adoptive effect on IQ and, at the same time, with the possibility that the differences in IQ between the biological and adoptive parents were attributable in part to genetic factors? If the parental IQ differences were, in fact, partially attributable to genetic influences, what would you expect to find if the IQs of the adopted children were compared with the IQs of biological children of the adoptive parents?

4. In Freud's concept of the Electra complex (p. 81) girls are said to be envious of males. The text (pp. 83, 92-93) mentions that Freudian theory has been criticized for its demeaning view of women. Consider two possible explanations for the negative Freudian view of females as embodied in the theory of the Electra complex. The traditional--and most likely--explanation is that the theory is simply one generated by men in a form that is flattering to males. In this explanation, the cultural context of having mostly male psychoanalysts, combined with a naturally self-serving bias in human beliefs, accounts for the negative view of females. A second possibility is that any disadvantaged group (in this case, women) will be envious of aspects of the dominant, powerful, and privileged group (in this case, males). From this perspective, it may be that Freud did find that female patients were envious of males, but that their reactions reflected male-dominated societal conditions rather than a universal developmental stage. According to this explanation, had Freud been living in a matriarchal society, he would have "discovered" that males were envious of women's ability to bear children and of other salient characteristics of women (e.g., breasts). Note that Malinowski found little evidence of Oedipal conflict among Trobriand Islanders, who do not live in a patriarchal family structure (p. 107), suggesting that Freud's findings were culture-bound.

5. In discussing the cognitive or cognitive-behavioral tradition, it is customary to contrast this tradition with the behavioral emphasis on overt behavior (e.g., pp. 87-89) in a mechanistic fashion (p. 87). Notice, however, that as time has passed even the behavioral tradition has become more cognitive: in classical conditioning "animals (and people) actively *acquire information* about what CSs allow them to predict, expect, or prepare for a biologically significant event (the US)" (p. 84, italics added) and in instrumental or operant conditioning "it is now believed that the person learns a *response-outcome expectancy*" (p. 84). Considering that even in these most basic behavioral paradigms the organism is theorized to

acquire information and to learn expectancies, how cognitive is the behavioral tradition? On the other hand, due to the presence of language in humans, what differences would you expect from a tradition that focuses largely on studies with non-human animals (classical and operant conditioning, learning theory) versus humans in psychotherapy (the cognitive-behavioral tradition in clinical psychology)?

◊ CHAPTER 3 QUIZ

Circle the best of the four answers provided and check them according to answers provided at the back of this study guide. Be sure you understand why each answer is correct.

1. A factor that increases the probability of developing a disorder without being either necessary or sufficient is a _____ cause. (p. 64)
   a. distal
   b. proximal
   c. reinforcing
   d. contributory

2. The specialized structure on the postsynaptic neuron at which the neurotransmitter exerts its effect is the _____. (Highlight 3.1, p. 70)
   a. synaptic cleft
   b. synaptic vesicle
   c. receptor site
   d. enzyme

3. After being released into the synaptic cleft, the neurotransmitter substance may be reabsorbed into the presynaptic axon button, a process called _____. (p. 69)
   a. re-uptake
   b. deactivation
   c. recapture
   d. active transport

4. In genetic studies the subject, or carrier, of the trait or disorder in question who serves as the starting point is known as the: (p. 72)
   a. proband.
   b. zygote.
   c. risk person.
   d. initiation point.

5. In studies of newborns the ways in which they react to different stimuli are called _____ _____, which are one component of temperament. (p. 75)
   a. fundamental reaction styles
   b. biological predispositions
   c. primary reaction tendencies
   d. stable reaction patterns

6. According to Freud's psychoanalytic perspective, the source of all instinctual drives is the: (p. 79)
   a. ego.   c. libido.
   b. id.   d. superego.

7. Which type of anxiety is a signal to the ego that the id's unacceptable impulse is threatening to break out? (p. 79)
   a. reality anxiety   c. moral anxiety
   b. neurotic anxiety   d. free-floating anxiety

8. Margaret Mahler focused on the process by which children come to understand that they are different from other objects. This process involves a developmental phase called: (p. 82)
   a. assimilation-accommodation.   c. introversion-extroversion.
   b. introjection-identification.   d. separation-individuation.

9. The form of learning where an individual learns to achieve a desired goal is: (p. 84)
   a. classical conditioning.   c. modeling.
   b. operant conditioning.   d. avoidance conditioning.

10. The ability to discriminate may be brought about by: (p. 85)
   a. classical conditioning.   c. differential reinforcement.
   b. shaping.   d. avoidance conditioning.

11. The behavioristic tradition has been criticized for: (p. 85)
   a. its precision and objectivity.   c. its failure to demonstrate effectiveness.
   b. its research orientation.   d. its overconcern with symptoms.

12. The major impact of the humanistic perspective on our views of psychopathology is its emphasis on: (p. 92)
   a. building one's courage to face frustration.
   b. moving people from maladjustment to adjustment.
   c. our capacity for full functioning as human beings.
   d. replacing negative self-talk with positive self-cognitions.

13. Harry Stack Sullivan noted that we sometimes screen out of consciousness some especially frightening aspect of our self-experience and perceive it as: (pp. 93-94)
   a. "bad me".   c. "not me".
   b. "good me".   d. "vulnerable me".

14. A basic goal of psychosocial therapies is _____. (p. 96)
    a. accommodation
    b. social skills training
    c. reduction of anxiety
    d. assimilation

15. Instead of Freud's concept of fixation at the oral stage of development, Erikson proposed that parental deprivation might interfere with the development of _____. (p. 98)
    a. high self-esteem
    b. tolerance for stimulation
    c. self-control
    d. basic trust

16. Bowlby found that when young children were separated from their parents during prolonged periods of hospitalization, their reaction upon reunion was: (p. 100)
    a. strong dependence.
    b. detachment.
    c. joy.
    d. anger.

17. A _____ parental style is likely to produce a child who is impulsive and aggressive, spoiled, selfish, inconsiderate, and demanding and who will exploit people for his/her own purposes. (pp. 102-103)
    a. authoritative
    b. authoritarian
    c. permissive-indulgent
    d. neglecting-uninvolved

18. Which of the following was *not* proposed as a strong factor in popularity among juveniles? (p. 105)
    a. parents' income
    b. intelligence
    c. being seen as friendly and outgoing
    d. physical attractiveness

19. Research by Malinowski and Benedict concluded that what is considered abnormal in one society may be considered normal in another. This led to a(an) _____ position concerning abnormal behavior. (p. 107)
    a. cultural relativism
    b. genetic transmission
    c. racial separatist
    d. universalized

20. Epidemiological studies that have linked psychopathology with social class are: (p. 111)
    a. based on controlled experimentation.
    b. correlational in nature.
    c. establishing a clear-cut cause-effect relationship.
    d. good examples of analogue studies.

21. According to the authors, the problematic proliferation of diverse viewpoints about psychopathology can best be solved by: (p. 114)
    a. adhering to a single point of view for consistency's sake.
    b. becoming an eclectic.
    c. developing a unified point of view.
    d. divorcing oneself from all major perspectives.

Chapter 4
Stress and Adjustment Disorders

◊ OVERVIEW

The chapter begins with a detailed discussion of stress, a topic of increasing concern as modern life becomes more and more pressured. An understanding of the potential sources of stress, the functional equivalence of biological, psychological, and sociocultural sources of stress, and the general strategies for coping with stressful demands is probably the single most relevant topic to the average person that is presented in this text. The reactions of individuals to war, concentration camps, and civilian disasters are described and can be viewed as case studies of human functioning under levels of severe stress. The chapter describes the coping techniques used by individuals in these situations and the symptoms that appear as coping techniques fail to eliminate the stress--leading in many cases to adjustment disorders. It will seem unbelievable when reading about some of the incidents that there were *any* people who could cope without developing severely abnormal behavior. The practical implications of this chapter are seen in applications such as preparing people to cope more effectively when they are about to face stressful situations (e.g., surgery).

◊ LEARNING OBJECTIVES

After studying this chapter, you should be able to:

1. Define the concepts of stressor, stress, and coping, describe the basic categories of stressors, and discuss factors that increase or decrease a person's vulnerability to stress. (pp. 119-126)

2. Contrast the two major categories of coping responses and outline the numerous negative consequences of a failure to cope successfully. (pp. 126-131)

3. Characterize the DSM-IV diagnosis of adjustment disorder and describe three major stressors and the consequences that increase the risk of adjustment disorder. (pp. 131-134)

4. List the diagnostic criteria for acute stress disorder and posttraumatic stress disorder and summarize what is known about the major features of reactions to catastrophic events. (pp. 135-138)

5. Identify the factors that influence the effects of rape on the victim and describe the typical immediate and long-term consequences of rape. (pp. 138-140)

6. Characterize the phenomenon of combat exhaustion and of posttraumatic stress disorder in connection with battlefield stress, outline the factors that appear to influence these reactions, and describe the long-term effects of PTSD. (pp. 140-145)

7. List and illustrate the long-term effects of being a prisoner of war or in a concentration camp and note the methodological problems associated with biased sampling. (pp. 145-147).

8. Describe the psychological problems associated with being tortured and with being a refugee. (pp. 147-150)

9. Summarize the approaches that have been used to treat or to prevent stress disorders and evaluate their effectiveness. (pp. 150-153)

10. Evaluate the pros and cons of using PTSD as a defense in criminal court cases or as a basis of requesting compensation in civil court cases. (p. 153-154)

◊ TERMS YOU SHOULD KNOW

---

stress (p. 120)

stressor (p. 120)

eustress (p. 120)

distress (p. 120)

frustration (p. 120)

conflict (p. 120)

posttraumatic stress disorder (pp. 134-135)

disaster syndrome (p. 135-136)

shock stage (p. 135)

suggestible stage (pp. 135-136)

recovery stage (p. 136)

combat exhaustion (pp. 140-141)

stress inoculation training (p. 152)

direct therapeutic exposure (p. 153)

◊ NAMES YOU SHOULD KNOW

Hans Selye (pp. 120, 128-130; Highlight 4.2, p. 129)

Scott Monroe (pp. 123, 125)

George Brown (p. 125)

◊ CONCEPTS TO MASTER

---

1. Compare and contrast the concepts of stressors, stresses, and coping strategies, noting particularly the interrelation among them. (p. 120)

2. Describe and illustrate three basic categories of stressors. (pp. 120-122).

3. Define an approach-avoidance conflict and list several examples from your own experience. (p. 120)

4. Differentiate between *chronic* and *acute* life stressors. (pp. 122, 124)

5. The concept of a stressful environment requires attempts to quantify the degree of stress. How did Holmes and his colleagues attempt to measure the cumulative stress associated with life events? What did they find happens as environmental stressfulness increases? (p. 125)

6. Life stress scales are a method to measure the number of life changes currently active in a person's life. Research on life events has been extensive, but the methodology employed in life stress scales has been severely criticized by Monroe and others. Summarize these limitations of life events measurements. (p. 125)

7. Differentiate between *task-oriented* and *defense-oriented* reactions to stress, and describe two ego-defense mechanisms that are examples of the latter. (pp. 127-128)

8. List three stages of the "disaster syndrome," indicate at which stage posttraumatic stress disorder may develop, and identify the three intense emotions that may complicate the picture. (pp. 135-136)

9. In the context of predicting who will develop posttraumatic stress disorder in response to traumas of varying severity, compare and contrast the views of Clark, Watson, & Mineka with those of McFarlane. (p. 138)

10. List the four stages of the coping behavior of rape victims and summarize the major features of each stage. (pp. 139-140)

11. Trace the evolution of the concept of combat exhaustion from World War I to the present. (pp. 140-141)

12. The twin methodology has been used extensively to examine genetic influences on psychopathology. How was it used by Goldberg et al. to demonstrate strong environmental effects on the etiology of PTSD and what were the results of this application? (pp. 141-142)

13. In spite of variations in experience, the general clinical picture of combat stress has been surprisingly uniform for those soldiers who develop it. Describe this common clinical picture, the effects of intermittent versus prolonged periods of shelling, the emotional components of PTSD, and the differences seen between soldiers hospitalized for wounds versus psychiatric problems. (pp. 142-143)

14. What is meant by the concept of *delayed* posttraumatic stress? How severe are the stresses associated with the onset of symptoms? (p. 145)

15. Explain how the concept of a representative versus a biased sample is critically important in evaluating the long-term pathogenic effects of the concentration camp experience. (pp. 146-147).

16. What is meant by a "dose-response effect" for psychological problems among disaster assistance workers? (p. 150)

17. Summarize Janis' research on psychologically preparing patients to undergo dangerous surgery with particular emphasis on the concept of the "work of worrying." (p. 152)

18. Describe a three-stage type of stress inoculation used by cognitive-behavioral therapists. (p. 152)

19. What is "direct therapeutic exposure," when is it used, and what traditional behavior therapy methods may be used in conjunction with it? (p. 153)

20. Describe ways in which the posttraumatic stress syndrome has been used in both criminal and civil court cases. (pp. 153-154)

◊ STUDY QUESTIONS

Stress and stressors

1. Adjustive demands, also known as _____, create effects within an organism that are known as stress. (p. 120)

2. The following is a list of types of stressors. Match each type with the example that correctly illustrates it. (pp. 120-121)

Example	Type of Stressor
_____	1. Frustration (p. 120)
_____	2. Approach-avoidance conflict (p. 120)

_____   3. Double-approach conflict (p. 121)

_____   4. Double-avoidance conflict (p. 121)

_____   5. Pressures (p. 121)

Example

a. A "mixed blessing dilemma" in which some positive and negative features must be accepted, no matter what the decision--such as an African-American judge who is offered a membership in a discriminatory club.

b. A plus-plus conflict, choosing between two desirable alternatives, such as deciding between a trip to Las Vegas or Reno.

c. Finals week with a part-time job, studying, and social obligations.

d. Finding out that the women's basketball team must travel four to a room, but the men's team has only two per room.

e. A minus-minus conflict, choosing between two undesirable alternatives such as being given the choice to go on a diet or die.

Factors influencing the severity of stress

3. How is the severity of stress gauged or measured? (p. 122)

4. The nature of the stressor is known to influence the degree of disruption that occurs. This impact, in turn, depends on many factors, such as the _____ of the stressor to the person, the _____ of the stress, the _____ of the stressors in the person's life, and whether or not the stressor is seen by the person as within or outside his or her own _____. (p. 122)

5. The severity of disruption experienced in response to a stressor is related to the individual's perception of the stressor, stress tolerance, and external resources and support. Indicate whether severe or minimal disruption may be expected under the following circumstances:

a. New adjustive demands that have not been anticipated by the individual and for which no ready-made coping patterns are available. (p. 123)

b. Adjustive demands placed upon a person with marginal previous adjustment. (p. 123)

c. Adjustive demands confronted by a person with a supportive spouse, close extended family, and strong religious traditions. (pp. 123-124)

Intense stress and the experience of crisis

6. Why are "crises" especially stressful? (p. 124)

7. How can the outcome of a crisis affect a person's subsequent adjustment? (pp. 124-125)

General principles of coping with stress

8. Place the following reactions to stress in the appropriate space to indicate the level at which they operate: (pp. 126-127)

a. Learned coping patterns
b. Immunological defenses against disease
c. Group resources such as religious organizations
d. Self-defenses
e. Damage-repair mechanisms
f. Support from family and friends

Levels of Coping	Reactions to Stress
Biological level	1. _____
	2. _____
Psychological-interpersonal level	1. _____
	2. _____
	3. _____

Sociocultural level   1. _____

9. What are the two challenges with which a person is confronted in coping with stress? (p. 127)

Defense-oriented reaction patterns

10. Two types of defense mechanisms are described in the text. What are they? (p. 127)

    1. _____ mechanisms such as crying and repetitive talking.

    2. _____ or _____ mechanisms that function to relieve anxiety.

11. In what three ways do defense mechanisms protect the individual from both internal and external threats? (p. 127)

    a.

    b.

    c.

12. Defense mechanisms are learned, automatic, habitual reactions designed to deal with inner hurt and anxiety. As such they may serve useful self-protective functions, but they can also be maladaptive. When are ego-defense mechanisms considered maladaptive? (p. 128)

13. Stress is a fact of life. However, stress can be damaging. Describe how severe stress:

    a. lowers adaptive efficiency. (p. 128)

    b. depletes adaptive resources and lowers tolerance to other stressors. (p. 128)

    c. causes wear and tear on the organism. (p. 128)

14. Davidson and Baum (1986) studied the effects of stress over a five-year period among residents at Three Mile Island and in a control community. Describe their findings. (p. 128)

15. Personality decompensation under extreme stress appears to follow a course resembling biological decompensation, which consists of three stages: alarm and mobilization, resistance, exhaustion and disintegration. Provide the missing information below that describes the behavior of the individual during each stage. (pp. 128-130)

Stage	Behavior of Organism
Alarm and mobilization	
Resistance	
Stage of exhaustion	

16. Over the past 20 years a great deal of research has been concerned with the link between stress and physiological changes. Schwartz and Perry conclude that the evidence demonstrates that the alarm reaction initiates a cascade of cellular and molecular processes that _____ to create an adaptive record of survival-related information. (p. 130)

17. Numerous studies have suggested that stress associated with grief, separation and divorce, and examination stress may produce changes in the _____ system that could affect health. (pp. 130-131)

Adjustment disorder: Reactions to common life stressors

18. The DSM-IV provides for the rating of current stress on Axis IV. In addition, it contains three relevant diagnostic categories: adjustment disorder, acute stress disorder, and posttraumatic stress disorder. All three of these disorders occur in response to identifiable stressors. What are the dimensions along which they differ? (p. 131)

19. List the different stressors associated with adjustment disorders versus posttraumatic stress disorders and indicate the way in which the two groups of stressors differ. (pp. 131, 134-135)

20. The impact of chronic unemployment on a person's _____, _____, and feeling of belongingness is shattering. (p. 132)

21. Often the first reaction to death of a loved one is _____. Then feelings of _____ frequently overwhelm us. (p. 133)

22. What is the upper limit of the duration of the normal grieving process and what factors associated with a death often lead to complicated or prolonged bereavement? (p. 133).

23. Many factors make a divorce or separation unpleasant and stressful for everyone concerned. List some of these factors. (p. 134)

24. What is the salient characteristic of the stressor associated with posttraumatic stress disorder? (pp. 134-135)

25. Give specific examples of symptoms for the first three and the fifth general symptom categories that typify posttraumatic stress disorder and list the fourth symptom category. (p. 135)

    a. Persistent reexperiencing of the traumatic event
       Example:

    b. Individual avoids stimuli associated with the trauma
       Example:

    c. Persistent symptoms of increased arousal
       Example:

    d.

    e. Feelings of depression
       Example:

26. What feature distinguishes between acute stress disorder and posttraumatic stress disorder? (p. 135)

27. What feature distinguishes between acute versus delayed posttraumatic stress disorder? (p. 135)

28. Over half of the survivors of the disastrous Coconut Grove nightclub fire required treatment for psychological shock. All of the survivors of the collision of two jet planes on Santa Cruz de Tenerife Island suffered from serious emotional problems. A "disaster syndrome" has been observed among victims that has been divided into three stages. Fill in the following chart with the behavior that is typical of each stage. (pp. 135-136)

Stage	Behavior Observed
Shock stage	
Suggestible stage	
Recovery stage	

29. Shore, Vollmer, and Tatum found the prevalence rates for posttraumatic stress reaction to be _____ percent for both men and women in the general population. However, a recent review by Rubonis and Bickman concluded that _____ percent of individuals who had experienced disasters showed psychological adjustment problems. (p. 137)

30. A general population survey by Breslau et al. found that _____ Americans have been exposed to significant traumatic events before the age of 30 and _____% of young adults meet the diagnostic criteria for PTSD. (pp. 137-138)

31. Women are said to be especially vulnerable to victimization. What is the evidence for this statement (as reported by Resnick et al.) with respect to rates of traumatic events, including crime, sexual assault, and multiple incidents? (p. 138)

32. Discuss how each of the following variables are thought to affect a woman's response to rape: (pp. 138-139)

    a. Relationship to the offender

    b. Age

    c. Marital status

33. With respect to long-term effects, comparisons of women who have been raped with those who have not generally find _____ in overall psychological adjustment. (p. 140)

Traumatic reactions to military combat

34. According to the government figures presented in your text, the percent of soldiers who suffered combat exhaustion decreased in each successive war from World War II to Vietnam. According to government claims, _____ percent of soldiers experienced combat exhaustion in Vietnam. (p. 141)

35. What are the reasons given to account for the decreases in the number of soldiers who experienced combat exhaustion in Vietnam? (p. 141)

36. How did the results of two studies in Israel strongly support the conclusion that levels of anxiety (and depression, in one case) among civilians were related to exposure to SCUD missile attacks? (p. 142)

37. Laufer, Brett, and Gallops (1985) surveyed 251 Vietnam veterans who varied in combat exposure. Having participated in abusive violence was found to be correlated with what symptoms? (p. 142)

38. What are usually the first symptoms of combat exhaustion (combat stress)? (pp. 142-143)

39. In terms of biological factors, constitutional differences probably do affect a soldier's resistance to combat, but we have more information about the conditions of battle that tax a soldier's _____. (p. 143)

40. What did Merbaum and Hefez (1976) find about the role of previous psychological adjustment in determining a soldier's vulnerability to combat exhaustion? (p. 144)

41. Clarity and acceptability of war goals, identification with the combat unit, esprit de corps, and quality of leadership are sociocultural factors that play an important part in determining a person's adjustment to combat. Describe how each of these has an effect. (p. 144).

42. DeFazio, Rustin, and Diamond found that there are residual, or long-lasting, effects of stress. Complete this list of the six most common complaints of combat veterans, which were reported twice as often compared with noncombat veterans: (p. 145)
   a.
   b. quick temper
   c.
   d.
   e. difficulties with emotional closeness
   f. quick fatigue

43. What is controversial about assessments of the frequency of diagnosis of delayed posttraumatic stress disorder? (p. 145)

The trauma of incarceration

44. Medical problems are commonly seen in those incarcerated in POW or concentration camps. About _____ of the American prisoners in Japanese POW camps during WWII died during imprisonment and an even higher number of prisoners of Nazi concentration camps died. Interpretation of seemingly psychological symptoms among survivors of Nazi concentration camps is problematic because they may be attributed to biological stressors, such as _____, _____, and serious infectious diseases. (p. 145)

45. What is the "re-entry" problem for former POWs and concentration camp survivors? (p. 145)

46. In a two-year follow-up of a representative sample of Vietnam War POWs, O'Connell found that the _____, the more likely a person was to develop psychiatric problems and that _____ and _____ while captured predisposed people to later problems. (p. 146)

The trauma of torture

47. List and illustrate the array of psychological symptoms experienced after torture. (Highlight 4.4, p. 149)

48. In the study of 55 former Turkish political prisoners who were tortured, what two variables were found by Basoglu & Mineka to have an important impact on the severity of the consequences of torture? (Highlight 4.4, p. 149)

The trauma of forced relocation

49. Refugees face not only the trauma of being uprooted from their home, but also the stress of adapting to a new and unfamiliar culture. Among those who come to the U. S., the Southeast Asians arriving after 1975 have had the most difficult adjustment. A ten-year longitudinal study of Hmong refugees from Laos found many signs of improvement after ten years in the U.S.: 55% were employed, the percentage on welfare dropped from 53% to 29%, and

symptoms of phobia, somatization, and low self-esteem had also improved. On the other hand, considerable problems remained. What were these? (p. 150)

◊ CRITICAL THINKING ABOUT DIFFICULT TOPICS

1. The text says that the concept of stressors refers to "adjustive demands" and that "all situations, positive and negative, that require adjustment can be stressful" (p. 120). Thus, such events as getting married, being promoted to a better position, graduating from college, and starting a new and attractive job all constitute positive stress or eustress, as opposed to negative stress or distress. Do you think such positive stressors are as pathogenic as negative stressors--e.g., contributing to the onset of depression, ulcers, etc.? Can you imagine a new marriage or a new job having negative consequences without first developing a component of negative stress (e.g., interpersonal conflict in the marriage, inability to cope with new obligations in the job)?

2. Chapter 3 focused on the diathesis portion of the diathesis-stress model, whereas this chapter focuses on "the role of stress as a precipitating causal factor" (p. 119). Psychiatrists with a strong biological orientation are skeptical about the contribution of stress, arguing that the person's stress response reflects greater vulnerability more than the external, objective features of the stressor. Psychologists, in contrast, want to provide unequivocal evidence of the causal contribution of external stressors. The problem arises because, as the text states, often "the severity of stress is gauged by the degree to which it disrupts functioning" (p. 122). The text then goes on to emphasize the importance of "person characteristics" in determining the severity of the stress response. These person characteristics include such factors as the importance of the stressor to a person, the cumulative effect of stressors (which might be secondary to whether or not the person copes adequately with the stressors), chronic difficult life situations (to which the person's personality might contribute), the person's perception of threat and tolerance of stress, and overall vulnerability to stress (pp. 122-123). All of these

100

factors point to the confounding of these person characteristics with the magnitude of the stress response and the degree to which the stressor disrupts functioning. This perspective is summed up in the statement that "However great a challenge, it creates little stress if a person can easily handle it" (p. 124). In view of this methodological difficulty, how would you prove to a skeptic that the external, objective stress designated in the diathesis-stress model does, in fact, act as a causal factor in the etiology of abnormal behavior? How could you assess the severity of stress without using the degree to which it disrupts functioning?

3. In the previous chapter, biological influences on abnormal behavior and on temperament were emphasized. An important theme of the present chapter is that psychological events in the form of stressors produce physiological changes that contribute to the onset of illness (e.g., heart disease and cancer, p. 130) and *even alter brain structure and function* (p. 130). How does this finding alter the interpretation of biological influences on abnormal behavior and temperament and of the origin of individual differences in biological influences?

4. The text states that in the case of delayed posttraumatic stress disorder "the frequency with which this disorder has recently been diagnosed in some settings suggests that its increased use is as much a result of its plausibility and popularity as of its true incidence" (p. 145). If this assertion is true, what does it tell you about the validity of diagnosis? If a diagnosis can be influenced so strongly by plausibility and popularity, should we view diagnoses with a bit of skepticism?

5. The evidence supporting the relationship between stress and psychopathology is "so substantial that the role of stressors in symptom development is now formally emphasized in diagnostic formulations" in DSM-IV (p. 131). Why did it take very strong evidence to incorporate such a plausible notion in the DSM? In thinking about this problem, consider that (a) the DSM largely reflects psychiatric thinking strongly influenced by the disease model and (b) in the disease model the source of the psychopathology is inside the person, not in the environment. When events such as bereavement over the death of a spouse or anxiety during battlefield conditions elicit emotional problems in a large minority of the population, does it seem right to refer to these individuals as having a psychiatric "disorder"? If not, what does this attitude imply about the cause of psychiatric disorders? Note that even though bereavement often produces the full symptom syndrome of a depressive disorder, DSM-IV excludes the diagnosis of depressive disorder.

6. Developing the point in question 5 further, the text notes that PTSD "bears such a close relationship to the experience of stress" (p. 135) that it is covered in this chapter (on stress) rather than in the chapter on anxiety disorders--implying that stress is a less obvious contributor to other anxiety disorders. What implicit model would allow you to conceptualize this distinction? In finding an answer, think about the concept of underlying liability for a

disorder and a threshold (or "breaking point" as mentioned on page 138) for appearance of symptoms. For example, in arbitrary units, it might take 100 points of liability to reach threshold for developing an anxiety disorder. If both diathesis and stress combine additively to produce total liability, what happens as one of these variables becomes more severe? In the case of the severe traumas reviewed in the present chapter (rape, battlefield stress, incarceration, being held hostage, and forced relocation) would it require less diathesis to reach threshold--e.g., if these potent environmental factors contributed 80 points of liability? In the absence of major stressors, would it take a lot of diathesis to reach threshold? (See the discussion of the contribution of personality factors citing the work of Clark, Watson, & Mineka and of Ursano, Bodystun, & Wheatley on page 138 for a clear statement of this model.) Does this model account for the greater knowledge of environmental factors than of personal characteristics in PTSD (p. 143)? How does this model affect your understanding of the concept of a psychiatric "disorder"? What would you do with intermediate cases, in which the diathesis and the stress each contribute equally?

◊ CHAPTER 4 QUIZ

Circle the best of the four answers provided and check them according to answers provided at the back of this study guide. Be sure you understand why each answer is correct.

1. A wedding is likely to cause which of the following? (p. 120)
   a. distress
   b. stress
   c. stressor
   d. eustress

2. Working at a job that was unfulfilling would probably lead to feelings of: (p. 120)
   a. conflict.
   b. frustration.
   c. pressure.
   d. defensiveness.

3. A person wants to accept a party invitation because he/she is very social but is concerned because there will be a lot of drinking and he/she is a member of AA (Alcoholics Anonymous). He/she is experiencing a(an): (pp. 120-121)
   a. mixed blessing dilemma.
   b. approach-avoidance conflict.
   c. double-avoidance conflict.
   d. double-approach conflict.

4. Life stress scales have been severely criticized by Monroe (and others) for numerous methodological problems. Which of the following was *not* one of his criticisms? (p. 125)
   a. the subjectivity of the scoring
   b. failure to take into account the relevance of items for the populations studied
   c. they do not assess specific types of disorders
   d. they measure reactions to specific environmental events

5. Which of the following defense-oriented behaviors is of the damage-repair type? (p. 127)
   a. denying   c. mourning
   b. intellectualizing   d. repressing

6. When we are faced with a stressor, we need to do two things. One thing is meet the requirements of the stressor, and the other is to: (p. 127)
   a. protect the self from damage and disorganization.
   b. change the way we think about the problem.
   c. protect the self from defense-oriented response.
   d. make sure that we do not face a stressor again.

7. When coping resources are already mobilized against one stressor, they are: (pp. 128)
   a. made stronger for coping with others.
   b. less available for coping with others.
   c. shifted immediately to the new stressors.
   d. unaffected by additional stressors.

8. In studying the effects of the nuclear incident at Three Mile Island, Davidson and Baum found even five years later a higher incidence (when compared to a control community) of: (p. 128)
   a. gastric ulcers.
   b. duodenal ulcers.
   c. elevated levels of urinary norepinephrine.
   d. posttraumatic stress disorder.

9. The alarm and mobilization stage of personality decompensation under excessive stress is characterized by: (p. 129)
   a. emotional arousal, increased tension, and greater alertness.
   b. exaggerated and inappropriate defense measures.
   c. lowering of integration.
   d. rigidity as the individual clings to accustomed defenses.

10. The normal grieving process in bereavement should last no longer than about: (p. 133)
    a. 4 months.   c. 12 months.
    b. 8 months.   d. 18 months.

11. Resnick et al. found high rates of traumatic events among women, suggesting that they are especially vulnerable to victimization. Which of the following was *not* found in their survey? (p. 138)
    a. One-fourth were abandoned by husbands with no support for their children
    b. 69% experienced at least one type of traumatic event
    c. One-third reported a crime such as physical or sexual assault
    d. Over 50% experienced multiple incidents

12. Which of the following is *not* a phase in the coping response of rape victims? (p. 139)
    a. anticipatory phase   c. posttraumatic recoil phase
    b. shock phase   d. reconstitution phase

13. In a study of 251 Vietnam veterans in 1985, Laufer, Brett, and Gallops concluded that the *most severe* psychopathology developed in those who: (p. 142)
    a. participated in abusive violence in combat.
    b. suffered debilitating physical injuries.
    c. were exposed to abusive violence in combat.
    d. were exposed to combat.

14. Which of the following causes of combat stress do we know the most about? (p. 143)
    a. constitutional differences in sensitivity
    b. differences in temperament
    c. differences in vigor
    d. the conditions of battle that tax a soldier's stamina

15. In a 1975 study of Vietnam veterans who were making a satisfactory readjustment to civilian life, DeFazio, Rustin, and Diamond found that the *most frequently* reported symptom was: (p. 145)
    a. difficulties with emotional closeness.
    b. frequent nightmares.
    c. many fears.
    d. worries about employment.

16. Why is it difficult to explicitly relate delayed cases of stress syndrome to combat stress? (p. 145)
    a. The biological effects will be gone
    b. Clinicians could not do anything anyway
    c. The psychological effects are not substantial
    d. There might be other adjustment problems involved

17. Definitively proving the existence of PTSD to the satisfaction of the legal system: (p. 154)
    a. would be scientifically unethical.
    b. is exceedingly difficult.
    c. has already been accomplished.
    d. will never be accomplished.

◊ OVERVIEW

This chapter covers several behavior patterns that had, in the past, been called *neuroses*. In keeping with the descriptive approach of DSM-IV, the behavioral problems grouped together as anxiety disorders all have in common an obvious contribution of anxiety--either as the prominent presenting symptom, as in generalized anxiety disorder, or as an easily elicited reaction--e.g., when phobic avoidance or compulsive behaviors are blocked. These disorders are usually of mild to moderate intensity. In most cases, the disorders are episodic in nature with dramatic symptoms occurring only during periods of high stress. However, between flare-ups of symptoms, these individuals are less happy and less effective than they could be if they learned more appropriate coping behavior. Individuals with these disorders usually respond well to psychotherapy or behavior therapy and rarely require hospitalization. The chapter contains a detailed description of the clinical picture, causal pattern, and treatment of anxiety disorders.

◊ LEARNING OBJECTIVES

After studying this chapter, you should be able to:

1. Compare and evaluate the merits of Freud's use of the concept of anxiety in the etiology of the neuroses versus the descriptive approach used in DSM since 1980. (pp. 157-158)

2. Distinguish between fear and anxiety. (pp. 158-159)

3. Describe the major features of phobias, identify and differentiate different subtypes of phobia, and explicate the major etiological hypotheses. (pp. 160-168)

4. List the diagnostic criteria for panic disorder, contrast panic attacks and other types of anxiety, explain the association with agoraphobia, and summarize the major developments over the last 15 years in theories of etiology. (pp. 168-176)

5. Summarize the central features of generalized anxiety disorder, distinguish among psychoanalytic, conditioning, and cognitive theories of etiology, and identify the central nervous system processes and structures associated with this type of anxiety. (pp. 176-182)

6. Describe the defining features of obsessive-compulsive disorder, summarize theories of etiology along with supporting evidence (or the lack thereof), and outline the treatment of OCD with exposure and response prevention techniques. (pp. 182-189)

7. Provide several examples of sociocultural effects on anxiety disorders. (pp. 189-190)

8. Critically evaluate the relative merits of biological and psychological treatments for anxiety disorders. (pp. 190-194)

◊ **TERMS YOU SHOULD KNOW**

---

neurotic behavior (p. 157)

neurosis (p. 157)

anxiety (p. 157)

anxious apprehension (pp. 158, 176)

fight or flight response (pp. 158, 160)

anxiety disorder (p. 159)

phobia (p. 160)

specific phobia (pp. 160-161)

social phobia (pp. 160, 166)

agoraphobia (pp. 160, 169)

blood-injury phobia (p. 161)

secondary gains (pp. 162-163)

immunization (p. 164)

inflation effect (p. 164)

behaviorally inhibited (p. 165)

preparedness (p. 165)

specific vs. *generalized social phobia* (p. 166)

panic disorder (pp. 168-169)

true alarms vs. *false alarms* (p. 169)

panic provocation agents (p. 172)

kindling (p. 173)

interoceptive fears (pp. 173-174)

interoceptive conditioning (pp. 173-174)

free-floating anxiety (p. 176)

worry (p. 176)

generalized anxiety disorder (pp. 176-177)

safety signals (p. 179)

benzodiazepines (pp. 181, 190)

GABA (p. 181)

obsessive-compulsive disorder (pp. 181-182)

obsession (p. 182)

compulsion (p. 182)

taijin kyofusho (TKS) (pp. 189-190)

tricyclic antidepressants (p. 191)

monoamine oxidase inhibitors (p. 191)

behavior therapy (p. 192)

systematic desensitization (p. 192)

cognitive-behavior therapies (pp. 192-193, Highlight 5.4, p. 194)

interoceptive exposure (p. 193)

multimodal therapy (p. 193)

◊ NAMES YOU SHOULD KNOW

Donald Klein (p. 172)

Martin Seligman (pp. 165, 180)

Arne Öhman (pp. 165-167)

Jeffrey Gray (pp. 158, 165, 169)

David Clark (pp. 168, 174-175)

◊ **CONCEPTS TO MASTER**

1. Freud's overall views on the nature of neurosis have come under attack as too theoretical. In what way is his use of the concept of anxiety to account for neurosis too theoretical? Why has the decision to adopt a different approach in editions of the DSM since 1980 resulted in greater reliability of diagnosis (with subsequent advances in understanding causes and in treatment)? (p. 158)

2. Compare and contrast the concepts of fear or panic, on the one hand, and anxiety, on the other hand. Be sure to note that both emotions involve cognitive/subjective, physiological, and behavioral components and that the emotions differ with respect to the present versus future orientation. (pp. 158-159)

3. Describe the major manifestations of phobias as a class and differentiate specific phobias and social phobias. (pp. 160-161)

4. Describe the classical conditioning hypothesis of the origin of phobias and explain how observational learning, immunization, and preparedness greatly expand the explanatory power of this hypothesis. (pp. 163-166)

5. Contrast the classical conditioning/vicarious conditioning/preparedness theory of the origin of social phobias with that for specific phobias. (pp. 167-168)

6. Explain the importance of a perception of uncontrollability in conditioning models of the acquisition of phobias. (pp. 164, 168)

7. Define panic disorder according to the DSM-IV definition. (pp. 168-169)

8. Differentiate between panic attacks and other types of anxiety in terms of intensity and the time course. (p. 169)

9. Define agoraphobia and explain its close association with panic disorder. (pp. 169-170)

10. How are the locus coeruleus, the limbic system, and the prefrontal cortex involved in the various phenomena of panic disorder? (pp. 172-173, 181)

11. Traditionally a key feature of panic attacks is that they seem to "come out of the blue." Recent evidence, however, suggests that panic attacks are, in fact, triggered by bodily sensations. Compare and contrast the closely related interoceptive conditioning and the cognitive models of panic with respect to the triggering of panic attacks and summarize the extensive evidence supporting the cognitive model. (pp. 173-176)

12. In the diagnosis of generalized anxiety disorder, what symptoms were included in previous DSMs but dropped in DSM-IV and why were they dropped? (p. 176)

13. Describe the attempt to apply a conditioning model to generalized anxiety disorders and indicate why this model has not fared well. Then summarize the more promising cognitive approach emphasizing uncontrollability and unpredictability, including the important study by Mineka et al. with infant rhesus monkeys. (pp. 179-181)

14. What are negative automatic thoughts and what evidence has shown their presence among patients with GAD? (p. 180)

15. What is the effect of being generally anxious on attending to threat cues, interpreting ambiguous information, and memory for threat cues? (p. 180-181)

16. What are benzodiazepines and why are they important in identifying brain structures associated with GAD? (p. 181)

17. Summarize the major manifestations of obsessive-compulsive disorders, and explain *why* they are considered maladaptive. (p. 182-183)

18. Obsessive-compulsive disorder frequently co-occurs with other mood and anxiety disorders and personality disorders. What issues are raised by this extensive co-morbidity? (pp. 183-184)

19. Describe the psychoanalytic theory of OCD and give two reasons why this theory cannot be considered to have any support. (pp. 185-186)

20. Summarize the behavioral view of OCD and explain how it has been revitalized by the addition of the preparedness hypothesis. (p. 186)

21. Compare and contrast the biological treatments for the anxiety disorders with the behavior therapies and the cognitive-behavior therapies. (pp. 190-191, 192-193; Highlight 5.4, p. 194)

Introduction

1. What was the original meaning of the term *neurosis* as introduced by Englishman William Cullen? (p. 157)

2. Later, Freud suggested that neurosis stemmed from intrapsychic conflicts. Complete the missing words in Freud's definition. Neurosis is the outcome of an internal conflict between some _____ _____ and prohibitions against its expression. (p. 157)

3. The DSM classification since 1980 is theoretically neutral and abandons the use of the term neurosis. In its place are three general classes of disorders--one of which is anxiety disorders. List the other two classes. (p. 158)

   a.

   b.

4. Historically, the most common way of distinguishing between fear and anxiety has been whether there is a _____ and _____ source of danger. When the source of danger is _____, the emotion has been called fear. The term anxious apprehension is applied to an unpleasant inner state in which we are _____ some dreadful thing happening that is not predictable from our actual circumstances. (p. 158)

5. Activation of the fight or flight response is associated with the basic emotion of _____ or _____. (p. 158)

6. The basic fear and anxiety response patterns are highly conditionable to previously neutral stimuli. These neutral stimuli may consist not only of external cues, but also of _____ sensations. (p. 159)

Anxiety disorders

7. What is the principal manifestation of anxiety disorders? (p. 159)

8. Anxiety disorders are relatively common. According to the results of the New Haven-Baltimore-St. Louis Epidemiologic Catchment Area program, one form of anxiety disorder was the most common psychiatric disturbance among women and the second most common among men. Which form of anxiety disorder was it? (p. 160)

9. Anxiety disorders, which include generalized anxiety, panic, phobic, and obsessive-compulsive disorders, are thought to have a lifetime prevalence rate of nearly _____ % of the entire U.S. population. (p. 160)

Phobic disorders

10. A phobia is a persistent fear of some specific object or situation that presents no actual danger to the person, but physiologically and behaviorally the phobic response is often identical to that which would occur in an encounter with an _____ situation. (p. 160)

11. The Epidemiological Catchment Study revealed a lifetime prevalence rate of over ____% for women and ____% for men for specific phobias. (p. 162)

12. Regardless of how they begin, phobias are reinforced in two ways. First, they are reinforced by the reduction in anxiety that occurs each time the individual avoids the feared situation. Second, phobias may be maintained by *secondary gains* which are . . . (pp. 162-163)

13. Experiencing an inescapable and _____ trauma seems to condition fear much more powerfully than the same intensity of trauma that one can to some extent _____. (p. 164)

14. The phenomenon in which a person who acquired a mild conditioned fear then develops a full blown phobia in response to a later traumatic experience even without the conditioned stimulus being present is called the _____ effect. (p. 164)

15. Evidence supporting the contribution of temperament in the etiology of phobias comes from Kagan's finding that _____ children were at higher risk for the development of multiple specific phobias at 7-8 years of age. (p. 165)

16. Fear of _____ by others may be the hallmark of social phobias. (p. 166)

17. Specific social phobias involve disabling fears of one or more discrete social situations. Complete the following list of three situations mentioned in the text: (p. 166)
    a. _____
    b. urinating in a public bathroom
    c. _____ or _____ in public

18. Individuals with generalized social phobia have significant fears of most social situations and often also share a diagnosis of _____ personality disorder. (p. 166)

Panic disorder and agoraphobia

19. Panic disorder is characterized by the occurrence of _____ panic attacks not triggered by an actual or threatened harm by another person, often seeming to come "out of the blue." (p. 168)

20. To qualify for the diagnosis of panic disorder, an individual must have recurrent, unexpected panic attacks and be persistently concerned about a future attack for a period of at least one month. To qualify as a panic attack, there must be _____ onset of at least _____ of 13 symptoms (such as shortness of breath, etc.). (p. 168)

21. Agoraphobia is a frequent complication of _____ disorder. Cases of agoraphobia without _____ are extremely rare in clinical settings but are not uncommon in _____ studies. The reasons for this discrepancy are unclear. (p. 169)

22. A recent and carefully conducted epidemiological study by Katerndahl and Realini estimated lifetime prevalence of panic disorder to be nearly _____%. (p. 170)

23. Panic attacks are only one component of panic disorder. Persons with panic disorder also experience _____ anxiety and those with agoraphobia also engage in _____ behavior. (p. 173)

Generalized anxiety disorder

24. Generalized anxiety disorders are characterized by chronic, unrealistic, excessive worry of at least six months duration that does not appear to be anchored to a specific object or situation. This type of anxiety was traditionally described as _____ anxiety. (p. 176)

25. Complete the following list of the symptoms characteristic of individuals suffering from generalized anxiety disorder, in addition to the core experience of excessive worry. (p. 176)

a. Restlessness or feelings of being _____

b. A sense of being easily _____

c. Difficulty _____ or mind going blank

d. _____

e. Muscle tension

f. _____ disturbance

26. A multi-site study found that patients diagnosed with GAD did not endorse symptoms of autonomic hyperactivity with much frequency, but it was found that they respond to laboratory stressors with high levels of _____ and _____ tension. (p. 176)

27. Although _____ also is part of other anxiety disorders, it is the essence of GAD, leading Barlow to refer to GAD as the "basic" anxiety disorder. (pp. 176-177)

28. Generalized anxiety disorder is experienced by approximately ____% of the population in any one-year period. (p. 178)

29. According to the psychoanalytic view, the primary difference between simple phobias and free-floating anxiety is that, in the phobias, defense mechanisms of _____ and _____ are operative, whereas in free-floating anxiety these defense mechanisms are not operative. (p. 179)

Obsessive-compulsive disorder

30. What are the one-year prevalence and lifetime prevalence of obsessive-compulsive disorder according to the Epidemiologic Catchment Area study? Is there an effect of gender on prevalence? (p. 182)

31. Obsessive thoughts may center around a variety of topics. A study by Jenike et al. found the most frequent themes of obsessions were _____ (55%), _____ (50%), the need for symmetry (37%), _____ _____ (35%), and sexual content (32%). (p. 182)

32. What are the three primary types of compulsive acts? (p. 183)

33. What seems consistent across all the different clinical presentations of OCD is: (a) _____ is the affective symptom, (b) people afflicted with OCD fear that something _____ will happen to themselves or others for which they will be responsible; and (c) compulsions usually _____, at least in the short term. (p. 183)

34. Give an example of each of the following forms of obsessive-compulsive symptoms: (Highlight 5.2, p. 184)

    a. Ruminations

    b. Cognitive ritual

    c. Motor ritual

    d. Avoidance

35. Steketee and Foa (1985) describe the treatment of obsessive-compulsive disorder as consisting of two phases: exposure treatment and response prevention. Describe what the therapist did during each phase. (Highlight 5.3, p. 187)

    a. Exposure treatment

    b. Response prevention

Treatment and outcomes

36. Many patients with anxiety disorders obtain symptom relief from drugs. However, for many persons, drugs merely mask the symptoms. How is this viewed as detrimental to patients by the authors of the text? (p. 191)

37. All traditional psychotherapies with anxious individuals aim to develop self-understanding, a realistic frame of reference, a satisfying pattern of values, and the development of effective techniques for coping with adjustive demands. Achievement of these objectives by psychotherapy faces a number of stumbling blocks. Complete the following list of obstacles: (pp. 191-192)

a. Establishing a relationship in which the anxious person feels safe enough to . . .

b. Provide opportunities for learning new . . .

c. Helping transfer what has been learned in therapy to . . .

d. Changing conditions in real life that may be . . .

38. Behavior therapies focus on (a) removing specific _____ or maladaptive behaviors; (b) developing needed _____ and _____ behaviors; and (c) modifying _____ that may be reinforcing and maintaining maladaptive behaviors. (p. 192)

39. The behavior therapy most commonly used in the treatment of many anxiety disorders involves controlled _____ to anxiety-producing circumstances. (p. 192)

Unresolved issues

40. Over the last fifteen years, great progress has been made in both biological and cognitive-behavioral approaches to the anxiety disorders. It is unfortunate that these two different lines of research have so often proceeded along relatively independent and unrelated paths. What we need to understand is how the events occurring at _____ (cognitive or behavioral) affect events occurring at another _____ (physiological) and vice versa. This leads us to the importance of developing a coherent _____ approach to understanding these disorders. (p. 196)

◊ CRITICAL THINKING ABOUT DIFFICULT TOPICS

1. If the causes of two diseases (e.g., cancer and ulcers) are truly independent, the probability of suffering from both of them is the product of their respective prevalences. Thus, if each has a prevalence of 2%, the probability of having both is .02 X .02 = .0004 or .04% (i.e., 4 cases in a population of 10,000). Traditionally, the DSM conceptualized psychiatric disorders as independent diseases. However, in recent years it has become increasingly clear that there is a great deal of co-morbidity--instances of dual diagnoses. For example, in the present chapter the text states that it is "very common for a person diagnosed with one anxiety disorder to be diagnosed with one or more additional anxiety disorders, as well as with a mood disorder" (p. 160) and that individuals with generalized social phobia (an anxiety disorder) "often lso share a diagnosis of avoidant personality disorder" (p. 166). What does the phenomenon of co-morbidity imply about the conceptualization of these supposedly independent disorders?

2. The text notes that in recent years many prominent researchers have proposed a fundamental distinction between fear or panic, on the one hand, and anxiety, on the other hand (pp. 158, 181). Further, this distinction proves important in understanding differences between phobias and panic, on the one hand, and generalized anxiety, on the other. Have you been making a similar distinction in your everyday usage of the concept of anxiety? If not, how would such a distinction affect your interpretation of your social environment? For example, in terms of personality traits, can you identify some individuals who show more anxiety (worry, preparation for future problems) while others show more fear or panic (acute anxiety)? Do some students worry about and prepare for exams in advance, whereas others do not prepare for them but become very anxious during them? Can a similar distinction be made for public speaking?

3. Both the interoceptive conditioning model and the cognitive model propose that panic attacks are triggered by internal bodily sensations (pp. 173-174). In the cognitive model, it is said that the person has a tendency to catastrophize about the meaning of bodily sensations but that the person is often not ware of making these catastrophic interpretations. The thoughts are often just barely out of the realm of awareness. In comparing the conditioning and the cognitive models, however, the difference between them is that the "cognitive model would predict panic only if this patient makes catastrophic interpretations about what it means that his heart is racing on a particular occasion" (p. 174). How could you test this hypothesized difference between the hypotheses if the catastrophic interpretations are not always conscious--i.e., how would you know whether the person makes a catastrophic interpretation? In answering this question, it may help to read the evidence supporting the cognitive hypothesis that involves manipulations of perceptions (as opposed to asking subjects about their conscious thoughts).

4. A key feature of the DSM approach to anxiety disorders since 1980 is that people with such disorders must "show prominent symptoms of anxiety" (p. 158). Consider what the following statement implies about the assessment of prominent symptoms of anxiety: Those with generalized anxiety disorder do not have any very effective anxiety-avoidance mechanisms, whereas victims of other anxiety disorders can to some extent allay their anxieties through avoidance behavior (p. 176). For those whose avoidance behavior is successful in allaying anxiety, how are prominent symptoms of anxiety to be demonstrated? Will avoidance behavior alone suffice to infer anxiety? What if the avoidance response is blocked (e.g., among phobics, agoraphobics, or obsessive-compulsives)?

◊ **CHAPTER 5 QUIZ**

Circle the best of the four answers provided and check them according to answers provided at the back of this study guide. Be sure you understand why each answer is correct.

1. In the New Haven-Baltimore-St. Louis Epidemiologic Catchment Area (ECA) program sponsored by the National Institute of Mental Health, _____ were the most common psychiatric disorders reported for women and the second-most common for men. (p. 160)
   a. obsessive-compulsive disorders   c. panic disorders
   b. generalized anxiety disorders   d. phobias

2. All phobic behaviors are reinforced by: (p. 162)
   a. increased self-esteem.   c. repetition.
   b. reduction in anxiety.   d. sympathy from others.

3. The concept that explains why phobias often are not learned in spite of the fact that we observe models responding fearfully is: (p. 164)
   a. counter-conditioning.   c. immunization.
   b. stimulus pre-exposure.   d. reciprocal inhibition.

4. In the Cook and Mineka study of the acquisition of phobias through observational learning in rhesus monkeys, it was found that the monkeys did not condition fears to: (pp. 165-166)
   a. toy snakes.   c. toy rabbits.
   b. toy crocodiles.   d. live snakes.

5. The two features of panic attacks that distinguish them from other types of anxiety are their characteristic _____ and their _____. (p. 169)
   a. focal stimulus, intensity
   c. focal stimulus, constancy
   b. brevity, mildness
   d. brevity, intensity

6. Biological psychiatrists such as Donald Klein concluded that panic disorder is qualitatively different from generalized anxiety because of an apparent finding that a _____ drug appeared to block panic attacks in agoraphobics without affecting their anticipatory anxiety. (p. 172)
   a. minor tranquilizer
   c. barbiturate
   b. tricyclic antidepressant
   d. monoamine oxidase inhibitor

7. The common mechanism underlying the effects of all the various panic provocation agents is that they: (p. 175)
   a. mimic the physiological cues that normally precede a panic attack.
   b. stimulate the locus coeruleus.
   c. interfere with processes that inhibit anxiety.
   d. increase activity in the anxious apprehension system.

8. Barlow refers to the fundamental process in generalized anxiety disorder as: (p. 176)
   a. the alarm reaction.
   c. anxious apprehension.
   b. the fight or flight response.
   d. prepared focal anxiety.

9. The benzodiazepines, minor tranquilizers that reduce generalized anxiety, probably exert their effects through stimulating the action of: (p. 181)
   a. acetylcholine.
   c. serotonin.
   b. GABA.
   d. norepinephrine.

10. An impulse the person cannot seem to control is called a(an): (p. 182)
    a. compulsion.
    c. hallucination.
    b. delusion.
    d. focal phobia.

11. Which of the following was the least frequent theme of obsessions? (p. 182)
    a. sexual content
    c. contamination
    b. need for symmetry
    d. aggressive impulses

12. The personality disorders with which OCD most often occurs are: (p. 184)
    a. narcissistic and antisocial.
    c. schizoid and schizotypal.
    b. borderline and histrionic.
    d. avoidant and dependent.

13. The techniques used by Steketee and Foa in the recommended treatment of obsessive-compulsive disorders are _____ and _____. (Highlight 5.3, p. 187)
    a. counter-conditioning, reciprocal inhibition
    b. exposure treatment, response prevention
    c. implosion, response prevention
    d. cognitive restructuring, exposure treatment

14. Which of the following is *not* a characteristic of the benzodiazepines used in the treatment of anxiety disorders? (pp. 190-191)
    a. they tend to lose their effectiveness after several weeks
    b. they can produce drowsiness and sedation
    c. they take several weeks before they have any beneficial effects
    d. the patient develops increasing tolerance for and persistent dependence on the drug

Chapter 6
Mood Disorders and Suicide

◊ **OVERVIEW**

Depression is the most common mood disorder clinicians encountered among persons who seek psychological help. Depression is also widespread among the normal population. Mild levels of depression are often resolved with support from family, friends, clergy, physicians, and even bartenders or hairdressers. The first half of the chapter begins with a differentiation between clinical depression and normal depression. Then the symptoms of several different clinically significant levels of depression are described. Finally, consideration is given to mania, which in bipolar disorder is an alternate phase to depression. The section concludes with a review of the causal factors and treatment approaches of both depression and mania.

Suicide is always a risk with depressed individuals. Well-known persons periodically capture the headlines by killing themselves at the height of success and in the midst of lives of luxury and recognition. From the outside, they do not seem to have a bad life or many insoluble problems. These deaths mystify and disturb most of us and raise questions about what makes life livable (or unlivable). This section presents information relevant to these questions--asking, for instance, whether all persons who commit suicide are mentally disordered. Data are also presented on the increasing problem of suicide among young people and college students. The section concludes with a discussion of some of the factors that characterize the person who is at high risk for suicide and a brief description of suicide prevention procedures.

◊ **LEARNING OBJECTIVES**

After studying this chapter, you should be able to:

1. Summarize the symptoms associated with normal depression, list the various causes of or contributors to normal depression, and characterize the phases of the grieving process. (pp. 202-203)

2. Compare and contrast the clinical features of dysthymia, adjustment disorder with depressed mood, and major depressive disorder, as well as of the various subtypes or subcategories of major depressive disorder. (pp. 204-209)

3. Compare and contrast Bipolar I disorder, Bipolar II disorder, and cyclothymia. (pp. 209-212)

4. List the features of schizoaffective disorder and discuss its relation to affective disorder and schizophrenia. (p. 212)

5. Describe the biological and psychosocial factors that are causally-related to mood disorders. (pp. 213-234)

6. Discuss how sociocultural factors affect the incidence of some of the mood disorders. (pp. 235-236)

7. Describe biological and psychosocial therapies that have been used to treat mood disorders and evaluate their effectiveness. (pp. 236-240)

8. Characterize the people who are most likely to commit suicide. List some of their motives for ending their lives, and explain how psychosocial and sociocultural variables influence the likelihood of suicide among depressed persons. (pp. 240-249)

9. Evaluate the ethical and legal issues involved in sanctioning and preventing suicide. (pp. 249-250)

◊ **TERMS YOU SHOULD KNOW**

mood disorders (p. 199)

affect (p. 199)

unipolar disorder or *unipolar major depression* (Highlight 6.1, p. 200; p. 201)

bipolar disorder (Highlight 6.1, p. 200; p. 201)

*hypomania (*Highlight 6.1, p. 200; pp. 206, 209)

cyclothymia (Highlight 6.1, p. 200; pp. 209-210)

dysthymia (Highlight 6.1, p. 200; p. 204)

adjustment disorder with depressed mood (Highlight 6.1, p. 200; p. 205)

mania (p. 201)

depression (p. 201)

anaclitic depression (p. 201)

normal depression (pp. 202-203)

major depressive disorder (p. 206)

psychotic symptoms (pp. 206-207)

severe major depressive episode with psychotic features (pp. 206-207)

mood-congruent (p. 207)

mood-incongruent (p. 207)

melancholic type (p. 207)

endogenous causation (pp. 207, 219)

double depression (p. 207)

recurrence (p. 208)

relapse (p. 208)

seasonal affective disorder (SAD) (p. 208, 216)

mixed bipolar disorder (p. 210)

Bipolar I versus *Bipolar II disorder* (p. 210)

bipolar disorder with a seasonal pattern (p. 211)

rapid cycling (p. 212)

full recovery (p. 212)

schizoaffective disorder (p. 212)

concordance rate (pp. 213-214, 231)

adoption method of genetic research (p. 214)

neurotransmitter (pp. 214-215)

monoamine hypothesis (pp. 214-215)

hypothalamic-pituitary-adrenal axis (p. 215)

cortisol (p. 215)

dexamethasone (p. 215)

dexamethasone suppression test (DST) (p. 215)

hypothalamic-pituitary-thyroid axis (p. 215)

limbic system (p. 217)

sociotropy (p. 220)

autonomy (p. 220)

dysfunctional beliefs (pp. 220-221, 223)

pessimistic attributional style (p. 221)

response contingent positive reinforcement (pp. 222-223)

negative cognitive triad (p. 223)

negative automatic thoughts (p. 223)

learned helplessness (pp. 225-226)

reformulated helplessness theory (pp. 226, 228)

hopelessness theory (pp. 226, 228)

antidepressants (pp. 236-237)

tricyclics (p. 236)

lithium carbonate (p. 237)

electroconvulsive therapy (ECT) (p. 237)

cognitive-behavioral therapy (pp. 238-239)

interpersonal therapy (IPT) (pp. 238-239)

suicide attempts versus *completed suicide* (p. 241)

"To be" group (p. 245)

"not to be" group (p. 245)

"To be or not to be" group (p. 245)

crisis intervention (pp. 247-248)

◊ NAMES YOU SHOULD KNOW

Peter Lewinsohn (pp. 201, 208, 219, 222-223)

Ian Gotlib (pp. 201, 203, 208, 221, 228, 230)

John Bowlby (pp. 201-203, 221-222)

Connie Hammen (pp. 201, 208, 221, 228, 230)

George Brown (pp. 202, 218-219, 221)

Scott Monroe (pp. 202, 218, 219)

Richard Depue (pp. 209, 232, 234, 244)

Hagop Akiskal (pp. 209, 234)

Bruce Dohrenwend (p. 218)

E. S. Paykel (pp. 217, 218)

Aaron T. Beck (pp. 217, 220-221, 223-225)

Lynn Abramson (pp. 221, 226, 228)

Martin Seligman (pp. 225-226)

Susan Nolen-Hoeksema (Highlight 6.2, p. 227)

◊ CONCEPTS TO MASTER

1. List the symptoms associated with "normal depression" and the eight types of psychological losses in addition to the death of a loved one that may trigger grief. (p. 202)

2. Characterize the four phases of response to the loss of a spouse or close family member (as described by Bowlby) and note when prominent anxiety and prominent depression are likely to appear. (p. 202)

3. Define postpartum depression and note the evidence for and against it. (p. 203)

4. List the two dimensions customarily used to differentiate the mood disorders, and give examples of unipolar mood disorders varying along these two dimensions. (pp. 201, 204-209)

5. Describe the clinical manifestations of major depressive disorder and note the more restricted features of the melancholic type of major depressive disorder. (pp. 206-207)

6. Explain the meaning of the term "double depression." (p. 207)

7. Distinguish between a recurrence of depression and a relapse. (p. 208)

8. Describe the clinical manifestations of cyclothymia and of bipolar disorder and note the relation between the two. (pp. 209-211)

9. Explain the difficulty of knowing whether a person showing only depression during an initial episode of affective disorder should be diagnosed as suffering from a bipolar disorder. (p. 211)

10. Describe the symptoms of a schizoaffective disorder, and explain why some psychologists find this diagnosis controversial. (p. 212)

11. Summarize the evidence for a genetic contribution to unipolar depression, including the variation in heritability with subtype of depression. (pp. 213-214)

12. Trace the history and current status of the monoamine hypothesis of depression. Note that the antidepressant drugs actually begin to have their clinical effects 2-4 weeks after initial administration and discuss the implications of this consideration for the interpretation of the effects of these drugs. (pp. 214-215)

13. Define the concepts of sleep stages, circadian rhythms, and seasonal variations in basic functions and review their possible involvement in unipolar depression. (pp. 216-217)

14. List the five major facts that support the hypothesis of biological involvement in major depression and note the central importance of the limbic system in this hypothesis. (p. 217)

15. Cognitive theories of depression postulate that depressed individuals have a distorted interpretation of events, and this distortion creates difficulties for research on the effects of life events on depression (since the depressed person's report of these events may be distorted). Indicate how George Brown and Bruce Dohrenwend each attempt to deal with this problem and summarize the results of research on life events and depression using their methodology. (pp. 218-219)

16. List the four factors found by Brown and Harris to be associated with *not* becoming depressed among women who experienced a severe life event. (p. 219)

17. Compare and contrast the diathesis-stress theories of depression based on (a) genetic or constitutional diathesis, (b) personality variables, (c) cognitive diathesis, and (d) parental loss or poor parental care. (pp. 220-222)

18. Differentiate between Beck's cognitive theory of depression involving dysfunctional beliefs and Abramson et al.'s reformulated learned helplessness and hopelessness theories involving the concept of a pessimistic attributional style. (pp. 220-221, 223-228)

19. Discuss the evidence for the conclusions that interpersonal problems and social skills deficits may play a causal role in depression *and* that depression creates many interpersonal difficulties. (pp. 228, 230)

20. Outline the evidence strongly supporting a genetic contribution to the etiology of bipolar disorders. Also, explain the conceptual difficulties created by the finding that among the relatives of bipolar patients there is a higher rate of unipolar than bipolar disorders (pp. 231-233)

21. A person goes on a round of parties to try to forget a broken love affair or tries to escape from a threatening life situation by restless action, occupying every moment with work, athletics, sexual affairs, and countless other activities--all performed with professed gusto but not necessarily with true enjoyment. What psychoanalytic concept do these anecdotes exemplify and what does it have to do with mania? (p. 234)

22. Marsella's comprehensive review found that even in those nonindustrialized countries where depressive disorders are relatively common, depression generally takes on a form different from that customarily described in our society. Describe these different forms. (pp. 235-236)

23. The two best-known of the depression-specific psychotherapies are Beck's cognitive-behavioral approach and the interpersonal therapy (IPT) developed by Klerman, Weissman, and colleagues. How do these differ from the usual approach in psychodynamic psychotherapy and how effective are these therapies? (pp. 238-239)

24. Summarize the data on the degree to which suicide is communicated directly and indirectly and to whom it is communicated. (p. 246)

25. Define the concept of a "right to suicide" and summarize the vexing ethical and legal issues surrounding the debate on this issue. (pp. 249-250)

◊ STUDY QUESTIONS

Introduction

1. The mood disorders are so named because they involve disturbances of mood that are intense and _____ enough to be clearly _____. (p. 199)

2. The two key states of mood disorder are depression and _____. (p. 201)

3. Mild depressions are so much a part of our lives that their incidence is difficult to estimate. However, the most recent results from the National Comorbidity Study found lifetime prevalence rates of *major depression* at nearly _____% for males and _____% for females. Fill in the following statements about the incidence of depression. (p. 201)

   a. Bipolar affective disorder is much less common than unipolar depression. Estimates of lifetime risk of bipolar disorder range from _____% to _____%, and there is no discernible sex difference in prevalence rates.

   b. Most mood disorder cases occur during _____ and _____ adulthood. However, about _____ of adults reported the first onset of unipolar depression in childhood or adolescence.

Unipolar mood disorders: Normal depression

4. Everyday depression is unpleasant, but it usually does not last very long and is self-limiting, turning off after a period or a certain intensity level has been reached. Mild depression may even be adaptive because much of its "work" seems to involve _____ images, thoughts, and feelings that would normally be avoided. (p. 202)

5. Normal depression is almost always the result of recent _____. (p. 202)

6. Grief is a psychological process one goes through following the death of a loved one. Clayton (1982) suggests that the process of grieving following bereavement is normally completed within _____. Depression continuing after this period calls for therapeutic intervention. (p. 202)

7. O'Hara et al. (1990) found that as many as ____% of women experience at least a mild attack of the blues following childbirth, but the once firmly held notion that women were at especially high risk for _____ in the postpartum was not upheld. (p. 203)

8. Blatt et al. (1976) concluded that depression in male and female college students was similar and was characterized by three psychological variables. List these dimensions. (p. 203)

   a.

   b.

   c.

Unipolar mood disorders: Mild to moderate depressive disorders

9. The point on the severity continuum at which mood disturbance becomes a mood disorder is a matter of clinical judgment. True or False? (p. 204)

10. The two main depressive disorders of mild to moderate severity recognized by DSM-IV are dysthymia and adjustment disorder with depressed mood. Place these disorders in the blank next to the correct clinical description: (pp. 204-205)
    a. _____ Symptoms essentially similar to major depression, but the nonpsychotic levels of depression last two years or more with no tendency toward hypomanic episodes and with intermittent normal moods lasting from a few days to no more than a few weeks.
    b. _____ Also characterized by nonpsychotic levels of depression developing within three months of an identifiable stressor and lasting no longer than six months.

11. Few, if any, depressions occur in the absence of another significant affect. This affect is _____. (p. 205)

Unipolar mood disorders: Major depressive disorder

12. To be diagnosed as suffering from major depression, the person must experience either depressed mood or loss of interest in pleasurable activities. In addition, at least four symptoms must have been present all day and nearly every day during two consecutive _____. (p. 206)

13. The most severe form of major depression is severe major depressive episode with _____ features. (pp. 206-207)

14. The person who has a major depressive disorder may have a loss of contact with reality. Ordinarily, any delusions or hallucinations present are _____; that is, they seem in some sense "appropriate" to serious depression. (p. 207)

15. The term major depression of the _____ type may be used for the person who develops a major depression that includes lost capacity for pleasure and whose other symptoms are likely to include depression being worse in the morning, awakening early in the morning, showing marked psychomotor retardation or agitation, significant loss of appetite and weight, and excessive guilt. Historically, endogenous (internal) causation was thought to be responsible for triggering this form of depression. (p. 207)

16. Major depression may coexist with dysthymia, a condition given the designation _____. (p. 207)

17. The average duration of an untreated episode of major depression is about _____ months, according to DSM-IV. (p. 208)

18. Based on an extensive review of studies done between 1970 and 1993, Piccinelli and Wilkinson estimated that ____% of patients experienced a recurrence of major depression within one year of recovery and ____% experienced a recurrence within 10 years of recovery. Approximately ____% to ____% show persistent depression over five and ten year follow-up. (p. 208)

19. Hooley and Teasdale (1989) determined that a substantial predictor of depression relapse was marital distress, especially perceived _____. (pp. 208-209)

Bipolar disorder

20. Nondisabling, cyclical mood alterations between depression and elation with no obvious precipitating circumstance and lengthy normal periods between episodes are indicative of _____, a milder variant of bipolar disorder (or, in other words, a sub-syndromal form). (p. 209)

21. Bipolar mood disorder is distinguished from major depression by at least one episode of _____. The features of the depressive form of bipolar disorder are clinically _____ from those of major depression. (p. 210)

22. Mixed cases of bipolar disorder are those in which the full symptomatic picture of both manic and major depression occur intermixed or alternating every few hours. True or False? (p. 210)

23. The DSM-IV system contains the implicit assumption that all mania-like behaviors must be part of a _____ or bipolar disorder. (p. 210)

24. The symptoms of mania and depression are compared in the following chart. Fill in the missing information. (pp. 210-211)

Area of Behavior	Depression	Mania
Activity level	Loss of interest in activities	
Mood	Sad	Euphoric
Mental activity	Diminished cognitive capacity	Flight of ideas
Verbal output	Reduced	
Self-esteem	Self-denunciation and guilt	
Sleeping	Hypersomnia or insomnia	

25. A person with bipolar disorder whose first episode is a depression cannot be correctly diagnosed until the time that a manic episode appears. True or False? (p. 211)

26. Compared to patients with unipolar major depression, patients with bipolar disorder have _____ episodes in the course of their lifetimes, have episodes that tend to be somewhat _____ in duration, and have a probability of being symptom-free for five years following recovery of about ____%, the same as for unipolar disorder. Even with lithium maintenance therapy, ___% percent of manic patients experienced another manic episode within 1.7 years after discharge according to Harrow et al. (pp. 211-212)

Schizoaffective disorder

27. Patients with a diagnosis of schizoaffective disorder have a mood disorder equal to anything seen in major depression or bipolar affective disorder but their _____ and _____ processes are so deranged as to suggest the presence of a schizophrenic psychosis. The latter must include at least _____ major symptoms of schizophrenia. Unlike schizophrenia, the schizoaffective pattern tends to be highly _____ with relatively lucid periods between attacks. (p. 212)

28. The diagnosis of schizoaffective disorder is controversial. Some clinicians believe these persons are basically _____; others believe they have primarily psychotic _____ disorders; and still others consider this disorder a distinct entity. (p. 212)

Causal factors in unipolar disorders: Biological factors

29. Perris reviewed eight studies examining family risk for unipolar depression and estimated that about ____% of first degree relatives also experienced unipolar depression, substantially higher than in the general population. Because of the difficulties of disentangling _____ and _____ influences, however, this result can never in itself be taken as conclusive proof of genetic causation. (p. 213)

30. A very large population-based twin study by Kendler et al. estimated heritability of depression to range from ____% to ____%, depending on the definition used. However, Katz and McGuffin found the evidence for a genetic contribution to be much less consistent for milder forms of unipolar depression, such as neurotic depression or _____. (p. 214)

31. The biological therapies often used to treat severe mood disorders--such as _____ therapy and _____ drugs--may affect the concentrations or the activity of _____ at the synapse. (p. 214)

32. One contemporary hormonal theory of depression has focused on the
_____ _____ axis, and in particular on the hormone cortisol. It
was found that a potent suppressor of plasma cortisol, _____, either
fails to suppress or fails to sustain suppression of cortisol in about _____% of seriously
depressed patients. This gave rise to the widespread use of the
_____ (DST), and it was found that
nonsuppression was correlated with clinical severity and _____ response to drug
treatment. However, recent evidence has called into question the _____ of the
nonsuppression and hence the diagnostic utility of the DST for depression. (p. 215)

Causal factors in unipolar disorders: Psychosocial factors

33. Harder and colleagues found no difference between more and less severely depressed people
in the magnitude of _____. (p. 217)

34. Beck (1967) has listed six events that he believes are the most frequently encountered
precipitating circumstances in depression. Complete the following list: (p. 217)
a. Events that lower self-esteem
b.
c. Physical disease that activates ideas of deterioration or death
d. Overwhelming stressors
e.
f. Insidious stressors

35. Brown and Harris concluded that depression often follows from one or more severely stressful
events, usually involving some _____ or _____ from one's social sphere. Interestingly,
events signifying danger or threat were found more likely to precede the onset of _____
disorders. (p. 218)

36. Several studies have suggested that loss events are associated with the onset of depression.
What is also important in determining the onset of depression among older persons according
to Phifer and Murrell and Dohrenwend et al.? (p. 218)

37. A very rigorous study conducted by Billings et al. (1983) compared 409 matched pairs of
normal people and unipolar depressive people. They found that depressed people had not only
a greater frequency of prior stressors but also more _____ of psychosocial strain.
(p. 219)

38. Barchas and his colleagues concluded that psychosocial stressors may play a role in the development of mood disorders by causing long-term changes in _____ functioning. (p. 219)

39. Perhaps the most important contribution of the psychodynamic approaches to depression has been to note the importance of _____ (both real, and symbolic or imagined) to the onset of depression and to note the striking similarities between the symptoms of _____ and the symptoms of depression. (p. 222)

40. A "negative cognitive triad" consists of negative views of the self, world, and the _____. (p. 223)

41. Such depression-producing beliefs are believed by Beck to develop during childhood and adolescence as a function of one's experiences with one's _____ and with _____ (_____, etc.). (p. 223)

42. Overlap between measures of anxiety and depression occurs at all levels of analysis. A recent very large twin study by Kendler et al. showed that the liability for generalized anxiety disorder and depression comes from the same _____ _____, and which disorder develops is a result of what _____ _____ occur. (Highlight 6.3, p. 229)

43. In the dominant theoretical approach to understanding the overlap between anxiety and depression, known as the tripartite model, the overlap between anxiety and depression is attributable to the broad mood and personality dimension of _____, depressed persons are specifically low on a second dimension of mood and personality known as _____, and anxious but not depressed individuals show high levels of yet another mood dimension known as _____. (Highlight 6.3, p. 229).

Causal factors in bipolar disorders: Biological factors

44. There have been challenges to the evidence developed by Egeland et al. among the Amish of genetic transmission of bipolar disorder on chromosome 11. Is there consistent support for *any* specific mode of genetic transmission of affective disorders? (pp. 231-232)

45. The early monoamine hypothesis for unipolar disorder was extended to bipolar disorder, suggesting that perhaps mania was caused by an excess of norepinephrine and/or serotonin. Although there is some support for increased _____ during manic episodes, _____ activity appears to be low in both phases of the illness. Moreover, a recent influential model by Depue and Iacono more strongly implicates _____ rather than norepinephrine or serotonin for bipolar disorder. (p. 232)

46. Administration of _____ hormone is known at times to make antidepressant drugs work better. However, this hormone can also precipitate manic episodes. (p. 233)

Causal factors in bipolar disorders: Psychosocial factors

47. In the best prospective study to date using sophisticated stress measurement techniques, Ellicott and colleagues followed 61 patients with bipolar disorder for one to two years. What did they find regarding the association between high levels of stress and the experience of manic, hypomanic, or depressive episodes? (pp. 233-234)

Causal factors for both unipolar and bipolar disorders: Sociocultural factors

48. As non-Western societies adopt the ways of Western culture, how do the rates of mood disorders change? (p. 235)

49. How do rates of unipolar and bipolar disorders correlate with social class in the U.S.? (p. 236)

Treatments and Outcomes

50. Traditionally, moderate to serious depression has been treated pharmacologically with a drug such as _____ (_____), which is an example of a tricyclic antidepressant. Because of problems with unpleasant side effects and with suicide potential due to high toxicity with the tricyclics, physicians are increasingly prescribing one of the new _____ or SSRIs, such as Prozac (fluoxetine). (pp. 236-237)

51. Electroconvulsive therapy is often used with severely depressed, suicidal patients because antidepressants often take _____ to _____ weeks to produce significant improvement. ECT is also used with patients who have not responded to other forms of _____ treatment. When selection criteria are carefully observed, a complete remission of symptoms occurs after about four to six treatments and usually within about two weeks in some _____ % of the cases treated. (p. 237)

52. Early studies indicated that lithium carbonate was considered an effective preventive for approximately ____% of patients suffering repeated bipolar attacks, but one large recent study found only _____% of patients remained free of episodes over a two-year follow-up. (p. 237)

53. What was the verdict regarding the relative effectiveness for depression of the Beck approach to cognitive-behavioral treatment and interpersonal therapy (IPT) according to the carefully designed, multisite study sponsored by the National Institute of Mental Health and reported by Elkin et al.? Circle the correct statement from the choices below: (p. 239)
    1. IPT is more effective than Beck.
    2. Beck is more effective than IPT.
    3. Drugs are more effective than psychotherapy.
    4. Drugs, IPT, and the Beck approach are equally effective for milder cases of major depression.

54. Even without formal therapy, the great majority of manic and depressed patients recover from a given episode within less than _____. At the same time, the mortality rate for depressed patients appears to be significantly higher than that for the general population, partly because of the increased risk of suicide. (p. 240)

Suicide

55. Fill in the missing information in the following questions about the risk of suicide: (p. 240)
    a. The vast majority of those who commit suicide do so during the _____ phase of depression.
    b. The risk of suicide is just _____ percent during the year a depressive episode occurs but rises to _____ percent over the entire lifetime of an individual who experiences recurrent episodes.
    c. Experts agree that the actual number of suicides is probably _____ times as high as the official number.

56. Women are about three times as likely to attempt suicide as are men, but three times more men than women die by suicide each year. True or False? (p. 241)

57. In recent years, disproportionate increases have occurred in the suicide rates among certain groups. However, the greatest increases have been among _____ year olds, where the rate has tripled. Some of this increase is attributed to drug abuse. (p. 242)

58. Which is the more frequent precipitant for suicide in college students, poor grades or the breakup of a romance? (Highlight 6.4, p. 243)

59. Suicide rates vary considerably from one society to another. The world's highest rate (44.9 cases per 100,000) is in _____. The United States has a rate of approximately _____% per 100,000. Among certain groups, such as the Aborigines of the western Australian desert, the rate drops to _____%. (p. 244)

60. Name two religions that strongly condemn suicide. How do religious attitudes influence suicide rates? (p. 244)

61. The French sociologist Emile Durkheim concluded that suicide rates during times of stress vary according to group _____. The greatest deterrent to suicide is a sense of involvement and identity with other people. (p. 244)

62. Farberow and Litman (1970) have developed a classification of suicidal intent. Fill in the missing information in the chart below concerning their inferences and observations about suicidal behavior. (p. 245)

Group	Feelings About Death	Method of Suicide
"To be" group (66% of suicidal people)	Do not wish to die	
"Not to be" group (3-5% of suicidal people)		
"To be or not to be" group (30% of suicidal people)		Tend to choose methods that are moderately slow acting to allow for the possibility of discovery

63. Long-term follow-up of those who have made a suicide attempt show that about _____% will eventually die by suicide. Moreover, of people who do kill themselves, about _____% have a history of one or more previous attempts. (p. 245)

64. Which is more common: a person commits suicide and leaves a note, or a person commits suicide and does not leave a note? (p. 246)

65. The primary objective of crisis intervention therapy is to help the individual with an immediate life crisis. When persons contemplating suicide are willing to discuss their problems at a suicide prevention center, it is often possible to avert an actual suicide attempt. The primary objective is to help individuals regain their ability to cope with their immediate problems. Emphasis is placed in five areas. Complete the following list of objectives in suicide crisis intervention: (p. 247)

a. Maintaining contact with the person for one to six contacts

b.

c.

d.

e. Help the person see that the present distress will not be endless

66. Farberow (1974) states that two types of people come to a suicide prevention center. (p. 248)

a. Describe the larger group (60-65 percent), and indicate the treatment they should receive.

b. Describe the smaller group (35-40 percent), and indicate the treatment they should receive.

◊ CRITICAL THINKING ABOUT DIFFICULT TOPICS

1. The text states that "many clinicians feel that cyclothymia is but a milder variant of bipolar disorder, and the evidence for this view has in recent years become quite compelling" (p. 483). This finding that there are milder versions of traditional diagnostic categories is quite common. What does it imply for the categorical approach to diagnosis, in which the disorder is viewed as either present or absent?

2. As in earlier chapters, the text indicates that psychosocial stressors "may cause long-term changes in brain functioning" (pp. 501-502). At the same time, person characteristics in the form of distorted cognitions (negative views of self and the world) may cause individuals to perceive the environment to be more stressful than it objectively is (pp. 498-499). Given that environmental events can produce long-term changes in brain functioning and that person characteristics, quite possibly influenced by individual differences in brain functioning, can alter the effects of the environment, how can researchers identify the independent contributions of biological and psychosocial influences in the etiology of psychopathology?

3. Among the first-degree relatives of a person with bipolar disorder, about 8% will have a bipolar disorder and another 11% a unipolar disorder (p. 231). This result can be compared with the 15% risk of unipolar depression among relatives of a person with unipolar disorder, which is described as "substantially higher than would be expected in the general population" (p. 213). This finding that among relatives of a person with bipolar disorder the risk of unipolar disorders is actually higher than that for bipolar disorders constitutes one of the theoretically most challenging puzzles in psychopathology. Attempts to think of bipolar disorders as simply more severe versions of unipolar disorders have not been able to fit the available data. Can you think of any model of the causal factors for unipolar and bipolar mood disorders that could account for this pattern of results?

4. A number of psychiatrists advocate the very long-term use of anti-anxiety drugs to correct what they view as a "chemical imbalance" and the recent popularity of the antidepressant drug Prozac has similarly raised questions about the appropriateness and ethics of "prescribing drugs to essentially healthy people because the drugs make them feel more energetic, outgoing, and productive" (p. 237). Consider for yourself under what conditions it would be legitimate to prescribe a psychoactive drug (such as an anxiolytic or an antidepressant) for many years. In reaching an answer, think about the following questions: (a) why is it wrong for an alcoholic to drink alcohol continuously; (b) does your answer depend on whether there are negative "side effects" of the drugs; (c) would it matter whether the drug was obtained "on the street" or via prescription by a physician, (d) is a person on medication fully responsible for what they do, or is there in some sense "diminished capacity" or altered judgment (e.g., it is common for a person who has been drinking to blame the alcoholic state for inadequate or inappropriate behavior), and (e) is the resistance to decriminalizing (legalizing) drugs of abuse based on an assumption that they have serious negative effects or on some other reason?

5. In the pharmacological treatment of depression, your text says that "discontinuing the drugs when symptoms have remitted may result in relapse--probably because the underlying depressive episode is still present and only its symptomatic expression has been suppressed" (p. 237). This statement reflects a typical view of pharmacological treatment of psychiatric disorders: symptoms are treated but the underlying "episode" is not eliminated, and the drug is

not expected to reduce the risk of future episodes once it is discontinued (i.e., there is no carry-over benefit of having had the drug in the past). Do you think about psychological treatments in the same way, or do you expect them to have a long-term benefit? How do you conceptualize the processes involved in psychotherapy and how would these relate to continued benefits after therapy is discontinued? For example, you might think of psychotherapy as providing only emotional and moral support that ameliorates a current state of demoralization but does not last beyond active treatment. Alternatively, you might think of psychotherapy as learning more adaptive ways of dealing with problems, which should have benefits in dealing with future problems even though therapy has been discontinued. How does the three year study by Frank et al. (p. 239) of once per month "maintenance" IPT treatments for prevention of depression fit with your way of thinking about psychological treatments?

6. Your text does an excellent job of discussing the ethical issues involved in the concept of the "right to suicide" (pp. 249-250). If you are like many people and feel some sympathy for the desire to commit suicide in the case of terminal debilitating and painful illnesses, think through your own position with respect to who should be involved in such a decision and what restrictions you would place on the right to suicide. What about a young person who is obviously depressed over some recent perceived failure or rejection? What about a person recently diagnosed as having Alzheimer's (a severe form of dementia) or schizophrenia (a disabling and *often* chronic psychotic disorder), or a person who has become paralyzed from the waist down? Try to articulate the concepts involved in granting or denying the right to suicide in each case.

◊ CHAPTER 6 QUIZ

Circle the best of the four answers provided and check them according to answers provided at the back of this study guide. Be sure you understand why each answer is correct.

1. The lifetime prevalence of major depression among men is nearly 8%. Among women it is nearly: (p. 201)
   a. 4%.
   b. 14%.
   c. 21%.
   d. 27%.

2. Which of the following is *not* one of Bowlby's four phases of response to the loss of a spouse or close family member? (p. 202)
   a. numbing and disbelief
   b. denial and rejection of the dead person
   c. disorganization and despair
   d. some level of reorganization

3. A disorder that involves mood swings between subclinical levels of depression and mania is: (p. 209)
   a. bipolar disorder.   c. dysthymic disorder.
   b. manic depression.   d. cyclothymic disorder.

4. Bipolar mood disorder is distinguished from major depression by: (p. 210)
   a. at least one episode of mania.   c. evidence of earlier cyclothymia.
   b. disturbance of circadian rhythms.   d. evidence of earlier dysthymia.

5. All of the following are symptoms of the manic phase of bipolar mood disorder *except:* (p. 210)
   a. notable increase in activity.   c. high levels of verbal output.
   b. euphoria.   d. deflated self-esteem.

6. In the original monoamine hypothesis depression was attributed to: (p. 215)
   a. an increase in norepinephrine and/or dopamine.
   b. an increase in acetylcholine.
   c. a depletion of norepinephrine and/or serotonin.
   d. a depletion of acetylcholine and/or GABA.

7. Behaviorists such as Ferster and Lewinsohn assert that depression results when: (p. 223)
   a. angry responses are inhibited by aversive conditioning.
   b. conditioned grief responses are reactivated.
   c. negative reinforcers overwhelm positive reinforcers.
   d. response contingent positive reinforcement is not available.

8. The original learned helplessness theory refers to the depressed patient's perception that: (p. 225)
   a. accustomed reinforcement is no longer forthcoming.
   b. there is no control over aversive events.
   c. reinforcement is inadequate.
   d. the world is a negative place.

9. In a study of genetic factors in bipolar mood disorders in the Amish, Egeland found that the disorder was transmitted on the _____ chromosome. (pp. 231-232)
   a. eleventh   c. X
   b. twelfth   d. Y

10. All of the following have been suggested as biological causes of bipolar affective disorder *except:* (pp. 231-233)
    a. abnormalities of the hypothalamic-pituitary-thyroid axis.
    b. genetic abnormality on chromosome 11.
    c. levels of biogenic amines.
    d. acetylcholine depletion.

11. While lithium therapy is routinely used in the treatment of manic episodes, it is believed that it is effective in treating depression only when: (pp. 236-237)
    a. electroconvulsive therapy has failed.
    b. the disorder is bipolar in nature.
    c. the disorder is melancholic in nature.
    d. used in tandem with psychedelic drugs.

12. In the NIMH multisite study, which of the following treatments has proven most effective in the treatment of milder cases of major depression? (p. 239)
    a. antidepressant drug treatment
    b. Beck's cognitive-behavioral approach
    c. interpersonal therapy
    d. all of the above are equally effective

13. Most hospitalized manic and depressed patients can now be discharged within _____ days. (p. 240)
    a. 10   c. 40
    b. 30   d. 60

14. In suicides associated with depression, most often suicide is committed during the _____ phase of a depressive episode. (p. 240)
    a. early onset   c. peak of depression
    b. late onset   d. recovery

15. A recent review of studies interviewing friends and relatives of people who committed suicide found that ____% had communicated their suicidal intent in very clear and specific terms, and another ____% had communicated a wish to die or a preoccupation with death. (p. 246)
   a. 40, 30
   b. 25, 15
   c. 15, 25
   d. 10, 20

Chapter 7
Somatoform and Dissociative Disorders

◊ **OVERVIEW**

This chapter contains a detailed description of the clinical picture, causal pattern, and treatment of somatoform and dissociative disorders. Like the anxiety disorders in Chapter 5, somatoform and dissociative disorders had, in the past, been called *neuroses*. In the descriptive approach adopted in DSM-IV, however, the anxiety disorders were grouped together because the contribution of anxiety was obvious in each case. In contrast, the somatoform and dissociative disorders appear to be ways of avoiding anxiety and stress, but the specific causal pathways in the somatoform and dissociative disorders remain to a large extent obscure and this *possible* contribution of anxiety is not so prominent or obvious as in the anxiety disorders. In the somatoform disorders the central presenting problem is physical complaints or physical disabilities in the absence of any physical pathology, presumably reflecting underlying psychological difficulties. In the dissociative disorders the central problem is a failure of certain aspects of memory due to an active process of dissociation, such as in dissociative amnesia in which individuals cannot remember their names, do not know how old they are or where they live, etc. Whereas our personal experience with anxiety and depression in everyday life is a considerable aid in understanding on an intuitive, empathic level the extreme deviations of these emotions discussed in the last two chapters, the disorders examined in this chapter will seem less familiar and less readily grasped as exaggerated forms of everyday psychological phenomena. These disorders seem to involve more complex and exotic mental operations than the disorders previously discussed.

◊ **LEARNING OBJECTIVES**

After studying this chapter, you should be able to:

1. Describe the major manifestations of somatoform disorders. (pp. 254-263)

2. List the primary presenting symptoms of somatization disorder and hypochondriasis and note the similarities of and differences between these closely related disorders. (pp. 254-257)

3. Explain what is meant by a pain disorder. Discuss the difficulties of determining that pain is of psychological rather than of physical origin and of reliably assessing an entirely subjective phenomenon. (pp. 257-258)

4. Characterize the symptoms of conversion disorder, trace the history of the concept of "conversion" from Freud to the present, and describe the likely cause and chain of events in the development of a conversion disorder. (pp. 258-263)

5. Explain the differences between "unconscious processes" in current experimental psychology and the Freudian concept of the unconscious as they relate to the dissociative disorders. (pp. 263-264)

6. Compare the major features of dissociative amnesia and fugue, dissociative identity disorder, and depersonalization disorder. (pp. 264-269)

7. Discuss the etiological contributions of biological, psychosocial, and sociocultural factors to the somatoform and dissociative disorders and note the critical difficulty caused by the fallibility of memory in determining the contribution of childhood abuse to these disorders. (pp. 269-274)

8. Describe the most appropriate treatments for the somatoform and dissociative disorders, as well as the limitations of biological and psychological treatments. (pp. 274-275)

9. Explain the conflict between DSM-IV's descriptive approach to classification and the authors' preference in the case of the somatoform and dissociative disorders for classification based on underlying processes. (pp. 275-276)

◊ **TERMS YOU SHOULD KNOW**

---

somatoform disorder (p. 253-254)

dissociative disorder (pp. 253, 263)

dissociation (pp. 253, 263)

malingering (pp. 254)

factitious disorder (p. 254)

somatization disorder (p. 254)

hypochondriasis (pp. 255-256)

pain disorder (p. 257)

hysteria (pp. 253, 258)

pseudoneurological symptoms (p. 258)

conversion disorder (pp. 253, 258)

secondary gain (p. 258)

anesthesia (p. 260)

astasia-abasia (p. 260)

aphonia (p. 260)

mutism (p. 260)

la belle indifference (p. 262)

mass hysteria (p. 262)

implicit memory (p. 263)

implicit perception (p. 263)

amnesia (p. 264)

psychogenic or dissociative amnesia (p. 265)

fugue state (p. 265)

dissociative identity disorder (p. 266)

multiple personality (p. 266)

host personality (p. 266)

alter personality (p. 267)

depersonalization disorder (p. 269)

derealization (p. 269)

traumatic childhood abuse (p. 270)

false memories (p. 271)

neuroticism (p. 271)

pseudomemories (Highlight 7.3, p. 273)

alexithymia (p. 274)

◊ NAMES YOU SHOULD KNOW

Pierre Janet (p. 253)

John Kihlstrom (pp. 263-264, 271, 275)

Elizabeth Loftus (Highlight 7.3, p. 273)

1. Compare and contrast somatization disorder with hypochondriasis. (pp. 254-257)

2. Explain why hypochondriasis may be viewed as a certain type of interpersonal communication. (p. 257)

3. Describe the clinical features of pain disorder, and explain what the authors of the text mean when they say that people with psychogenic pain disorders may adopt an invalid life style. (pp. 257-258)

4. Describe the major manifestations of a conversion disorder, and describe some sensory, motor, and visceral symptoms that often appear. (pp. 258-262)

5. What are the four criteria that help to distinguish between conversion disorders and organic disturbances? (p. 262)

6. How can you distinguish a person with conversion symptoms from a *malingerer*, that is, a person who is consciously faking an illness? (p. 262)

7. Compare and contrast the concept of unconscious processes in implicit memory and implicit perception with the psychodynamic concept of the unconscious. (p. 263)

8. Describe the similarities and differences in the psychological functions of somatoform disorders and dissociative disorders. (p. 264)

9. List and describe four types of psychogenic amnesia, and explain why fugue is considered in the same section. (p. 265)

10. Explain in what way dissociative amnesia and conversion symptoms are similar. (p. 265)

11. How do the authors of the text describe the personalities of people who experience psychogenic amnesia? (p. 266)

12. Describe the symptoms of dissociative identity disorder (formerly multiple personality disorder), and explain the complexity of determining whether some may be considered genuine and others fraudulent. (pp. 266-268)

13. Describe the symptoms of a depersonalization disorder, and note the diagnostic problem that arises because feelings of depersonalization sometimes occur with personality deterioration. (p. 269)

14. Review the evidence in support of a strong contribution of traumatic childhood abuse, especially sexual abuse, to the etiology of DID (dissociative identity disorder). (pp. 270-271; Highlight 7.3, pp. 272-273)

15. Summarize the view that ordinary memory is fallible and is a constructive act employing multiple associational cues of diverse origins. Explain how this view makes it difficult to know for sure that memories of sexual abuse in childhood are valid. (Highlight 7.3, pp. 272-273)

16. DSM-IV (like DSM-III that preceded it) allocates the somatoform and dissociative disorders to separate categories. The evident intent was to follow the descriptive principle embraced by DSM-IV and gather together as somatoform disorders "all disorders involving physical disabilities or complaints for which no organic basis could be established." How does your text argue that examination of "potential underlying mechanisms" would lead to a different organization of these disorders? (pp. 275-276)

◊ STUDY QUESTIONS

Somatoform disorders

1. Sincere somatic symptoms that are thought to represent an expression of psychological difficulties and for which no organic basis can be found are referred to as _____. (p. 253)

2. Complete the following list of the four distinct somatoform patterns covered in the text: (pp. 254-263)
   a. Somatization disorder
   b. Hypochondriasis
   c.
   d.

Somatization disorder

3. This disorder is characterized by multiple complaints of physical ailments over a long period, beginning before age _____, that cannot be attributed to physical disorder, illness, or injury. (p. 254)

4. In making a diagnosis of somatization disorder, the diagnostician need not be convinced that the claimed illnesses actually existed in a patient's background history; the _____ is sufficient. (p. 254)

Hypochondriasis

5. A hypochondriac's visit to the doctor has been humorously called an "organ recital." Describe the characteristic behavior of such individuals. (p. 256)

6. Describe the typical attitude among hypochondriacal patients toward their illnesses. (p. 256)

7. The authors believe that hypochondriasis can be viewed as an interpersonal strategy which results when an individual has learned to view illness as way to obtain special consideration and avoid responsibility. Complete the following statements typical of hypochondriacal adults: (p. 257)
   a. I deserve your attention and concern.
   b.

Somatoform pain disorder

8. In approaching the phenomenon of pain, it is important to underscore that it is always in essence a sensation registered in a patient's mental experience; there is not a perfect correlation between the occurrence or intensity of pain (as reported in the general population) and _____ or _____. This partial independence of _____ and psychological experience evidently makes possible the considerable effectiveness of purely _____ treatment for pain that has a definite physical basis. (p. 257)

9. Because pain is ultimately always _____, we have no way of gauging with certainty the actual extent of a patient's pain. This fundamental lack of clarity is wholly insufficient to justify the conclusion that a patient is _____ or _____ his or her pain. (p. 257)

10. Freud used the term conversion hysteria because he believed that the symptoms were an expression of repressed sexual energy that was converted into a bodily disturbance. This view is no longer accepted. Rather, the physical symptoms are now viewed as serving a defensive function, enabling the individual to _____ without having to _____. (p. 258)

11. Compared to the higher incidences in the past, how frequent are conversion disorders today? (p. 259)

12. Why are these disorders decreasing in frequency? (p. 259)

13. Ironside and Batchelor studied hysterical visual symptoms among airmen in World War II. They found that the symptoms of each airman were closely related to his _____. (p. 260)

14. Hysterical motor symptoms such as paralysis are usually confined to a single limb. True or False (p. 260)

15. Mutism is one of the two most common speech-related conversion disorders. True or False (p. 260)

16. Place the following events in the development of a conversion disorder in the proper causal sequence: (a) Under continued stress, the symptoms of illness appear; (b) a desire to escape an unpleasant situation; (c) a wish to be sick to avoid the situation. (p. 262)
    First   _____
    Second   _____
    Third   _____

17. What determines the particular symptoms the person prone to conversion disorder will develop? (p. 262)

18. Can a conversion reaction occur after an accident in which the victim hopes to obtain compensation? (p. 263)

Dissociative disorders

19. Dissociative disorders, like somatoform disorders, are ways of avoiding anxiety and stress in a manner that permits the person to deny personal _____ for his or her behavior. (p. 264)

Psychogenic amnesia and fugue

20. Amnesia is partial or total inability to recall or identify past experience. If it is due to brain disorder, the amnesia usually involves an actual failure of retention. In such cases, the memories are truly lost. In _____ amnesia, the forgotten material is still there beneath the level of consciousness and can be recalled under hypnosis or narcosis. (pp. 265)

21. Label the following descriptions of four forms of dissociative amnesia using the following terms: localized amnesia, selective amnesia, generalized amnesia, continuous amnesia. (p. 265)

Forms of Psychogenic Amnesia	Definition
_____	In this form of amnesia, the individual remembers nothing that happened during a specific period--usually the first few hours following some traumatic event.
_____	In this form of amnesia, the individual forgets some but not all of what happened during a given period.
_____	In this form of amnesia, an individual cannot recall events beyond a certain point in the past.
_____	In this form of amnesia, the individual forgets his or her entire life history.

22. Dissociative amnesia is highly selective. What type of material is most likely to be forgotten? (p. 265)

23. In typical dissociative amnesic reactions, only episodic or autobiographical memory is affected. The types of memory that are not affected are: (p. 265)
a. semantic
b.
c.
d. short-term storage

24. Kiersch (1962) found _____ out of 98 amnesia cases among military personnel were due to deliberate suppression of memories. (p. 266)

Dissociative identity disorder

25. Dissociative identity disorder is rare. Until approximately the last quarter century, only about 100 cases had been described, but, oddly, the prevalence of this disorder seems to be increasing. Dissociative identity disorder is a dramatic dissociative pattern, usually due to stress, in which the individual manifests two or more complete _____ _____. (p. 266)

26. Describe the various types of relationships that may exist between the different personalities in an individual who exhibits multiple personalities. (p. 267-268)

Depersonalization disorder

27. In mild forms, depersonalization, or the loss of the sense of self, is a common experience and no cause for alarm. In individuals who experience depersonalized states, functioning in between episodes is usually _____. (p. 269)

Causal factors in somatoform and dissociative disorders

28. In contrast to the anxiety disorders (discussed in Chapter 5), the specific causal pathways in the somatoform and dissociative disorders remain to a large extent _____. Those holding to the psychodynamic viewpoint contend that _____ is the central problem, and in view of the widespread reports of childhood abuse it is reasonable to support that some

form of _____ or _____ may be involved in the development of somatoform and dissociative symptoms. Even so, much remains unexplained with respect to the development of these particular modes of coping. (p. 270)

Sociocultural factors

29. The incidence and prevalence of dissociative disorders are strongly influenced by the degree to which such phenomena are accepted or tolerated as legitimate mental disorders by the surrounding cultural context. Spanos has criticized the acceptance of DID, arguing that the abrupt rise in incidence in recent years is attributable to the _____ of both patients and clinicians. (p. 274)

30. In many instances, the best treatment for somatoform disorders turns out to be no treatment at all, but rather the provision of _____ _____. With the exception of conversion disorder and pain syndromes, the prognosis for full recovery from somatoform disorders is _____. (p. 274)

31. Kluft offered a three-stage "consensus model" for the treatment of DID. These three stages are: (pp. 274-275)
    a.
    b.
    c. Postintegration therapy

◊ CRITICAL THINKING ABOUT DIFFICULT TOPICS

1. There are many phenomena that seem to emphasize the importance of conscious processing of psychologically important stimuli. Two examples will illustrate this point. First, in Chapter 6 you read about cognitive theories of depression from Beck (schemata, dysfunctional beliefs) and from Abramson et al. (internal, stable, and global attributions), both of which might be thought to involve conscious thought processes. Second, in theories about the emotional impact of psychological stimuli (e.g., the difference between "innocent" and "guilty" at the end of a trial or the difference between "I love you" and "I hate you" in an interpersonal context), it

is obvious that there must be a process of appraisal of the meaning of the stimuli in order for them to have an emotional impact, and one might think this appraisal involves conscious processing. On the other hand, your text describes the new recognition in experimental psychology "that much (most) mental activity, much processing of information, occurs outside and independent of conscious awareness" (p. 263). How does this new perspective affect your understanding of the theories in the two examples just given? How would this new perspective affect the way in which you might conduct research on these hypotheses--e.g., if people are unaware of these attributional and appraisal processes and cannot tell you about them?

2. Your text nicely presents the conflicting issues surrounding the recovery of "repressed memories" of childhood sexual abuse. These may be true memories or "false memories" (p. 271). Think of the process of attempting (in psychotherapy) to determine whether a client actually suffered childhood sexual abuse as a process of assessment in which there are two types of errors: false positives (untrue "memories" of sexual abuse) and false negatives (failure to find evidence of sexual abuse when, in fact, it occurred). The problem of false negatives and false positives is characteristic of all attempts at assessment, and how one deals with these depends on the costs and benefits of each outcome. An extreme example would be the failure to detect a life-threatening illness such as cancer (a false negative with a fatal outcome) versus a false positive (incorrect detection of a life-threatening illness). If the false positive outcome results only in a more expensive and more accurate but safe additional test, then false negatives are very much more serious than false positives. Look at the discovery of "repressed memories" from this perspective (Highlight 7.3, pp. 272-273). How costly is a false accusation of childhood sexual abuse? How costly is the failure to detect abuse that actually occurred? In our judicial system, we set the threshold for assigning guilt very high by requiring strong proof of guilt and assuming that a person is innocent until proven guilty. Would you apply this standard to accusations of sexual abuse, or do you feel that failure to detect guilt is too serious to adopt the same standard?

3. Over time it has become clear that human memory is quite fallible and involves a constructive act that incorporates a variety of false information (Highlight 7.3, pp. 272-273). How does this information affect your attitude toward research that involves the extensive use of self-report tests in which people are asked to provide information based on their recollections?

4. Freud found that a number of his female patients reported childhood sexual abuse, and initially he reported this finding as evidence that such events had actually occurred. He received a chilly reception for these reports from his professional colleagues, at least in part because high rates of childhood sexual abuse were unthinkable in the Vienna of his time, and Freud eventually concluded that most such reports by patients "were merely libidinally inspired fantasies" (p. 271). Now, it is estimated that in the United States there may well be hundreds of thousands of instances of sexual abuse each year (p. 271). Does this information alter your

view of the validity of such reports by Freud's patients, or do you think cultural factors may make the incidence and prevalence of sexual abuse vastly higher in the U. S. today than in Freud's Vienna? Do you think there is any way Freud could have ascertained the truth of his patients' reports? If not, what does this tell you about the value of reports by patients in psychotherapy as evidence in support of any given theory?

◊ CHAPTER 7 QUIZ

Circle the best of the four answers provided and check them according to answers provided at the back of this study guide. Be sure you understand why each answer is correct.

1. Which of the following is characterized by multiple complaints of physical ailments over a long period that are inadequately explained by independent findings of physical illness? (p. 254)
   a. somatization disorder   c. pain disorder
   b. hypochondriasis   d. conversion disorder

2. A hidden message in the complaints of the hypochondriacal adult is: (p. 257)
   a. "I am terribly anxious about dying."
   b. "I can do things as well as you even though I'm sick."
   c. "I deserve your attention and concern."
   d. "You make me sick."

3. Aphonia is: (p. 260)
   a. inability to speak.
   b. ability to talk only in a whisper.
   c. a grotesque, disorganized walk.
   d. pseudopregnancy.

4. La belle indifference would be expected in cases of: (p. 262)
   a. malingering.
   b. hypochondriasis.
   c. conversion disorder.
   d. psychogenic pain disorder.

5. All of the following are part of a chain of events in the development of a conversion disorder except: (p. 262)
   a. a conscious plan to use illness as an escape.
   b. a desire to escape from an unpleasant situation.
   c. a fleeting wish to be sick in order to avoid the situation.
   d. the appearance of the symptoms of some physical ailment.

6. Dissociative disorders are methods in which individuals avoid stress by: (p. 264)
   a. escaping from their personal identity.
   b. projecting blame for their "sins" on others.
   c. separating themselves from significant others.
   d. withdrawing from stressful situations.

7. In _____ amnesia, the individual forgets his/her entire life history. (p. 265)
   a. localized   c. generalized
   b. selective   d. continuous

8. Alter personalities would be expected in cases of: (p. 267)
   a. psychogenic pain disorder.   c. conversion disorder.
   b. hypochondriasis.   d. dissociative identity disorder.

9. The strongest evidence implicates _____ as a risk factor for dissociative disorders. (p. 270)
   a. death of a parent during childhood
   b. traumatic childhood abuse
   c. low self-esteem developed during childhood
   d. parental use of strict discipline with excessive punishment

10. One of the difficulties in establishing that childhood sexual abuse occurred is that: (Highlight 7.3, pp. 272-273)
   a. repression keeps patients from recalling the event.
   b. therapists are too reluctant to help patients recover repressed memories.
   c. many abuses occurred too early in development to be remembered.
   d. memory is a constructive act.

	Chapter 8
	Psychological Factors in Physical Illness

◊ OVERVIEW

Emotional factors occupy a central position in our understanding of physical disease. The chapter presents the view that all physical disease is related to stress to some degree. At one end of the continuum are diseases that are primarily due to the invasion of body cells by a potent virus. However, the degree of stress a person is experiencing influences the efficiency with which the individual resists the virus and how rapidly he or she recovers. At the other end of the continuum are diseases such as eating disorders ulcers that mainly represent the direct results of psychological factors. This type of disease would not be seen in an individual unless high levels of stress were present. Chapter 8 first discusses the interrelationship of health, attitudes, life-style, and coping resources, followed by a description of the functioning of both the autonomic nervous system and the immune system. Then, specific data on the clinical picture and treatment of diseases such as coronary heart disease, anorexia/bulimia, essential hypertension, and recurrent headaches are presented. Finally, general etiological issues and methods of treatment are considered.

◊ LEARNING OBJECTIVES

After studying this chapter, you should be able to:

1. Describe the field of behavioral medicine and the way in which psychological factors in physical medicine are handled in DSM-IV. (pp. 279-280)

2. Review evidence that the following factors influence the risk of physical illnesses:
   - Health, attitudes and coping resources. (pp. 281-282)
   - Cannon's fight/flight response and chronic overarousal of the autonomic nervous system. (pp. 282-283)
   - Effects of psychological stress and depressed mood on the immune system. (pp. 283-287)
   - Various habits and aspects of life-style. (pp. 287-288)

3. Describe the three chief clinical manifestations of coronary heart disease and evaluate the evidence for an etiological contribution of Type A personality. (pp. 288-292)

4. Describe anorexia and bulimia, explain some of the psychosocial factors that may be responsible for these disorders, and list some of the serious physical conditions that often result. (p. 292-297)

5. Characterize the changes in blood flow that increase blood pressure, define essential hypertension and its consequences, and review the psychological contributors to its development. (pp. 297-298)

6. Distinguish among migraine, cluster, and tension headaches and both theories of etiology and approaches to treatment. (pp. 298-300)

7. Explain the "problem of specificity" in psychogenic illness and summarize the biological, psychosocial, and sociocultural factors contributing to these illnesses. (pp. 300-305)

8. Characterize the biological and psychosocial approaches to treatment of psychogenic illness, as well as sociocultural approaches aimed at prevention. (pp. 306-309)

9. List the reasons for the impending AIDS epidemic health catastrophe and explain why we are likely to fail in efforts to prevent this catastrophe. (pp. 309-310)

◊ **TERMS YOU SHOULD KNOW**

---

behavioral medicine (p. 279)

psychogenic (p. 279-280)

health psychology (p. 280)

etiology (p. 280)

host resistance (p. 280)

disease mechanisms (p. 280)

patient decision-making (p. 280)

compliance (p. 280)

intervention (p. 280)

psychophysiologic disorders (p. 280)

Type A (p. 282)

placebo effect (p. 282)

flight or fight response (p. 283)

diseases of civilization (p. 283)

autonomic nervous system arousal (pp. 283)

immune system (p. 284)

serum (p. 284)

white blood cells, or *leukocytes* (p. 284)

B-cells, or *humoral immune functioning* (p. 284)

T-cells, or *cellular immune functioning* (p. 284)

macrophages (p. 284)

natural killer cells (p. 284)

humoral branch (of the immune system) (p. 284)

cellular branch (of the immune system) (p. 284)

antigen (p. 284)

antibodies (p. 284)

immunocompetence (p. 285)

simple tension headaches (p. 299)

biofeedback (p. 299)

stomach reactor (p. 301)

weakest link (p. 301)

corticovisceral control mechanisms (p. 301)

broken heart syndrome (p. 303)

secondary gains (p. 304)

acupuncture (p. 306)

North Karelia Project (p. 308)

◊ NAMES YOU SHOULD KNOW

Walter Cannon (p. 283)

Meyer Friedman and Ray Rosenman (p. 289)

◊ CONCEPTS TO MASTER

1. What is the relationship between the concepts of behavioral medicine and health psychology? (pp. 279-280)

2. What did Walter Cannon mean by "diseases of civilization" and what physiological mechanism is involved? (pp. 282-283)

3. List and describe the component parts of the two main branches (humoral and cellular) of the immune system and explain the functions of each of the component parts. (pp. 284-285)

4. Summarize the research findings that point to psychosocial effects on the immune system, and describe the recent evidence that the relationship between stress and compromised immune function is causal. (p. 285)

5. Explain what is meant by the field of psychoneuroimmunology and summarize the major evidence supporting its major premise. (pp. 286-287)

6. List several aspects of the way we live that may produce severe physical problems. Explain why conclusive proof of these allegations is difficult to obtain and why even when the proof is conclusive (e.g., cigarette smoking) healthy individuals find it difficult to change their habits. (pp. 287-288)

7. What is meant by the Type A personality? Summarize the evidence linking it to coronary heart disease (CHD). (pp. 288-289, 291-292; Highlight 8.2, p. 292)

8. Describe the family dynamics that seem to contribute to anorexia, the life changes at which anorexia begins, and the behavior out of which it develops. (p. 293)

9. Fallon and Rozin used figure drawings as stimuli to be judged by men and women. Compare men's and women's perceptions of the ideal woman's figure and explain how these results help to explain the gender difference in prevalence rates of anorexia nervosa. (p. 294)

10. An example of the psychoanalytic approach to the contribution of emotional factors to physical illness was the hypothesis that asthma is caused by "suppressed crying." What is wrong with this hypothesis? (pp. 296-297)

11. Define *essential hypertension*, list some physical diseases that it causes, and explain McClelland's variation of the suppressed-rage hypothesis about the cause of essential hypertension. (pp. 297-298)

12. Differentiate between the physical causes of migraine and simple tension headaches, and summarize the research findings more strongly implicating psychosocial factors in tension headaches. (pp. 298-300)

13. Describe the psychological treatments for tension headaches. (p. 299)

14. Define the "problem of specificity" in the etiology of psychogenic illnesses and indicate (a) why it is important enough to be the particular concern of the discussion of etiologic considerations and (b) what etiological factors are inevitably involved in addition to psychogenic factors. (p. 300)

15. Wolf suggested that people can be classified as "stomach reactors," "pulse reactors," "nose reactors," and so on. Explain the theoretical importance of this concept and the related concept of the "weakest link" in accounting for the prediction of which psychogenic disease a person develops. (p. 301)

16. Dunbar (1943, 1954) thought that there were specific personality characteristics associated with particular psychophysiologic disorders. Later research, such as Kidson's (1973) cast doubt on this view. Describe Kidson's comparison of hypertensive patients' personalities to the personalities of a group of nonhypertensive people. (p. 302)

17. What theoretical explanation for the high rate of heart disease in industrialized societies is offered in the book, *The Broken Heart*? (p. 303)

18. Explain why psychogenic illnesses must be treated by a combination of medical and psychological measures, and describe how such combinations have been used to treat anorexia nervosa. (p. 308)

19. Indicate the major objectives of sociocultural efforts to reduce psychogenic diseases, and describe the five-pronged North Karelia Project and some of its early results. (pp. 308-309)

20. Explain why it is abundantly clear that we must expect a health catastrophe in the near future as a result of the AIDS epidemic and discuss reasons why the authors of the text are pessimistic about the success of efforts to stop this epidemic. (pp. 309-310)

◊ STUDY QUESTIONS

Introduction

1. Although an illness may be primarily physical or primarily psychological, it is always a disorder of the whole person, not just of the body or the psyche. The interdisciplinary approach to treatment of physical disorders thought to have psychological factors as major aspects of their causal patterns is known as _____. Psychologists who are interested in psychological factors that induce or maintain disease specialize in _____ which includes research on etiology, host resistance, disease mechanisms, patient decision-making, compliance, and intervention. (pp. 279-280)

2. In DSM-IV, when a "general medical condition" is coded on Axis III, Axis I provides a major category called Psychological Factors Affecting Medical Condition. The suspected contributing factors are specified under six subcategories: (p. 280)

   a. mental disorder
   b.
   c.
   d.
   e.
   f. other/unspecified

Health, attitudes, and coping resources

3. Why are some surgeons reluctant to operate unless the patient has a reasonably optimistic attitude about the outcome? (p. 281)

4. What has been learned by researchers such as Rahe (1974) and Payne (1975) about the likelihood of illness under increasing levels of stress? (p. 282)

5. What difference might it make if a cancer patient, for example, believed in his or her doctor, had faith in the treatment, and had an overall positive mental outlook compared to a patient who had lost hope? (p. 282)

183

Autonomic excess and tissue damage

6. Describe how autonomic nervous system arousal, adaptive among lower animals, leads to diseases of civilization among human beings. (p. 283)

Psychosocial factors and the immune system

7. The application of cold for minor burns is an example of counteracting the ``adaptiveness without intelligence'' of the body's defensive resources. Explain. (pp. 283-284)

8. The _____ system is responsible for defending bodily health against an intrusion of foreign substances such as bacteria, viruses, and tumors. The primary components of this system are the blood, thymus, bone marrow, spleen, and lymph nodes. The blood _____, made up of large protein molecules and water, is the medium by which the body transports its defenses. (p. 284)

9. The organism has been invaded by an antigen--that is, a substance recognized as foreign. Once this foreign substance has been detected, B- and T-cells become activated and _____, deploying the various forms of counterattack mediated by each type of cell. (p. 284)

10. B-cells, which are formed in the _____, perform their defensive function by producing antibodies that circulate in the blood _____. B-cell functioning is involved chiefly with protection against the more common varieties of _____ infection. (p. 284)

11. T-cells develop to maturity in the _____ and mediate immune reactions that, while slower, are far more _____ and _____ in character. These cells mainly generate an attack that is _____ to a given invading antigen. (p. 284)

12. Psychosocial factors were originally thought to play little or no role in the pervasive immune breakdown characteristic of AIDS (HIV-1). More recent research suggests that behavioral interventions, such as _____, had positive psychological and _____ effects among groups of uninfected high-risk and early-stage infected gay men. More recently, Kemeny and colleagues presented evidence that a _____ mood was associated with enhanced HIV-1 activity among infected gay men, confirming in this group the more general point that psychological _____ compromises _____. (p. 285)

184

13. Many stressors such as sleep deprivation, marathon running, space flight, and death of a spouse have been shown to reduce _____ blood cell production, which affects immunity. Until recently, researchers were convinced that the _____ _____ axis was the pathway by which stress affected the immune response. However, recent research has turned up a number of competing paths. We now know that a number of other hormones, including growth hormone, _____, and _____, respond to stress and also affect immune competence. The same is true of a variety of neurochemicals, including _____. There may even be direct neural control of the secretion of immunologic agents, as suggested by the discovery of nerve endings in the _____. (p. 286)

14. In a surprising result, it was found that immunosuppression can be _____ _____--that is, it can come to be elicited as an acquired response to previously neutral stimuli. (p. 286)

Life-style as a factor in health maintenance

15. Numerous aspects of the way we live significantly affect the risk of developing physical illnesses. These include: (p. 287)

   a. _____
   b. lack of _____
   c. _____
   d. excessive _____ and _____ use
   e. constantly facing high-stress situations
   f. ineffective ways of dealing with day-to-day problems

16. Some of the data regarding life-style and disease is correlational and relatively weak. Even when the evidence for causation is extremely strong, it is difficult for many people to change their life-styles to reduce their risk of disease--an incentive that may be _____ for healthy people. (p. 288)

Coronary heart disease and the "Type A" behavior pattern

17. Coronary heart disease (CHD) is the nation's number one killer. It is a potentially lethal blockage of the arteries supplying blood to the heart muscle (called the myocardium). The clinical picture of CHD includes (a) _____, which is severe chest pain and signals that insufficient blood is getting to the heart muscle; (b) _____, which is complete blockage of a section of the blood supply to the heart and leads to death of

heart muscle tissue; and (c) disturbance of the heart's _____ conduction consequent to arterial blockage, resulting in interruption or stoppage of pumping action and leading to sudden death. (p. 289)

18. The Type A behavior pattern as conceptualized by Friedman and Rosenman is characterized by excessive competitive drive, time urgency, and hostility manifested in accelerated speech and motor activity. Type B behavior is the absence of Type A characteristics. Respond true or false to the following questions about Type A and Type B behaviors. (p. 289, 291-292)

a. The most popular questionnaire measure of Type A behavior is the Jenkins Activity Survey. True or False

b. The alternative approaches to measuring Type A behavior are highly correlated, which suggests widespread agreement on the definition of this concept. True or False

c. Not all components of Type A behavior are equally predictive of CHD. The hyper aggressivity/hostility component of the pattern is most correlated with coronary artery deterioration. True or False

d. The Western Collaborative Group Study (WCGS) typed people for A-B type and followed their health for over 8 years. The strong virtue of this study is that it was retrospective. True or False

e. In the WCGS, Type A personalities were approximately twice as likely as Type B personalities to have developed CHD by the end of the study. True or False

f. The Framingham Heart Study is a prospective study that has been ongoing for more than 40 years. It has demonstrated that the Type A-CHD correlation holds for women as well as for men. True or False

g. Some aspect of the Type A behavior pattern, most likely general negative affect that remains unexpressed, contributes to the development of potentially lethal CHD. True or False

19. What is the cause of atherosclerosis? (Highlight 8.1, p. 290)

20. List the warning signs of heart attack. (Highlight 8.1, p. 290)
   a.
   b.
   c.
   d.

The anorexic and bulimic syndromes

21. Anorexia nervosa and bulimia are coded as adult Eating Disorders in DSM-IV. In fact, both syndromes are rare before adolescence and onset after age _____ is rare. They occur at

least nine times more frequently in women than men. Anorexia is considered both difficult to treat and dangerous; the death rate approaches _____ percent overall. (p. 292)

22. The central features of anorexia are: (pp. 292-293)
    a. Intense fear of _____ and the irrational belief that one is fat
    b. Weight loss of more than _____ percent of original body weight
    c. Refusal to maintain weight within the lower limits of normal
    d. Absence of three consecutive _____
    e. Marked overactivity
    f. Binge eating with or without voluntary _____

23. Anorexic girls often describe their mothers in unflattering terms as excessively dominant, intrusive, and overbearing. Why must we be cautious in interpreting these reports? (p. 293)

24. Bulimia nervosa involves recurrent episodes of seemingly uncontrollable _____ with full awareness of the abnormality of this eating pattern. Bulimic young women normally have pronounced fears that they will be unable to _____ voluntarily; are preoccupied with _____; and engage in frequent, inappropriate attempts to lose weight by _____, overuse of _____ and _____. (p. 294)

25. The estimated frequency (point prevalence) of bulimia among women of college age is as high as _____ percent. (p. 294)

26. Most anorexics and bulimics come from socioeconomically advantaged homes. Researchers consider that both anorexics and bulimics are dealing with similar problems but that the typical _____ is at a more advanced stage of identity development. The establishment of independent selfhood and mature _____ remains a difficult hurdle for both groups of women. (p. 296)

Essential hypertension

27. What changes in blood distribution take place when an individual is subjected to stress? (p. 297)

28. Preexisting organic factors account for only some _____ to _____ percent of hypertension cases; the large remainder are given the designation _____ hypertension. (p. 297)

29. About _____ percent of Americans suffer from hypertension. Hypertension is the primary cause of more than 60,000 deaths each year and a major predisposing factor in another million or more deaths a year from strokes and cardiovascular disease. The incidence among blacks is about _____ high as among whites. (p. 297)

30. Why are so many people unaware that they have hypertension? (p. 297)

31. The "suppressed rage" hypothesis of hypertension suggests that hypertensives often must keep their anger to themselves and outwardly appear submissive and controlled. McClelland has developed a variant of the suppressed rage hypothesis that attributes hypertension to the need to inhibit the expression of power motives. However, the text suggests the more general concept that the common factor is the _____ of strong _____ to perform acts poorly tolerated by society. (p. 298)

Recurrent headaches

32. More than ____ million Americans suffer from tension or migraine headaches. Among college students, one study reported that _____ percent reported headaches at least once or twice a week. (p. 298)

33. The typical migraine occurs in two phases. Complete the following description of the physiological changes associated with each stage of migraine headache. (pp. 298-299)
   a. First phase: alterations in the brain's electrical activity--may cause victims to experience an aura.
   b. Second phase:

34. Do stressors play an important role in cluster headaches? (p. 299)

35. Are the physiological changes that lead to tension headaches indisputably different from the changes that lead to migraine headaches? (p. 299)

36. At what life period do tension and migraine headaches typically begin? (p. 299)

37. According to the study by Andrasik and colleagues, are tension or migraine headaches more indicative of psychological problems? (p. 300)

Psychogenic physical disease: Biological factors

38. The three general biological causal factors involved in all disease are genetic factors, differences in _____ reactivity and _____ weakness, and disruption of _____ mechanisms. (pp. 300-301)

39. In Liljefors and Rahe's twin study of the role of life stress in coronary heart disease, what was the critical difference between the twins in each pair? What are the implications of their findings? (pp. 300-301)

40. In the autonomic reactivity/somatic weakness theory, if a stomach reactor were to develop a psychogenic illness, which one would it likely be? (p. 301)

41. Sometimes a particular organ is especially vulnerable because of heredity, _____, or prior _____. (p. 301)

42. Some individuals appear to have a hypothalamus that overstimulates the pituitary that, in turn, leads to overstimulation of the adrenal gland and, ultimately, to oversecretion of adrenocortical hormones. An excess of these hormones can cause an organism to function the majority of time as if it were under stress. The authors label this sequence of events an inadequate _____ control mechanism. (p. 301)

Psychogenic physical disease: Psychosocial factors

43. What are the three major psychosocial factors that play a prominent role in causing many diseases? (pp. 301-302)

44. When people are subjected experimentally to frustrating experiences, their blood pressures rise and their hearts beat more rapidly. If they are then given an opportunity to _____ _____, their blood pressures and heart rates rapidly return to normal. (p. 302)

45. How is the incidence of illness related to the following stressors:
    a. Marital problems, divorce (Bloom et al.) (p. 302)
    b. Bereavement (Parkes et al., Aiken) (p. 302; Highlight 8.4, p. 303)

46. Explain how the overprotectiveness and tendency to reject the child that has been observed in asthmatic children's mothers could just as easily be viewed as both a *cause* of the child's asthma and an *effect* of the child's asthma. (p. 303)

47. Regardless of how a physical symptom may have been developed, it may be elicited by suggestion and maintained by the reinforcement provided by secondary gains. The ability of suggestion to elicit a physical symptom was demonstrated by Blecker (1968) among asthmatics. What did this experiment involve, and how were the results interpreted? (p. 304)

Psychogenic physical disease: Sociocultural factors

48. How common are psychophysiologic illnesses among nonindustrialized peoples? (p. 304)

49. Which psychogenic illness shows large effects on prevalence of both social classes and gender in our own society? (p. 305)

Treatment and outcomes

50. The following are the biological treatments used for psychogenic illnesses. Briefly indicate what each treatment accomplishes. (p. 306)
    a. Mild tranquilizers
    b. Antidepressant medication
    c. Acupuncture

51. In the treatment of psychosocially medicated illness, one-to-one, verbally oriented psychotherapies have been relatively ineffective. On the other hand, _____ therapy has shown promising results. (p. 306)

52. _____ treatment for psychogenic diseases had until recently generally failed to live up to the enthusiasm it generated when first introduced some 25 years ago. Its effects rarely exceeded those that could be obtained in simpler and cheaper ways, as by providing systematic _____ training. That situation may be changing, although it is still not entirely clear that _____ is anything more than an elaborate means to teach patients to _____. There have been increasingly favorable reports in recent years regarding efficacy for _____ in the control of musculoskeletal pain. Similarly, some work on _____ in respect to the muscle tonus of _____ in cases of asthma looks promising. (p. 306)

53. On what assumption is behavior therapy for physical disorders based? (p. 306)

54. How successful are relaxation techniques in the treatment of simple tension headaches and hypertension? (p. 307)

55. Some cognitive behavior therapists have worked to modify maladaptive behaviors such as rushing, impatience, and hostility--characteristics of Type A personalities. Others such as Kobasa (1985) have been experimenting with methods to increase _____, which is defined as the ability to withstand stressful circumstances and remain healthy in the face of them. (p. 307)

56. As reported by Halmi et al., in anorexia nervosa, choice of treatment does not seem to be a factor in successful weight gain for hospitalized patients, who typically gain weight regardless of the treatment technique employed. Why may therapy for psychological adjustment still be important? (p. 308)

57. Describe the treatment approach used by Lucas et al. (1981) at the Mayo Clinic to meet the physiological and psychological needs of anorexic patients. (p. 308)

58. Sociocultural treatment measures are targeted more toward preventive efforts and are typically applied to selected populations or subcultural groups. Within these groups, efforts are made to alter certain _____ to reduce the overall level of susceptibility to a disorder. (p. 308)

59. The North Karelia Project was aimed at reducing atherosclerotic disease in an entire Finnish province. Describe the following aspects of the program: (pp. 308-309)

a. Overall goal

b. Activities undertaken by project staff

c. Early results

◊ CRITICAL THINKING ABOUT DIFFICULT TOPICS

1. As you have seen in previous chapters, unequivocal demonstrations of the contributions of stress to psychopathology are difficult to produce. In contrast, the present chapter offers undeniable evidence of the role of stress in physical illness. What accounts for this difference? In thinking about your answer, consider that the immune system is known to be involved in the resistance to physical illnesses and that many components of the immune system response to stress can be measured (e.g., p. 286). That is, it is possible to measure the *immediate* effects of stress on an *underlying process* (the immune response), which allows a more definitive determination of causal relationships. Can you think of any similar underlying processes for anxiety disorders and depression that could unequivocally show the causal effects of stress?

2. The methodologies of family, twin, and (more rarely) adoption studies together provide clear evidence for a role of genetic factors in psychopathology and physical illnesses. This conclusion tells us nothing, however, about *what* is inherited--leaving unanswered many of the most interesting questions. Regarding genetic contributions to psychogenic diseases, for example, your text notes the difficulty of determining whether a genetic contribution acts through "an underlying physical vulnerability for acquiring the disease in question" or "the psychological makeup of the individual and his or her stress tolerance" (p. 300). In the first case, there might be an "organ weakness," in which, for example, the cardiovascular system is prone to development of atherosclerosis (see Highlight 8.1, p. 290). In the second case, the person may be anxiety-prone or unduly sensitive to stress, as a result of which the person responds with a stress response to many minor irritations, thereby working a hardship on the cardiovascular system. Can you apply this train of thought to psychopathology? Given that we have evidence for a strong genetic contribution to schizophrenia and to bipolar affective disorder and for a moderate genetic contribution to depression and anxiety disorders, what underlying processes might be inherited?

3. To pursue the previous question further, the processes mediating a genetic influence on global behavior and functioning might be very complex. Consider two examples. First, a person's physical attractiveness has an important effect on his or her social interactions--i.e., on the way the world responds to him or her. Imagine that research first showed an important genetic contribution to the personality trait of "sociability," but that as time passed it was determined that much of the genetic effect was on the person's physical attractiveness--i.e., those who inherited physical attractiveness became more sociable. Thus, the apparent causal pathway involved a genetic effect on the person's physical attractiveness, an effect of physical attractiveness on the social environment (positive reactions, greater popularity), and an effect of a positively responsive social environment on the personality trait of sociability. Would you consider this a genetic or an environmental influence? Second, there is a substantial (estimates vary, but probably about 50%) genetic influence on IQ, and low IQ carries with it a number of

disadvantages: a person with low IQ is likely to experience school failure with subsequent occupational and economic disadvantage and may even suffer in peer relations. These disadvantages may cumulate to make the world more stressful for a person with an IQ of 75 than for a person with an IQ of 125. In view of this, when considering evidence for an effect of genetic factors on any stress-related illness or form of psychopathology, is it possible that some of the genetic effect is mediated by inheritance of lower IQ?

4. In discussing the immune system, your text states that "while efforts to relate specific stressors to specific physical diseases have not generally been successful, stress is becoming a key underlying theme in our understanding of the development and course of virtually all organic illness" (p. 287). In discussing "the problem of specificity" (p. 300) your text discusses a model that elsewhere has been called the "organ weakness" hypothesis--the hypothesis that which organ system breaks down in response to stress will depend on which organ is "weak" (p. 301). For example, a "stomach reactor" may have problems with peptic ulcers, whereas a "pulse reactor" may develop problems in the cardiovascular system. Consider three different explanations for why a person develops essential hypertension. (a) The person is exposed to an environment that specifically induces reactivity of the cardiovascular system and, therefore, works a hardship on the mechanisms regulating blood pressure. (b) The person is a blood pressure responder--i.e., when stressed the person reacts most strongly with an increase in blood pressure but normal response in other organ systems. This excessive blood pressure reactivity works a hardship on the mechanisms regulating blood pressure. (c) The person has a weakness in the mechanisms regulating blood pressure, which break down under normal levels of stress. Evidence for option (a) is difficult to find, although not altogether absent. On the whole, options (b) and (c)--the organ weakness models--seem likely to be more important. In options (b) and (c) there is a psychological contribution in the sense that the stress response is activated by psychological stimuli, but do you see any component of personal maladjustment or emotional disturbance in those models? In those models, would the likelihood of illness be increased as a result of the person's being in a particularly stressful environment or by being strongly anxiety-prone? What if you think of quantitative individual differences in the organ weakness? Would some individuals require greater stress or anxiety-proneness to produce hypertension if there is only a modest degree of "organ weakness"? Can you think of ways to apply these models to psychopathology--e.g., bipolar affective disorder and schizophrenia?

5. The text nicely summarizes the stark realities of the AIDS epidemic, in which without a major change in our behavior "a health catastrophe will be upon us." For individuals, the risk of failing to take precautions is exposure to an almost certain, slow, and painful death. The adaptive behavior required is "modest levels of forethought, judgment, restraint, and perhaps the risk of embarrassment" (p. 310), yet the authors are correctly pessimistic about our ability to effect these changes in behavior. Why is it so difficult to change human behavior? Note the implications for the efficacy of psychological interventions. It is not that psychological factors

are not important in the etiology of psychopathology and physical illness, but rather that psychological interventions must deal with resistance to change that is so strong that individuals readily risk death rather than change their habits. Does this explain the great popularity of biological treatments?

◊ CHAPTER 8 QUIZ

Circle the best of the four answers provided and check them according to answers provided at the back of this study guide. Be sure you understand why each answer is correct.

1. Health psychology deals with the diagnosis, treatment and prevention of: (pp. 279-280)
   a. anxiety disorders.
   b. physical disorders.
   c. stress disorders.
   d. psychogenic physical disorders.

2. In behavioral medicine, a search for the predisposing causes of a disease is a problem of: (p. 280)
   a. ecology.
   b. entymology.
   c. epidemiology.
   d. etiology.

3. Which of the following is not one of the six subcategories of Psychological Factors Affecting Physical Illness on Axis I of DSM-IV? (p. 280)
   a. repressed anger
   b. personality traits or coping style
   c. mental disorder
   d. stress-related physiological response

4. A patient who shows improvement after a trusted physician gives him/her an injection of sterile water is demonstrating: (p. 282)
   a. the Hawthorne effect.
   b. the placebo effect.
   c. demand characteristics
   d. faith healing.

5. The immune function is divided into two branches which are: (p. 284)
   a. blood-related and lymph-related.
   b. glandular and nervous.
   c. humoral and cellular.
   d. red cell-mediated and white cell-mediated.

6. B-cells produce antibodies which are involved chiefly with protection against the more common varieties of: (p. 284)
    a. bacterial infection.
    b. cancerous growth.
    c. cellular dysfunction.
    d. viral infection.

7. Psychosocial factors were originally thought to play little or no role in the pervasive immune breakdown characteristic of AIDS (HIV-1). More recent research suggests that behavioral interventions, such as _____, had positive psychological and immunocompetence effects among groups of uninfected high-risk and early-stage infected gay men. (p. 285)
    a. treatment of depression
    b. aerobic exercise
    c. relaxation training
    d. group therapy

8. The finding of nerve endings in the thymus suggests that: (p. 286)
    a. the thymus is centrally involved in the General Adaptation Syndrome.
    b. the HPA interpretation is correct.
    c. there is direct neural control of immunological agents.
    d. the placebo effect is mediated by the pons.

9. Severe chest pain resulting from too little oxygenated blood being delivered to the heart muscle is called: (p. 288; Highlight 8.1, p. 290)
    a. angina pectoris.
    b. arrhythmia.
    c. myocardial infarction.
    d. tachycardia.

10. According to Friedman and Rosenman, all of the following indications are involved in the Type A behavior pattern *except:* (p. 289)
    a. excessive competitive drive with poorly defined goals.
    b. hostility.
    c. impatience or time urgency.
    d. decelerated speech and motor activity.

11. In the Framingham Heart Study, all of the following groups showed Type A associations *except:* (p. 291)
    a. blue collar men.
    b. blue collar women.
    c. white collar men.
    d. white collar women.

12. The mortality rate for anorexia nervosa approaches _____ percent. (p. 292)
    a. 3
    b. 5
    c. 7
    d. 9

13. The estimated frequency (point prevalence) of bulimia among women of college age is as high as _____ percent. (p. 294)
    a. 5
    b. 10
    c. 15
    d. 20

14. Essential hypertension, in which preexisting organic factors do not account for the hypertension, is seen in _____ to _____ percent of all hypertension. (p. 297)
    a. 20, 25
    b. 45, 50
    c. 65, 70
    d. 85, 90

15. A variably experienced but painless disturbance having odd sensory (particularly visual), motor, and/or mood components is associated with: (pp. 298-299)
    a. tension headaches.
    b. essential hypertension.
    c. migraine headaches.
    d. asthma.

16. Some individuals appear to have a hypothalamus that overstimulates the pituitary that, in turn, leads to overstimulation of the adrenal gland and, ultimately, to oversecretion of adrenocortical hormones. This sequence of events is due to a failure of _____ (p. 301)
    a. the corticovisceral control mechanism.
    b. the pituitary to respond to circulating progesterone.
    c. cholinergic pathways in the CNS to control the hypothalamus.
    d. integration of the autonomic nervous system and the hypothalamic-pituitary-adrenal axis.

17. Sociocultural treatment of psychogenic diseases is targeted *most often* toward: (p. 308)
    a. encouraging diseased individuals to seek help.
    b. obtaining social support after treatment.
    c. preventing pathogenic life-style behaviors.
    d. raising money for research.

Chapter 9
Personality Disorders

◊ OVERVIEW

In this chapter several specific disorders of personality are discussed. With these disorders we encounter, for the first time, behavior that is not episodic and that, generally, is not exacerbated by stress. Rather, the personality disorders represent ingrained "life-styles" or characteristic patterns that are maladaptive of meeting the individual's needs. Often, the person with a personality disorder ends up imposing on other people's rights in order to obtain his or her goals. Chapter 9 includes descriptions of the various types of personality disorders, their causal patterns, and their treatment. Special treatment is given to one particular personality disorder--antisocial personality and psychopathy--because of the extensive research on this topic.

◊ LEARNING OBJECTIVES

After studying this chapter, you should be able to:

1. List the clinical features of the personality disorders and problems associated with diagnosis. (pp. 314-316)

2. Compare and contrast the different types of personality disorders and identify the three clusters into which most personality disorders are grouped. (pp. 316-330)

3. Summarize what is known about the biological, psychological, and sociocultural causal factors of personality disorders. (pp. 330-332)

4. Discuss the difficulties of treating individuals with personality disorders and describe the approaches to treatment that have been tried. (pp. 332-335).

5. Compare and contrast the DSM-IV concept of antisocial personality and Cleckley's concept of psychopathy. (pp. 335-337)

6. List the clinical features of psychopathy and antisocial personality. (p. 337)

7. Summarize the biological and psychosocial causal factors in psychopathy and antisocial personality and the integrated developmental perspective. (pp. 341-346)

8. Explain why it is difficult to treat psychopathy and antisocial personality and describe the most promising of the as yet unproven approaches to treatment. (pp. 346-349)

◊ TERMS YOU SHOULD KNOW

---

personality (p. 313)

personality disorder or *character disorder* (p. 313)

prototype (pp. 316, 349)

paranoid personality (p. 316)

schizoid personality (p. 318)

schizotypal personality (p. 319)

histrionic personality (p. 320)

narcissistic personality (p. 321)

antisocial personality (p. 322)

borderline personality (p. 323)

avoidant personality (p. 324)

dependent personality (p. 326)

obsessive-personality (pp. 326-327)

passive-aggressive personality (p. 328)

depressive personality (p. 328)

schemas (p. 333)

psychopathy or *sociopathy* (p. 335)

Psychopathy Checklist (p. 336)

behavioral inhibition system (p. 342)

passive avoidance learning (p. 342)

behavioral activation system (p. 342)

stimulation seeking (p. 343)

oppositional defiant disorder (p. 345)

burned-out psychopath (p. 349)

◊ NAMES YOU SHOULD KNOW

Thomas Widiger (pp. 315, 316, 319, 322-326, 328, 330-332, 350, 351)

Lee Anna Clark (pp. 315, 316,350, 351)

Otto Kernberg (pp. 322, 331)

Heinz Kohut (pp. 322, 331)

Theodore Millon (pp. 331-332)

George Vaillant (pp. 332, 338, 348)

Hervey Cleckley (pp. 335-337)

Robert Hare (pp. 336, 339, 342, 344, 349)

David Lykken (p. 342)

Hans Eysenck (p. 342)

Lee Robins (p. 345)

◊ CONCEPTS TO MASTER

1. Define *personality disorder* and explain three broad reasons for the high frequency of misdiagnosis of the personality disorders. (pp. 314-315)

2. List and describe the general characteristics of three clusters of personality disorders, and note two additional disorders that appear in DSM-IV. (p. 316; Highlight 9.1, p. 317)

3. Describe and differentiate among the following personality disorders in Cluster I: paranoid, schizoid, and schizotypal. (Highlight 9.1, p. 317; pp. 316-320)

4. Describe and differentiate among the following personality disorders in Cluster II: histrionic, narcissistic, antisocial, and borderline. (Highlight 9.1, p. 317; pp. 320-324)

5. Describe and differentiate among the following personality disorders in Cluster III: avoidant, dependent, and obsessive-compulsive. (Highlight 9.1, p. 317; pp. 324-328)

6. Beck and Freeman argue that personality disorders can be characterized in terms of interpersonal strategies they use, patterns of behavior they have underdeveloped or overdeveloped, and their characteristic core dysfunctional beliefs. Use this scheme to compare the personality disorders. (pp. 329-330; Highlight 9.2, p. 329)

7. Explain why we know comparatively little about the causal factors in personality disorders, and summarize what we do know about the biological, psychological, and sociocultural factors that seem implicated. (pp. 330-332)

8. Herman, Perry, and van der Polk found that 57% of borderline personality disorder patients reported some combination of physical abuse, sexual abuse, or witnessing of domestic violence before age seven, compared with only 13% of a control group of patients with other related disorders. Explain the shortcomings of these studies that make the results only suggestive. (p. 331)

9. List several reasons why personality disorders are especially resistant to therapy, and describe treatment strategies for persons who are already too dependent or who are hypersensitive to any perceived criticism from the therapist. (pp. 332-334).

10. Describe three criteria, in addition to being 18 or older, that must be met before an individual is diagnosed as an antisocial personality, according to DSM-IV. (p. 335)

11. List personality traits that help to define psychopathy that are not included in the DSM-IV criteria for antisocial personality disorder. (p. 335)

12. Identify the two dimensions of psychopathy found in Hare's Psychopathy Checklist based on Cleckley's criteria and indicate how they relate to the DSM-IV concept of antisocial personality disorder. Which group of psychopaths is not detected by the DSM-IV diagnosis of antisocial personality disorder, even though the latter concept is broader than the former? (p. 336)

13. Summarize Fowles' application of Gray's theory to psychopathy, including the roles of the behavioral inhibition system, the behavioral activation system, and the fight/flight system. (pp. 342-343)

14. Explain the concept of stimulation seeking or sensation seeking and review the evidence supporting this trait as a feature of psychopaths. (pp. 343-344)

15. Describe Robins' findings from her classic prospective longitudinal study with respect to the two independent factors during childhood that predicted who will develop an adult diagnosis of psychopathy or antisocial personality. How do these findings relate to the current diagnoses of conduct disorder and oppositional defiant disorder? (p. 345)

16. Outline the major psychosocial and sociocultural variables identified by Capaldi and Patterson as contributing to poor and ineffective parenting. Given poor parenting, what is the causal pathway to an antisocial life-style? (p. 346; Figure 9.1, p. 346)

17. Explain why most individuals with antisocial personalities seldom come to the attention of mental hospitals and clinics, and evaluate the success of traditional psychotherapy in treating this disorder. (pp. 346-347)

18. List and describe three steps that Bandura recommends to modify antisocial behavior of individuals with antisocial personalities. (p. 347)

19. According to Vaillant, what conditions are, and are not, effective in the treatment of individuals with antisocial personalities? (p. 348)

20. Identify and explain two major problems that make Axis II diagnoses quite unreliable. (pp. 350-351)

21. What do the authors of the text suggest to resolve the difficulties with Axis II? (p. 351)

◊ STUDY QUESTIONS

Introduction

1. Healthy adjustment throughout life is primarily a matter of flexibly adapting to _____ _____, _____, and _____ associated with each life stage. (p. 313)

2. Personality disorders typically do not stem from debilitating reactions to stress. Rather, they stem largely from the gradual development of _____ and _____ personality patterns, which result in persistently maladaptive ways of _____, _____, and relating to the world. (p. 313)

3. The actual prevalence of personality disorders is unknown, in part because many individuals never come in contact with mental health or legal agencies. However, estimates available from a very large epidemiological study (Robins et al.) suggest that the prevalence of antisocial personality is between _____ and _____ percent, which is consistent with more recent estimates (Weissman) of about _____ to _____ percent in the U.S. and Canada. (p. 314)

Personality disorders

4. Respond true or false to the following statements about personality disorders. (p. 314)
   People with personality disorders:
   a. Cause as much difficulty for others as for themselves. True or False
   b. Show bizarre behavior that is out of contact with reality. True or False
   c. Almost always experience a good deal of emotional suffering. True or False
   d. Experience significant occupational or social impairment. True or False
   e. Show persistent behavioral deviations that are intrinsic to their personality. True or False
   f. Learn from their previous troubles. True or False

Clinical features of personality disorders

5. In the DSM-IV the personality disorders are coded on a separate axis, _____, because they are regarded as being different enough from the standard psychiatric syndromes to warrant separate classification. These reaction patterns are so deeply embedded in the personality structure that they are extremely resistant to _____. (p. 315)

Types of personality disorders

6. List the personality disorders that belong to each cluster: (p. 316)
   a. Cluster I: odd or eccentric individuals
   b. Cluster II: dramatic, emotional, and erratic individuals
   c. Cluster III: anxious, fearful individuals

7. Fill in the clinical description in the following personality disorders:

Personality Disorder	Clinical Description
Paranoid (p. 316)	Suspicious, distrustful, hypersensitive, bearing grudges, blaming others for their own mistakes.
Schizoid (p. 318)	
Schizotypal (p. 319)	Socially isolated and withdrawn. Oddities of thought, perception, and speech: highly personalized and superstitious thinking, magical thinking, magical rituals, and ideas of reference.

Histrionic (p. 320)

Narcissistic (p. 321)   Exaggerated sense of self-importance (grandiosity), preoccupied with being admired, lacking in empathy, not uncommonly take advantage of others, often envious of others.

Borderline (p. 323)

Avoidant (p. 324)   Extreme social inhibition, hypersensitive to criticism, lonely and bored, experience acute distress, low self-esteem.

Dependent (p. 326)

Obsessive-compulsive (p. 326)   Excessively concerned with maintaining order, perfectionistic, very careful in order to avoid making mistakes, preoccupied with trivial details, devoted to work to the exclusion of leisure activities, excessively conscientious and inflexible about moral issues, have difficulty delegating tasks to others, rigid and stubborn.

Passive-aggressive (p. 328)

Depressive (p. 328)

Causal factors in personality disorder

8. Research on the causal factors of personality disorders is difficult. One major problem in studying the causes of personality disorders stems from the high level of _____. Widiger and Rogers found that ____ percent of patients with a diagnosis of personality disorder also qualified for at least one more diagnosis of personality disorder. Even in a nonpatient sample, Zimmerman and Coryell found that almost ____ percent showed _____. An additional problem is that many people with these disorders are never _____, with the consequence that only _____ study is possible. (p. 330)

9. Theories that link physique or constitutional reaction tendencies to the development of personality disorders are hypothetical, that is, are not supported by evidence. True or False (p. 330)

10. Suggestions that early learning contributes to personality disorders are speculative and inferential. True or False (pp. 330-331)

11. The incidence of personality disorders has increased in recent years. Research has indicated that this increase is due to our present emphasis on impulse gratification, instant solutions, and pain-free benefits, which lead more people to develop self-centered life-styles. True or False (p. 332)

Treatment and outcome

12. Under what circumstances do persons with personality disorders generally get involved with psychotherapy? (p. 333)

13. How do the difficulties personality disordered people have with personal relationships, acting out, and avoiding problems affect the course of psychotherapeutic treatments? (p. 333)

14. For personality disordered individuals who become identified with their therapy group, or who are sufficiently "hooked" into couples therapy that they do not flee the sessions when their behavior comes under scrutiny, the intense feedback from _____ or _____ often is more acceptable than confrontation by a _____ in individual treatment. (p. 333)

15. What are schemas and what is their relevance to Beck and Freeman's cognitive approach to treating the personality disorders? (p. 333)

16. For the pharmacological treatment of borderline personality disorder Gitlin concluded that low doses of _____ medication have modest but significant effects that are broad-based, _____ antidepressants are ineffective, but that antidepressant drugs from the same class as _____ are promising. (p. 334)

17. Probably the most promising treatment for borderline personality disorder is the recently developed _____ behavior therapy. (p. 334)

18. Linehan's dialectical behavior therapy for borderline personality disorder involves a problem-focused treatment in which the hierarchy of goals includes: (p. 334)
    a.
    b. decreasing behaviors that interfere with therapy
    c.
    d.
    e. other goals the patient chooses

Antisocial personality and psychopathy

19. With its strong emphasis on behavioral criteria that reasonably can be measured objectively, DSM-III and IV have broken from the tradition of psychopathy researchers, in an attempt to increase the reliability of the diagnosis. However, much less attention has been paid to its _____--that is, whether it measures a _____ construct and whether that construct is the same as psychopathy. (pp. 335-336)

20. In the study by Harris, Rice, and Cormier, following release from an intensive therapeutic community program psychopaths were almost _____ times more likely to commit a _____ offense than nonpsychopaths. (p. 336)

21. Whichever diagnosis is used, individuals with antisocial personality disorder or psychopathy include a mixed group of individuals: (p. 337)
    a. unprincipled business professionals
    b.
    c. crooked politicians
    d.
    e.
    f. assorted criminals

22. The prevalence of antisocial personality in American men is approximately _____ percent according to several large epidemiological surveys. Among women, the prevalence is approximately _____ percent. (p. 337)

23. Describe Widom's (1977) approach to recruiting research participants and the type of people who volunteered. (Highlight 9.3, p. 337)

Clinical picture in antisocial personality and psychopathy

24. Fill in the missing information on the following chart that summarizes the personality characteristics of antisocial persons: (pp. 338-339)

Area of Functioning	Behavior Typical of the Antisocial Person
Conscience development	
Feelings of anxiety and guilt	Act out tension rather than worrying: apparent lack of anxiety and guilt combined with appearance of sincerity allows them to avoid suspicion
Impulse control	
Frustration tolerance	Seldom forego immediate pleasure for future gains; live in the present; unable to endure routine jobs or accept responsibility
Ability to accept authority	
Profit from experience	Despite difficulties they get into and the punishments they receive, they continue to behave as if they are immune from the consequences of their actions
Interpersonal and sexual relationships	
Ability to manipulate others	

25. Results of twin and adoption studies show a modest heritability for antisocial or criminal behavior and probably for psychopathy. However, researchers also note that _____ _____ factors interact with genetic predispositions to determine which individuals become criminals or antisocial personalities. List the unfavorable conditions that tend to promote poor outcome among adopted children whose biological parents are criminals: (p. 341)
   a. unfavorable conditions in infancy
   b.
   c. low social status
   d.
   e.

26. Many investigators--e.g., Lykken, Eysenck, and Hare--have found that antisocial individuals seem to lack normal fear and anxiety reactions. What appears to happen in the development of antisocial persons as a result of their lack of anxiety and fear? (p. 342)

27. Patrick and his colleagues found that psychopaths did not show a larger startle response as a result of being in a fearful state. To which of Hare's dimensions of psychopathy did these differences in startle response relate? (p. 342-343)

28. Gorenstein suggested that antisocial individuals have deficits in cognitive processes such as attention to detail that could reflect dysfunctioning in the frontal lobes of the brain. On what grounds has Hare disputed these results? (p. 344)

29. Although the loss of a parent during childhood was more common among antisocial subjects than normal controls, the authors of the text conclude that this factor can only be a partial or interactive cause of antisocial personality. Why did Hare suggest that parental loss per se is not the factor of key significance? (p. 344)

30. McCord and McCord concluded that severe _____ by parents was a primary cause of antisocial personality. (p. 344)

Treatment and outcomes

31. In general, traditional psychotherapeutic approaches have not proven very effective in altering the personality problems of psychopaths. Among the factors inherent in the psychopathic individual's personality that make the prognosis for psychotherapy very poor are the inability to trust, to _____, to fantasize, and to learn from _____. (p. 347)

32. Perhaps the most promising therapeutic approach is _____ therapy. (p. 347)

33. Is psychotherapy with antisocial persons usually successful when attempted on an outpatient basis? (p. 348)

34. Is one-to-one, as opposed to group, therapy usually more effective? (p. 348)

35. Why do many antisocial persons seem to improve after age 40? (p. 349)

Unresolved issues

36. Skodol and colleagues found that patients were given an average of _____ personality disorder diagnoses. (p. 349)

37. Axis II diagnoses (the personality disorders) are more unreliable than diagnoses made for Axis I (mental disorders). The authors of the text suggest the following two reasons for the unreliability: (p. 350)

a. DSM-IV assumes that we can make a clear distinction between _____ and _____ of a personality disorder when, in fact, the personality processes classified on Axis II are _____ in nature.

b. There are enormous _____ in the kinds of symptoms that people can have who nevertheless obtain the same diagnosis. For example, for borderline personality, a person had to meet _____ out of eight possible symptom criteria, and this means that there are ___ different ways to meet the criteria for this diagnosis. The DSM-IV is not based on mutually _____ criteria. Many of the traits are correlated with other traits and may also be seen as symptoms of various mental disorders.

◊ CRITICAL THINKING ABOUT DIFFICULT TOPICS

1. In the field of psychometrics, it is axiomatic that reliability sets the upper limit of validity. That is, if you are trying to assess constructs such as "intelligence" or "psychopathy," the meaningfulness (validity) of the construct is to be found in the nonrandom variation in test scores (reliability) and not in the random variation (error variance). Thus, an extremely unreliable assessment cannot be valid. Taking this principle to heart, DSM IV has emphasized reliable measurement. In the case of psychopathy, however, your text implicitly raises the possibility that validity may have been sacrificed: "much less attention has been paid to validity- -that is, whether it measures a meaningful construct and whether that construct is the same as psychopathy" (pp. 335-336). Can you explain how validity might be sacrificed in emphasizing reliability? Think about concepts such as "social class" or "standard of living" and whether they might be reliably indexed by measuring a family's electric power consumption. Over a wide range of incomes, power consumption probably does show a positive correlation with both income and social class, and it can be measured quite reliably. However, these concepts usually refer to a broader set of variables that are not adequately indexed by power consumption. Can you think of other examples where inappropriate use of highly reliable measures may undermine validity?

2. In the case study of Donald S. (pp. 339-341), the following statements express Donald's view: "Although his behavior is self-defeating in the long run, he considers it to be practical and possessed of good sense. Periodic punishments do nothing to decrease his egotism and confidence in his own abilities, nor do they offset the often considerable short-term gains of which he is capable" (p. 341). Thus, Donald thinks his behavior reflects a rational hedonism. Read his case history again and see whether you agree, or whether you can attribute some of his behavior to deficits. For example, is it rational to break out of prison with only one month left to serve, when recapture means automatic conviction (there is no difficulty in proving who escaped from prison)? Donald's "short-term gains are invariably obtained at the expense of someone else" (p. 341). Would a rational hedonism lead one to this degree of indifference to others, or does his behavior reflect a deficit in attachments?

3. The text articulates two theories of psychopathy: a deficit in the behavioral inhibition system and stimulation seeking (pp. 342-343). The behavioral inhibition deficit would impair the ability to resist reward-seeking behavior that may result in punishment. Stimulation seeking is attributed to low levels of arousal that cause the individual to engage in stimulating activities. However, the text notes that "to some extent this high level of sensation seeking may also stem from the psychopath's underactive behavioral inhibition system; normal levels of activity in the behavioral inhibition system would lead a person to inhibit approach to a novel and potentially dangerous stimulus" (p. 343). Can you think of ways to distinguish between poor avoidance of punishment (weak behavioral inhibition system) versus pursuit of stimulating activities (stimulation seeking)? Consider the sport of sky diving, in which individuals parachute from planes. Jumping from a plane is certainly a stimulating activity. Can it also be viewed as a dominance of reward-seeking (development of an unusual skill, beautiful scenery while flying and parachuting, and most importantly considerable admiration from peers) over passive avoidance of punishment (fear of heights, risk of injury)?

4. Your text nicely states the problem of using a categorical approach to Axis II diagnoses when "the personality processes classified on Axis II are dimensional in nature" (p. 350). At the same time, as you have seen in earlier chapters, it can be difficult to make categorical distinctions with Axis I disorders: they vary quantitatively in the degree of severity and do not show a "point of rarity" that would make it easy to distinguish between the presence and absence of the disorder. What possible difference between some Axis I disorders and Axis II disorders could make applying a categorical model even more problematic with personality disorders? In developing your answer, note that personality is usually assumed to be normally distributed in the population and that Morey found that changing the cut-points (or threshold) for a diagnosis of a personality disorder "can have drastic effects in the apparent prevalence rates of a particular personality disorder diagnosis" (p. 350). In contrast, we usually would not think that bipolar affective disorder or schizophrenia is normally distributed in the population-- with the result that small changes in the cut-point for diagnosis would not have drastic effects

on estimates of prevalence. Thus, there are two components to this issue: (a) whether the phenomenon in question is dimensional in the sense that there is a continuum of severity, and (b) whether it is normally distributed with huge numbers of the milder forms in the "normal" population (personality disorders) or whether it is relatively rare in the "normal" population with only a small number of milder forms (bipolar affective disorder). What do you think is the distribution of other Axis I disorders, such as anxiety disorders and unipolar depression?

◊ CHAPTER 9 QUIZ

Circle the best of the four answers provided and check them according to answers provided at the back of this study guide. Be sure you understand why each answer is correct.

1. Personality disorders are: (p. 313)
   a. reactions to stress.
   b. intrapsychic disturbances.
   c. episodic in nature.
   d. maladaptive ways of perceiving, thinking, and relating.

2. According to a very large epidemiological study (Robins et al.), the prevalence of antisocial personality disorder is about _____ percent of our population. (p. 314)
   a. 3   c. 23
   b. 13   d. 33

3. Personality disorders are coded on Axis _____ of DSM-IV. (p. 315)
   a. I   c. III
   b. II   d. IV

4. Which of the following is not one of the three reasons given for the high rate of misdiagnoses of personality disorders? (p. 315)
   a. the diagnostic criteria are often not very precise or easy to follow
   b. the diagnostic categories are not mutually exclusive
   c. the personality characteristics that define personalities are dimensional in nature
   d. clinicians often do not receive sufficient training in the diagnosis of personality disorders

5. Individuals with this personality disorder typically show oddities of thought, perception or speech: (Highlight 9.1, p. 317; p. 319)
   a. schizoid
   b. schizotypal
   c. histrionic
   d. antisocial

6. Which of the following is characterized by loneliness and boredom? (p. 324)
   a. avoidant
   b. schizotypal
   c. schizoid
   d. paranoid

7. An individual is frequently late for work and meetings, misses appointments, forgets about assignments, refuses to follow instructions, and seems unmotivated. This is an example of _____ personality disorder. (p. 328)
   a. passive-aggressive
   b. avoidant
   c. narcissistic
   d. borderline

8. Establishing the causal factors of personality disorders hasn't progressed very far for all the following reasons except: (p. 330)
   a. there is a high level of co-morbidity.
   b. affected individuals do not seek professional help.
   c. only *prospective* studies have been possible so far.
   d. the personality disorders have only received consistent attention since 1980.

9. A history of some combination of physical abuse, sexual abuse, or witnessing domestic violence before age seven is most strongly implicated in _____ personality disorder: (p. 331)
   a. antisocial
   b. obsessive
   c. borderline
   d. schizoid

10. Several large epidemiological studies found that the prevalence of antisocial personality disorder is: (p. 337)
    a. about equal for males and females.
    b. higher for females than for males.
    c. higher for males than for females.
    d. higher in prepubertal females than in prepubertal males.

11. Research evidence indicates that a primary reaction tendency typically found in psychopathic individuals is: (pp. 341-342)
    a. deficient aversive emotional arousal.
    b. hyperactive reflexivity.
    c. oversensitivity to noxious stimuli.
    d. phlegmatic temperament.

12. According to Fowles' application of Gray's motivational theory, psychopaths are deficient in: (p. 342)
    a. reactivity of the fight\flight response.
    b. reactivity of the behavioral activation system.
    c. active avoidance learning.
    d. reactivity of the behavioral inhibition system.

13. While a number of early studies linked antisocial personality formation with losing a parent at an early age, Hare suggested that the key factor was the: (p. 344)
    a. age at which the loss occurred.
    b. emotional family disturbance before the parent left.
    c. length of the marriage before the loss.
    d. sex of the parent who left.

14. In the Capaldi and Patterson model, the key factor that mediates the influence of the others and increases the probability of antisocial behavior in the child is: (p. 346)
    a. parental antisocial behavior.
    b. divorce and other parental transitions.
    c. parental stress and depression.
    d. ineffective discipline and supervision.

15. Vaillant believes that antisocial individuals can be effectively treated only: (p. 348)
    a. as a part of family therapy.
    b. by outpatient psychotherapy.
    c. in a one-to-one therapeutic relationship.
    d. in controlled situations.

◊ OVERVIEW

It has been estimated that a major proportion of America's health problems are due to self-injurious practices such as excessive drinking, smoking, and overeating. They are all considered forms of addiction, along with drug use and compulsive gambling. These problems are explored in Chapter 9. A great deal of background information is presented to help document the extent of the various addictive behaviors and their costs to society. Treatment approaches that have been developed for each specific addiction are then described.

◊ LEARNING OBJECTIVES

After studying this chapter, you should be able to:

1. Outline the major divisions of psychoactive substance-related disorders, define alcohol abuse and alcohol dependence, summarize the many negative consequences of alcohol for both the individual and society, and indicate the prevalence and gender ratio of excessive drinking. (pp. 355-357)

2. Describe the clinical picture of alcohol abuse, including the biological and psychological effects of chronic consumption of alcohol. (pp. 357-363)

3. Review the biological, psychosocial, and sociocultural contributors to alcohol abuse and dependence. (pp. 363-369)

4. Summarize the research findings on the results of treatment and relapse prevention for alcohol-dependent persons. (pp. 369-374)

5. List the specific drugs and their effects, summarize theories of causal factors, and review treatments for the following drugs of abuse: Opium and its derivatives (pp. 377-381), cocaine and amphetamines (pp. 381-384), barbiturates (pp. 384-385), LSD and other hallucinogens (pp. 385-386), marijuana (pp. 386-388), and caffeine and nicotine (pp. 388-389).

◊ TERMS YOU SHOULD KNOW

---

addictive behavior (p. 355)

psychoactive (p. 355)

organic impairment (p. 355)

toxicity (p. 355)

alcohol abuse dementia disorder (formerly Korsakoff's syndrome) (p. 355)

psychoactive substance abuse (pp. 355-356)

psychoactive substance dependence (p. 356)

tolerance (p. 356)

withdrawal symptoms (p. 356)

alcoholism (p. 356)

alcohol dependence syndrome (p. 356)

blackouts (p. 360)

hangover (p. 360)

alcoholic psychoses (p. 362)

alcohol withdrawal delirium (p. 362)

alcohol amnestic disorder (p. 363)

snorting (p. 378)

skin popping (p. 378)

mainlining (p. 378)

rush (p. 378)

withdrawal symptoms (p. 378)

receptor sites (p. 379)

endorphins (p. 379)

methadone hydrochloride (p. 380)

bupenorphine (p. 381)

cocaine (p. 381)

crack (p. 381)

cocaine bug (p. 381)

amphetamines (p. 383)

Benzedrine (*amphetamine sulfate*) (p. 383)

Dexedrine (*dextroamphetamine*) (p. 383)

Methedrine (*methamphetamine hydrochloride*) (p. 383)

narcolepsy (p. 384)

Schedule II substances (p. 384)

amphetamine psychosis (p. 384)

barbiturates (p. 384)

silent abusers (p. 385)

potentiates (p. 385)

hallucinogens (p. 385)

model psychoses (p. 385)

LSD (*lysergic acid diethylamide*) (p. 385)

bad trip (p. 386)

flashbacks (p. 386)

mescaline (p. 386)

psilocybin (p. 386)

marijuana (p. 386)

hashish (p. 386)

caffeinism (p. 386)

nicotine withdrawal (p. 388)

hyperobesity (p. 389)

adipose cells (p. 390)

developmental obesity (p. 390)

reactive obesity (p. 390)

TOPS and *Weight Watchers* (p. 391)

anorexigenic drugs (p. 391)

pathological or compulsive gambling (p. 392)

Gamblers Anonymous (p. 395)

◊ NAMES YOU SHOULD KNOW

G. Alan Marlatt (pp. 367, 371, 374)

Kelly Brownell (p. 391, 392)

◊ CONCEPTS TO MASTER

1. Psychoactive substance-induced organic mental disorders and psychoactive substance-abuse and -dependence disorders are the two major divisions of "addictive or psychoactive substance-related disorders." Define what it means to be included in each of these two divisions. (pp. 355-356)

   a. Psychoactive substance-induced organic mental disorders

   b. Psychoactive substance-abuse and -dependence disorders

2. Describe three major physiological effects of alcohol. (p. 360)

3. Describe some physical ailments that can result from chronic alcohol use, and explain how these may lead to interpersonal and occupational problems. (pp. 360-362)

4. Alcohol withdrawal delirium is a form of psychosis that may occur following a long drinking spree when the person is in a state of withdrawal. List the symptoms and indicate how long they last and how dangerous they are. (p. 362)

5. Describe the memory deficit that occurs in alcoholic amnestic disorder. (p. 363)

6. Your text says, "once this point is reached, each drink serves to reinforce alcohol-seeking behavior because it reduces the unpleasant symptoms" (p. 363). What condition produces this effect?

7. Describe the mesocorticolimbic dopamine pathway and indicate what it has to do with addiction to psychoactive drugs. (Highlight 10.5; pp. 364-365)

8. List and describe five major psychosocial factors that may be partially responsible for the development of alcohol dependence. (pp. 366-368)

9. What are the rates of alcoholism among Muslims, Mormons, and orthodox Jews? How much of the world's consumption of alcohol takes place in Europe and European-influenced countries? What do these facts tell us about the power of sociocultural factors on drinking? (pp. 368-369).

10. List the strengths and limitations of Disulfiram (Antabuse) treatment. (p. 370)

11. Describe three psychosocial interventions excluding AA that have been used to treat alcohol-dependent persons. (pp. 370-372)

12. Briefly describe how AA and Al-Anon family groups operate and explain why one should be skeptical about the effectiveness of this form of treatment. (p. 372-373)

13. Discuss the controversy over controlled drinking treatment programs and review the empirical findings regarding controlled drinking outcomes. (pp. 371-374)

14. Summarize the history of the use of opium and its derivatives over the last 5000 years. (pp. 375-378)

15. Describe the major physical and psychosocial effects of ingesting morphine and heroin. (pp. 378-379)

16. List and explain three major causal factors in the development of opiate dependence. (pp. 379-380)

17. Describe some psychosocial and biological treatments that have been used as therapy for opiate dependent individuals, and evaluate the success of using methadone hydrochloride-- with and without psychotherapy or psychosocial support. (pp. 380-381)

18. Describe some physical and psychological effects of ingesting cocaine and some symptoms that are experienced in withdrawal. (pp. 381-383)

19. Describe some causes and effects of amphetamine abuse, and note some physical and psychological effects of withdrawal. (pp. 383-384)

20. Describe some of the effects of barbiturate abuse, list some of its causes, and summarize the dangers of withdrawal from this class of drugs. (pp. 384-385)

21. Describe the physical and psychological effects of using LSD, and note the treatment used for the acute psychoses induced by its use. (pp. 385-386)

22. Compare the effects of using mescaline and psilocybin with those of ingesting LSD. (pp. 386)

23. Define hyperobesity, and list some biological, psychosocial, and sociocultural factors that may underlie its development. (pp. 389-391)

24. Describe and evaluate several biological and psychosocial interventions that have been used to treat hyperobesity. (pp. 391-392)

25. Define pathological gambling and describe its symptoms. (pp. 392-394)

26. Summarize what is known about the causes of and treatments for pathological gambling. (pp. 394-396)

27. Summarize the evidence both for and against a strong genetic link in alcoholism. (p. 396)

Alcohol abuse and dependence: Definition, prevalence, significance

1. The World Health Organization prefers the term _____ syndrome to the term alcoholism. It defines this syndrome as ". . . a state, _____ and usually also physical, resulting from taking alcohol, characterized by behavioral and other responses that always include a _____ to take alcohol on a continuous or periodic basis in order to experience its _____ effects, and sometimes to avoid the discomfort of its _____; _____ may or may not be present. (p. 356).

2. A large NIMH epidemiological study reported that the lifetime prevalence of alcoholism is _____ percent. (p. 356)

3. Complete the following lists of some of the ways in which alcoholism harms the individual and is a drain on society: (pp. 356-357)

   Individual harm
   a. Leads to a _____ shorter life span
   b. Is the _____ major cause of death--after coronary heart disease and cancer
   c. _____ impairment, including _____ shrinkage, occurs in a high proportion
   d. About ___ percent commit suicide

   Harm to others:
   a. Related to ___ percent of all deaths
   b. Related to _____ of deaths and major injuries in auto accidents
   c. Related to ___ percent of all murders
   d. Related to ___ percent of all assaults
   e. Related to ___ percent or more of all rapes
   f. Related to one out of every _____ arrests
   g. Costs the economy over _____ billion per year

4. What is the ratio of male alcoholics to female alcoholics? (p. 357)

5.   Alcohol is a depressant. Indicate how alcohol: (p. 357)

1. affects higher brain centers

2. affects behavior

6. If the percent of alcohol in the blood reaches _____ percent, the person is intoxicated. When the blood alcohol reaches _____ percent the individual passes out, and concentrations of blood alcohol above 0.55% usually cause death. (p. 359)

7. Does alcohol help a person sleep more soundly? (Highlight 10.1, p. 358)

8. Does alcohol produce a true addiction in the same sense that heroin does? (Highlight 10.1, p. 358)

9. The legal level of intoxication, 0.1% blood alcohol level, would be reached after a 150-pound man had drunk _____ bottles of beer in one hour. It would require _____ hours for the alcohol to leave the body before it was safe to drive. (Highlight 10.2, p. 359)

10. When is frequent desire to drink a warning sign of drinking problems? (Highlight 10.3, p. 360)

11. How commonly are birth defects related to alcohol abuse? (Highlight 10.4, p. 361)

12. The liver works on assimilating alcohol into the system. How is it affected by large amounts of alcohol? (pp. 360-361)

13. How can excessive intake of alcohol lead to malnutrition? (p. 361)

14. According to Lishman, evidence is beginning to show that an alcoholic's brain could be accumulating _____ even when no extreme organic symptoms are evident. (p. 362)

15. Alcoholic amnestic disorder is considered to be caused by _____ deficiency and other dietary inadequacies associated with chronic alcohol consumption. (p. 363)

Causes of alcohol abuse and dependence

16. Cotton completed a review of 39 studies of families of alcoholics and nonalcoholics. He found that almost _____ of alcoholics had at least one parent with an alcohol problem. (p. 363)

17. Cloninger et al. found strong evidence for the inheritance of alcoholism. They found the following rates of alcoholism: _____ percent among women with no alcoholic parents, _____ percent among women with one alcoholic parent, and _____ percent among women whose parents were both alcoholics. (p. 363)

18. Finn (1990), studying persons at risk for alcoholism, has described an "alcohol risk personality." Some characteristics are: someone who is impulsive, prefers taking _____, is emotionally _____, has difficulty planning and _____ _____, finds that alcohol is helpful dealing with _____, and does not experience hangovers. (p. 364)

19. Fenna et al. (1971) and Wolff (1972) suggested that a hypersensitive reaction to alcohol occurs among Oriental and Eskimo persons. However, Shafer (1978) has challenged this conclusion. State Shafer's criticisms. (p. 366)

20. What do the authors of the text mean by the expression alcoholic personality? (p. 366)

21. About 75-80% of the studies of alcoholic personalities have shown an association between alcoholism and _____ personality. (p. 366)

22. What is the only characteristic common to the backgrounds of most problem drinkers? How well does this characteristic predict alcoholism? Is it a cause or an effect? (p. 366)

23. In Cox and Klinger's motivational model of alcohol use, alcohol is consumed to bring about _____ changes, such as _____ effects, and even indirect effects, such as peer approval. In short, alcohol is consumed because it is _____ for the individual. (p. 367)

24. Many treatment programs try to identify personality or life-style factors in a relationship that serve to _____, _____, or to _____ drinking behavior. (p. 368)

25. How important is alcoholism as a cause of marital discord? (p. 368)

26. Bales (1946) described three cultural factors that determined whether a specific group would have a high or low rate of alcoholism. What were these factors? (p. 307)
    a.
    b.
    c.

27. Europe and six countries that have been influenced by European culture make up less than 20 percent of the world's population yet consume 80 percent of the alcohol. Thus, it appears that religious sanctions and social customs can determine whether alcoholism is one of the _____ commonly used in a given group or society. (pp. 368-369)

Treatment and outcomes

28. A _____ approach to the treatment of drinking problems appears to be most effective. It once was considered essential for treatment to take place in an institutional setting. However, an increasing number of problem drinkers are being treated in _____ clinics. There is some indication that the more _____ the inpatient treatment the better the results. The objectives of treatment programs include detoxification, _____, control over _____ behavior, and development of an individual's realization that he or she can _____ and lead a much more rewarding life without alcohol. (p. 369)

29. Why are drugs such as Valium (a minor tranquilizer) used during the detoxification process? (p. 369)

30. Antabuse (disulfiram) is not considered a complete treatment for alcoholism. When might Antabuse be used? (p. 370)

31. Sometimes spouses and children of alcoholics are included in group therapy. Complete the list of reasons why this is done. (pp. 370-371)
   a. The alcoholic is part of a disturbed family in which all members have a responsibility for cooperating in the treatment.
   b.
   c. Members of the family may unwillingly encourage an alcoholic to remain addicted.

32. Relapses and continued deterioration are generally associated with a lack of _____ or with living in a stressful environment. (p. 371)

33. There are several behavior approaches to treating alcoholism. One involves injecting an emetic (i.e., a drug that causes the person to become extremely nauseated and to vomit). How does this treatment work and what is the purpose of repeating this procedure over several days? (p. 371)

34. One of the promising procedures for treating alcoholics is the cognitive-behavioral approach recommended by Marlatt (1985). Often referred to as a skills-training procedure, the program is aimed at younger problem drinkers who are considered to be at risk for developing more severe drinking problems on the basis of their family history of alcoholism or their current heavy consumption. The procedure has four components. Complete the following list: (p. 371)
   1. Teaching facts about alcohol
   2. Developing coping skills in situations where alcohol is typically abused
   3.
   4.

35. Brandsma et al. (1980) suggested that AA had a high dropout rate. Why? (p. 372-373)

36. Polich et al. (1981) studied the course of alcoholism after treatment. Fill in the percentages they reported among treated alcoholics with serious drinking problems: (p. 373)

_____ percent abstained for four years.

_____ percent showed alcohol-related problems.

_____ percent maintained alcohol dependency.

_____ percent had alcohol-related adverse consequences.

37. Under what conditions is treatment for alcoholism likely to be most effective? (p. 373)

38. Define the following components of a cognitive-behavioral approach to relapse prevention. (p. 375)

a. Indulgent behaviors

b. Mini-decisions

c. Abstinence violation effect

Drug abuse and dependence

39. The psychoactive drugs most commonly associated with abuse and dependence in our society are: narcotics, _____, _____, antianxiety drugs, and hallucinogens. (p. 375)

40. Drug abuse and dependence may occur at any age but are most common during _____ and _____ and vary according to metropolitan area, race, and _____, _____ status, and other demographic characteristics. (p. 375).

41. In a study of applicants for employment at a large teaching hospital in Maryland, Lange et al. found that _____ percent had detectable amounts of illicit drugs in their tests. Marijuana was detected among _____ percent of those who tested positively, followed by cocaine (_____ percent) and opiates (_____ percent). After implementing a formal drug-screening program, only _____ percent of those applying for the job tested positively for drugs. (p. 375)

236

42. Complete the following table that summarizes psychoactive drug abuse: (Highlight 10.6, pp. 376-377)

Classification	Sample drug	Effect
Sedatives	Alcohol	Reduce tension, facilitate social interaction, blot out feelings
Sedatives	Nembutal	
Stimulants		
	Heroin	Alleviate physical pain, induce relaxation and reverie, alleviate anxiety and tension
Psychedelics		Induce changes in mood, mind expansion
Antianxiety		

Opium and its derivatives (narcotics)

43. What happened to the rate of heroin addiction during the 1960s, and what has happened since 1975? (p. 378)

44. What happens if a person takes heroin repeatedly for 30 days? (p. 378)

45. What is likely to happen if this person now stops taking the heroin abruptly? (p. 378)

46. Is withdrawal from heroin dangerous and painful? (p. 378)

47. What are the effects of heroin use during pregnancy? (p. 378)

Causal factors in opiate abuse and dependence

48. What is the single most common cause for heroin use given by addicts? (p. 379)

49. The human body produces its own opium-like substances, called _____, in the brain and pituitary gland. These substances are believed to play a role in an organism's reaction to _____. (p. 379)

50. What were the distinguishing features found among a large number of addicts studied by Gilbert and Lombardi? (p. 379)

51. What changes are seen in the young addict who has joined the drug subculture? (p. 380)

Opiate abuse: Treatment and outcomes

52. As reported by Stephens & Cottrell, how successful were English hospitals at curing addiction with group and individual counseling? (p. 380)

53. Has psychotherapy been found to add significant benefit to that achieved through the use of methadone alone according to Woody et al.? (p. 380)

Cocaine and amphetamines (stimulants)

54. What are the effects of taking cocaine? (p. 381-382)

55. What is the "cocaine bug"? (p. 381)

56. Does tolerance to cocaine develop? (p. 382)

57. Why is crack cocaine believed to be the most dangerous drug introduced to date? (p. 382)

58. What are the legitimate medical uses of amphetamines? (p. 384)

59. Are amphetamines addicting? (p. 384)

60. Does one build up tolerance to them? (p. 384)

61. What are the major physiological effects of taking amphetamines? (p. 384)

62. When does amphetamine psychosis occur? (p. 384)

63. What happens when an established user of amphetamines abruptly stops taking the drug? (p. 384)

Barbiturates (sedatives)

64. How can barbiturates cause death? (p. 384)

65. What are the side effects of chronic use of barbiturates? (p. 384-385)

66. What age group is most often found to be addicted to barbiturates? Why? (p. 385)

67. Describe the typical symptoms of barbiturate withdrawal. (p. 385)

68. How can these symptoms be minimized? (p. 385)

69. Name four hallucinogenic drugs: (p. 385)
    a.
    b.
    c.
    d.

70. What effects does LSD have on sensory perception? (p. 385)

71. Is there evidence that LSD enhances creativity? (p. 386)

72. How difficult is it to treat dependence on LSD? (p. 386)

Marijuana

73. What is the difference between marijuana and hashish? (p. 386)

74. During the early 1970s, what proportion of teenagers and young adults experimented with marijuana? (pp. 386-387)

75. Describe the following effects of marijuana: (p. 387)

    a. Psychological effects

    b. Short-range physiological effects:

76. Does marijuana lead to physiological dependence? (pp. 387-388)

77. Does marijuana lead to psychological dependence? (p. 388)

Caffeine and nicotine

78. Respond with true or false to the following statements regarding caffeine and nicotine: (p. 388)
    a. They both are considered health problems today. True or False
    b. It is easy to stop using them. True or False
    c. "Caffeinism" is included in DSM IV. True or False

Hyperobesity

79. Weiss defined hyperobesity as 20 percent in excess of desirable weight. According to Kuczmarski, what percent of men and women are obese? (p. 389)

80. The text defines hyperobesity as _____ pounds or more above ideal body weight. (p. 389)

81. How does obesity put a person at greater risk for death? (p. 389)

82. What similarity between obesity and personality disorders makes it reasonable to consider obesity in the context of addictive disorders? (p. 389)

83. Obesity in adults is related to the number and size of the adipose cells (fat cells) in the body. People who are obese have markedly more adipose cells than people of normal weight. What happens when weight is lost? (p. 390)

84. How might overfeeding a child predispose him or her to obesity in adulthood? (p. 390)

85. What is the cognitive-behavioral explanation for obesity? (p. 390)

86. Is weight related to social class? (p. 390)

87. What is the average outcome of diets according to Stuart (1967)? (p. 391)

88. What do the authors of the text conclude about the effectiveness of the following methods of losing weight? (pp. 391-392)

   a. TOPS and Weight Watchers

   b. Fasting or starvation diets

   c. Anorexigenic drugs

   d. Behavioral management methods

Pathological gambling

89. In what ways can gambling be considered an addictive disorder? (pp. 392-393)

90. An estimated ___ to ___ million Americans get hooked on gambling. (p. 393)

91. How can compulsive gambling be explained by the principle of intermittent reinforcement? (p. 394)

92. How did Rosten (1961) characterize the compulsive gambler? (p. 394)

93. Work by Aronoff has pinpointed Laotian refugees as very high risk group for compulsive gambling. What four factors are thought to account for the problem of gambling in this group of people? (p. 395)
   a.
   b.
   c.
   d.

94. If a gambler joins a Gambler's Anonymous group, how likely is it that he/she will overcome the addiction to gambling? (p. 395)

95. List the treatment approaches used to assist compulsive gamblers at the Brecksville, Ohio, Veteran's Administration Medical Center. (p. 395)

◊ **CRITICAL THINKING ABOUT DIFFICULT TOPICS**

1. The World Health Organization defines alcohol dependence syndrome as ". . . a state, psychic and *usually* also physical, resulting from taking alcohol, characterized by *behavioral* and other responses that *always* include a compulsion to take alcohol on a continuous or periodic basis in order to experience its *psychic* effects, and sometimes to avoid the discomfort of its absence; tolerance *may or may not* be present. (p. 356). Point out the instances of an emphasis on psychological rather than biological aspects in this definition.

2. The abuse of alcohol "has killed more people, sent more victims to hospitals, generated more police arrests, broken up more marriages and homes, and cost industry more money than has the abuse of heroin, amphetamines, barbiturates, and marijuana combined" (pp. 356-357). What is your own reaction to this statistic? Does it imply that these other drugs are less destructive than alcohol and should be legalized? Alternatively, does it imply that we should bring back prohibition and outlaw alcohol?

3. Your text says that once cells adapt to the presence of alcohol to the extent that withdrawal symptoms appear when it is absent, "each drink serves to reinforce alcohol-seeking behavior because it reduces the unpleasant symptoms" (p. 363). Highlight 10.5 (pp. 364-365) discusses activation of the "pleasure pathway" and "the brain reward system" by addictive drugs. Can you explain the difference between these two sources of reinforcement? (Compare termination of punishment versus consumption of food when hungry.)

4. Alcoholics Anonymous tries to "lift the burden of personal responsibility" by helping alcoholics to "see themselves as not as weak-willed or lacking in moral strength, but rather simply as having an affliction" (p. 372). Can you see in these comments the issue concerning free will versus determinism raised in this section in Chapter 2?

5. The primary purely biological theory of substance abuse assumes that "addiction" derives from a state of physiological dependency that causes addicts to consume the drug in order to avoid the horrors of withdrawal. Consider the following statements from the text concerning abuse of opioids:

   - "Central to the neurochemical process underlying addiction is the role the drug plays in activating the 'pleasure pathway' .... Drugs that activate the brain reward system obtain reinforcing action and, thereby, promote further use" (Highlight 10.5, pp. 364-365).
   - "Among the immediate effects of mainlined or snorted heroin is a euphoric spasm (the rush) lasting 60 seconds or so, which many addicts compare to a sexual orgasm" (p. 378).
   - ". . . withdrawal from heroin is not always dangerous or even very painful" (p. 378).
   - "The ill health and general personality deterioration often found in opium addiction do not result directly from the pharmacological effects of the drug, but are usually products of the sacrifice of money, proper diet, social position, and self-respect as an addict becomes more desperate to procure the required daily dosage" (p. 379).
   - ". . . the three most frequently cited reasons for beginning to use heroin were pleasure, curiosity, and peer pressure. Pleasure was the single most widespread reason--given by 81 percent of addicts" (p. 379).
   - ". . . addicts on methadone [an opioid similar to heroin] can function normally and hold jobs . . ." (p. 380).

   After reading these statements can you see why the purely biological theory of substance abuse does not fit the facts well? Can you articulate a psychobiological theory consistent with the view held by many that substance abuse is "abuse of a reinforcer"?

CHAPTER 10 QUIZ

Circle the best of the four answers provided and check them according to answers provided at the back of this study guide. Be sure you understand why each answer is correct.

1. A person who shows tolerance for a drug or withdrawal symptoms when it is unavailable illustrates: (p. 356)
   a. psychoactive substance abuse.
   b. psychoactive substance dependence.
   c. psychoactive substance toxicity.
   d. psychoactive substance-induced organic mental disorders and syndromes.

2. The life of the average alcoholic is about _____ years shorter than that of the average citizen. (p. 356)
   a. 3   c. 12
   b. 6   d. 18

3. A person is considered intoxicated when the alcohol content of the bloodstream reaches _____ percent. (p. 359)
   a. 0.1   c. 1.0
   b. 0.5   d. 1.5

4. Maynard is 75 and has been an alcoholic for 15 years. He has a lot of trouble remembering things that just happened. In order to avoid embarrassment, he often makes up things so others won't know he forgot. Maynard's disorder is probably: (p. 363)
   a. alcohol amnestic disorder.
   b. alcohol idiosyncratic intoxication.
   c. alcohol withdrawal delirium.
   d. chronic alcoholic hallucinosis.

5. The only personality characteristic that appears common to the backgrounds of most problem drinkers is: (p. 366)
   a. general depression.   c. inadequate sexual adjustment.
   b. emotional immaturity.   d. personal maladjustment.

6. A cultural attitude of approbation and permissiveness toward drinking, such as exists in France, generally: (p. 369)
   a. is correlated with a low rate of alcoholism and problem drinking.
   b. is a sign that alcoholism has been accepted as a normal behavior pattern.
   c. is associated with the common use of alcohol as a means of coping with stress.

d. has no significant effect on either alcoholism or drinking behavior.

7. Extinction of drinking behavior by associating it with nausea is a procedure called: (p. 371)
   a. Antabuse.
   b. systematic desensitization.
   c. covert sensitization.
   d. aversive conditioning.

8. In an extensive comparative study of several different treatments for alcoholism, Brandsma found that the Alcoholics Anonymous treatment was: (p. 372-373)
   a. better than some treatments and worse than others.
   b. equally as effective as all others.
   c. less effective than all others.
   d. more effective than all others.

9. In their four-year follow-up of a large group of treated alcoholics, Polich et al. (1981) found that _____ percent continued to show alcohol-related problems. (p. 373)
   a. 7
   b. 18
   c. 36
   d. 54

10. According to Marlatt's cognitive-behavioral view, alcoholic relapse is typically based upon: (p. 374)
    a. accidental "falling off the wagon."
    b. an overpowering psychological craving.
    c. small, apparently irrelevant decisions.
    d. sudden increases in stressor strength.

11. The human body produces its own opium-like substances called _____ in the brain and pituitary gland. (p. 379)
    a. antibodies
    b. dopamines
    c. endorphins
    d. phagocytes

12. Which of the following personality disorders has the *highest* incidence among heroin addicts? (p. 379)
    a. antisocial
    b. avoidant
    c. compulsive
    d. dependent

13. Cocaine is classified as a(an): (p. 381)
    a. hallucinogen.
    b. narcotic.
    c. sedative.
    d. stimulant.

14. The drug that once was thought to be useful for inducing "model psychoses" is: (p. 385)
    a. cocaine.   c. heroin.
    b. LSD.   d. marijuana.

15. Apparently, adipose cells (fat cells): (p. 390)
    a. increase in number and size when an adult gains weight.
    b. have no relation to obesity.
    c. decrease in size, but not number, when an adult loses weight.
    d. change chemical structure in obese adults.

16. Goodwin and his colleagues concluded that which of the following situations put a son at *greatest* risk of becoming alcoholic? (p. 396)
    a. being born to an alcoholic parent
    b. being born to nonalcoholic parents
    c. being raised by an alcoholic parent
    d. being raised by nonalcoholic parents

Chapter 11
Sexual Variants, Abuse, and Dysfunctions

◊ OVERVIEW

In addition to an introduction discussing sociocultural influences on sexual practices and cultural attitudes toward those practices, Chapter 11 contains three separate sections that are related to sexual behavior: sexual variants, sexual abuse, and sexual dysfunctions. Thus, the chapter discusses a wide range of sexual behavior per se, not all of which is considered as reflecting a psychiatric disorder. Indeed, many of these behaviors may be seen in otherwise normal and healthy individuals.

The introduction discusses the enormous variability within and between cultures in sexual behaviors, especially emphasizing varying cultural effects on and attitudes toward homosexuality. Homosexuality is not viewed as a mental disorder in DSM-IV. The first of the three sections on sexual behavior discusses paraphilias, in which unusual objects, rituals, or situations have become centrally important to the person's full sexual satisfaction. It also discusses gender identity disorders, in which the person strongly rejects his or her biological sex and wishes to be of the opposite sex. Some of these behaviors are considered minor criminal offenses--e.g., exhibitionism or voyeurism--as well as being included as mental disorders in DSM-IV. The next section treats the major crimes of sexual abuse: childhood sexual abuse, pedophilia, incest, and rape. Only one of these (pedophilia) is listed as a mental disorder in DSM-IV, though the victims of the crimes are, of course, at increased risk for mental disorders. The last section concerns the sexual dysfunctions. These are problems that may interfere with an individual's full enjoyment of sexual relations. The sexual dysfunctions are not mental disorders but are simply problems that interfere with full sexual enjoyment and almost always can be changed.

◊ LEARNING OBJECTIVES

After studying this chapter, you should be able to:

1. Provide a number of examples of sociocultural influences in sexual practices and cultural standards and values. (pp. 400-404; Highlight 11.1, pp. 405-406)

2. Define, give examples of, and describe the clinical features of the following paraphilias: fetishism, transvestic fetishism, voyeurism, exhibitionism, sadism, and masochism. (pp. 404-413)

3. Summarize causal factors implicated in the etiology of the paraphilias. (pp. 413-414)

4. Define and describe the clinical features and treatment of the gender identity disorders (gender identity disorder of childhood, transsexualism). (pp. 414-416)

5. Review what is known about the frequency and nature of childhood sexual abuse. Discuss the controversies surrounding both childhood testimony regarding sexual abuse and adult "recovered memories" of childhood sexual abuse. (pp. 416-422)

6. Define pedophilia and summarize what is known about pedophiles. (pp. 422-423)

7. Review what is known about the frequency and nature of incest. (pp. 423-424)

8. Summarize what is known about rape and rapists, discuss the issues regarding the frequency of rape and the motivation of rapists, and describe the attempts to treat sex offenders. (pp. 424-430)

9. Define the sexual dysfunctions, describe their general features, review etiological theories, and summarize the major approaches to treatment. (pp. 430-439)

10. Knowledgeably discuss the difficulty of deciding whether childhood sexual abuse causes borderline personality disorder. (pp. 439-440)

◊ TERMS YOU SHOULD KNOW

---

homosexuality (pp. 402-403)

sexual variants (p. 404)

paraphilia (p. 404)

fetishism (p. 407)

transvestic fetishism (pp. 407-408)

voyeurism (p. 409)

exhibitionism (p. 410)

sadism (p. 411)

pathological sadists (p. 411)

masochism (p. 412)

autoerotic asphyxia (p. 412)

gender identity disorder (p. 414)

cross-gender identification (p. 414)

gender dysphoria (p. 414)

transsexualism (p. 415)

surgical sex reassignment (p. 416)

"recovered" memories (p. 418)

pedophilia (p. 422)

incest (p. 423)

rape (pp. 424-425)

statutory rape (p. 425)

"victim-precipitated" rape (p. 426)

covert sensitization (p. 429)

Depo-Provera (*medroxyprogesterone acetate*) (p. 430)

sexual dysfunction (p. 430)

sexual desire disorders (p. 431)

hypoactive sexual desire disorder (p. 431)

sexual aversion disorder (p. 431)

male erectile disorder (formerly *impotence*) (p. 432)

female sexual arousal disorder (formerly *frigidity*) (p. 432) *premature ejaculation* (p. 433)

male orgasmic disorder (p. 433)

female orgasmic disorder (pp. 433-434)

vaginismus (p. 434)

dyspareunia (p. 434)

◊ NAMES YOU SHOULD KNOW

John Money (pp. 401, 402, 406, 407, 414, 429)

Ray Blanchard (pp. 414, 415, 416)

Kurt Freund (pp. 414, 415, 422)

Richard Green (pp. 414, 415, 430, 432)

David Finkelhor (pp. 417, 418, 422, 424, 426)

Stephen Ceci (p. 418; Highlight 420, pp. 420-421)

Raymond Knight (p. 426)

William Masters and *Virginia Johnson* (pp. 430, 432-438)

◊ CONCEPTS TO MASTER

1. Explain how the case histories of (a) homosexuality in Melanesia and (b) homosexuality and American Psychiatry illustrate that opinions about acceptable and normal sexual behavior vary over time and across cultures. (pp. 402-404)

2. Explain why Kinsey found that homosexuality had a prevalence of 10% whereas more recent studies suggest a rate of 2 to 6 percent? (Highlight 11.1, pp. 405-406)

3. What is the role of androgen in the most influential etiological model of sexual orientation? (Highlight 11.1, pp. 405-406)

4. Define paraphilias and list eight examples recognized in DSM-IV. (p. 406)

5. Define fetishism and give several examples. (p. 407)

6. Define transvestic fetishism and summarize what is known about the personalities of transvestites. (pp. 407-408)

7. Define voyeurism, list two other terms that are synonyms, and describe its clinical features. (pp. 409-410)

8. Define exhibitionism, describe its clinical features, and indicate how its frequency varies with culture. (pp. 410-411)

9. Define sexual sadism and describe its varied manifestations. (p. 411)

10. Define sexual masochism and describe its varied manifestations. (pp. 412-413)

11. Describe Money's attempt to account for the fact that almost all paraphilics are male. (p. 414)

12. What do Freund and Blanchard mean by "erotic target location"? How does this concept help to account for the fact that people with paraphilias often have more than one? (p. 414)

14. List the short-term consequences of childhood sexual abuse and explain why knowledge about the long-term consequences is more uncertain. (pp. 417-418)

15. Critically evaluate the validity of children's testimony regarding sexual abuse. (p. 418; Highlight 11.2, p. 419; Highlight 11.3, pp. 420-421)

16. Describe the methods and results of the "Sam Stone Study" and explain the implications for preschool children's testimony. (Highlight 11.3, pp. 420-421)

17. Summarize the issues surrounding "recovered" memories of sexual abuse. (pp. 418-422)

18. Define pedophilia and describe its clinical features, including the subtype distinction between fixated and regressed pedophiles. (pp. 422-423)

19. Koss and colleagues found that 15% of randomly selected college women had been raped, and an additional 12% had experienced attempted rape. Why have these figures been criticized as misleading and what evidence from Koss's own study supports this criticism? What is the solution to this argument? (p. 425)

20. On what basis do the authors reject the hypothesis that sexual desire is not involved at all in rape? (pp. 425-426)

21. What is the evidence in support of the hypothesis that rape should be considered a category of paraphilia? (pp. 427-428)

22. List the three goals of therapies for sex offenders and describe the approaches taken to achieve these goals. (pp. 429-430)

23. Compare and contrast dysfunctions of sexual arousal with orgasmic disorders in men and women. (pp. 432-434)

25. Summarize the contrasting etiological theories of sexual dysfunction proposed by Masters and Johnson, on the one hand, and Beck and Barlow, on the other hand. (p. 436)

26. Summarize the causes of "lack of emotional closeness and poor communication" that can lead to erectile or orgasmic problems. (pp. 436-437)

27. How do the authors of the text suggest that changes in the social roles of women have affected men's sexuality? How have these changes affected women's sexuality? (p. 437)

28. Discuss the complexities (in terms of methodological issues) of attempting to determine whether childhood sexual abuse causes borderline personality disorder. (pp. 439-440)

◊ STUDY QUESTIONS

Introduction

1. Few people are always happy with their sex lives, but a significant minority have psychological problems that make sexual fulfillment especially difficult. The three general sets of difficulties considered in the chapter are problematic sexual _____, sexual _____, and sexual _____. (p. 399)

Sociocultural influences on sexual practices and standards

2. Although some aspects of sexuality and mating are cross-culturally universal, others are quite variable. For example, all known cultures have taboos against sex between _____, but attitudes toward _____ vary considerably. (p. 400)

3. Recent large, carefully selected samples from the United States, France, and England suggest that the rate of adult homosexual behavior is between ___ and ____ percent, with the rate of exclusively male homosexuality between ___ and ____ percent. The analogous rates for female homosexuality are approximately _____ those for males. (Highlight 11.1, p. 405-406)

4. What explanation is offered by Symons for the high number of sexual partners reported by gay men? (Highlight 11.1, pp. 405-406)

The paraphilias

5. These are a group of persistent sexual behavior patterns in which unusual objects, _____, or _____ are required for sexual satisfaction to occur. (p. 404)

Fetishism

6. In fetishism, sexual interest centers on some body part or an inanimate object. Describe how fetishists get their desired objects and what they do with them once obtained. (p. 407)

7. What is most arousing to the fetishist, the fetish or the illegal act of obtaining the object? (p. 407)

8. How can fetishes be developed through conditioning? (p. 407)

Transvestic fetishism

9. Transvestic fetishism involves obtaining sexual excitement by wearing the clothes of the opposite sex. Do transvestites see themselves as homosexuals? (p. 408)

10. Bentler and colleagues administered a standardized psychological inventory to a large sample of transvestites and to a matched control group. Describe their findings. (p. 408)

11. Gosslin and Eysenck (1980) asked male transvestites to take personality tests while wearing men's clothes and again when dressed as a woman. Describe their results. (p. 408)

Voyeurism

12. Voyeurism, also known as scotophilia and inspectionalism, refers to obtaining sexual pleasure through looking at other people undressing or having sex. What age group commits the majority of voyeuristic acts? (p. 409)

13. Many men enjoy looking at women. Under what conditions does this normal behavior become voyeurism? (pp. 409-410)

14. If a voyeur is married, how well adjusted would he be expected to be in his sexual relationships with his wife? (p. 410)

15. Why doesn't pornography seem to satisfy most voyeurs? (p. 410)

Exhibitionism

16. Exhibitionism involves obtaining sexual pleasure from exposing the genitals to others under inappropriate conditions such as in a public place. How common is exhibitionism in the following: (p. 411)
    a. United States, Canada, and Europe
    b. Argentina
    c. Japan
    d. Burma and India

Sadism

17. Sadism refers to the achievement of sexual gratification through the infliction of physical pain, psychic pain, or humiliation on a sexual partner. Sometimes sadistic activities are associated with objects other than human beings such as _____. (p. 411)

18. What is a "pathological sadist"? (p. 411)

Masochism

19. Explain how the clinical picture in masochism is similar to that in sadistic practices. (p. 412)

20. What does it mean to say that sadism and masochism require a "shared complementary interpersonal relationship"? (p. 412)

261

21. Two facts about paraphilia are likely to be etiologically important: (p. 413)
    a. Almost all paraphilics are _____.
    b. People with paraphilias often _____.

Gender identity disorders

22. Gender identity disorder is characterized by two components: (p. 414)
    a.
    b.

23. Although mere tomboys frequently have many or most of the traits of (a) preferring boys' clothing and hair styles and (b) engaging in activities seen in girls with gender identity disorders, tomboys differ in that they do not desire to _____, or to grow up _____. (p. 414)

24. Has psychotherapy been successful in altering gender identity in transsexuals? (p. 416)

25. Describe what procedures are involved in the following surgical changes of sex: (p. 416)

    1. Male-to-female

    2. Female-to-male

26. What do follow-up studies reviewed by Green and Fleming reveal about the satisfaction of persons who have had sex-change surgery? (p. 416)

27. Why is it required that a person seeking sex-change therapy spend a period of time cross-dressing and taking hormones? (p. 416)

Sexual Abuse

28. In a probability sample of 3,000 persons, Russell found that ____ percent of women and ____ percent of men reported forced sexual contact during childhood. In a sample of 900 women, ____ percent reported having been sexually abused by a relative and ____ percent by a nonrelative before age 14. (p. 417)

30. The conviction of Kelly Michaels was overturned because of concerns about the manner in which child abuse "experts" _____, especially the concern that the adults asked _____ and otherwise _____ reports of abuse. (p. 418)

31. In children's testimony regarding sexual abuse, the use of sexually anatomically correct dolls _____ increase the accuracy of the reports of where (or even if) they were touched. (p. 418)

32. Stephen Ceci found that preschoolers are not deficient at distinguishing between whether they performed an act or whether someone else performed the act, but they do have a deficit in distinguishing between _____ versus _____ acts when both were done by themselves. (Highlight 11.3, pp. 420-421)

Pedophilia

33. Most pedophiles are men. By a ratio of 2 to 1, _____ are most often victimized. (p. 422)

34. In pedophilia the sex object is a _____, and the sexual contact frequently involves _____. (p. 422)

35. Respond to the following questions: (p. 422)
    a. Are most pedophiles known to their victims?
    b. Do most pedophiles use force?
    c. Do most pedophiles show sexual arousal only to children?
    d. Is the most common type of pedophile drawn to children because he feels in control with them?

36. There has been a rash of pedophilia among the Catholic clergy: at least _____ priests were charged with sexual abuse during the 1980s. (p. 423)

Incest

37. Culturally prohibited sexual relations between family members, such as a brother and sister or a parent and child, are known as incest. Describe the consequences of inbreeding among 12 brother-sister and 6 father-daughter matings as studied by Adams and Neel. (p. 423)

38. Incest is thought to be grossly underreported to authorities, but Williams and Finkelhor found almost _____ cases of "intrafamilial sexual abuse" in 1985. In two studies, brother-sister incest was 5 times more common than father-daughter incest. (p. 424)

39. How common is mother-son incest compared to father-daughter? (p. 424)

40. Incestuous fathers tend to be of lower _____ than other fathers, but they do not typically evidence serious _____. Indeed, they are often _____, _____ and claim devotion to their families. Most incestuous fathers are not _____. (p. 424)

41. The wives of men who commit incest were often _____ themselves as children, and in more than _____ of such cases the wife often _____ even if she knows about the incest. (p. 424)

Rape

42. What happened to the incidence of reported rape from 1979 to 1990 according to the National Crime Survey data? (p. 425)

43. Using data from the National Crime Survey, which draws on a probability sample of 59,000 households, the authors estimate that the lifetime risk of total (reported and unreported) rapes or attempted rapes is _____ to _____ percent. (p. 425)

44. Respond to the following questions: (p. 426)
    a. Is rape a repetitive activity?
    b. Are most rapes planned?
    c. Do a third of rapes involve more than one offender?
    d. Does a close relationship between victim and offender mean the victim is more likely to be brutally beaten?

45. Far from being a seductress, the woman repeatedly victimized by rape is often quite _____ and _____. (p. 427)

46. How old is the typical rapist? (p. 427)

47. Unfortunately, most sexual assaults are not reported and, of those that are, less than _____ percent result in conviction. Convictions often bring _____. (p. 428)

264

48. What are the two concerns about the practical effectiveness of therapies that attempt to modify sexual arousal patterns via aversion therapy? (p. 429)

Sexual dysfunctions

49. The term *sexual dysfunction* refers to impairment either in the desire for sexual gratification or in the ability to achieve it. With some exceptions, these impairments are based on faulty _____ and _____. (p. 430)

50. How is sexual desire disorder, which can affect either men or women, different from sexual arousal disorders? (pp. 431-432)

51. Explain the distinction between lifelong and situational erectile disorder. (p. 432)

52. Circle the correct term. Prolonged or permanent erectile insufficiency before the age of 60 is relatively: Common or Rare (p. 432)

53. More recent data suggest that somewhere around _____ percent of cases of erectile insufficiency have some organic involvement, including vascular disease, diabetes, neurological disorders, kidney failure, etc. (p. 432)

54. Can insufficiency due to organic causes be differentiated from psychogenic insufficiency by the presence of nocturnal erections? (p. 432)

55. LoPicolo's (1978) rule for determining when a male is a premature ejaculator is an inability to tolerate as much as _____ minutes of stimulation without ejaculation. Younger men are notorious for their "quick trigger," and longer periods of abstinence increase the likelihood of premature ejaculation. (p. 433)

56. It is thought that many more men experience retarded ejaculation than the number who seek the help of sex therapists. Why don't men seek help for this problem? (p. 433)

58. Vaginismus is an involuntary spasm of the muscles at the entrance to the vagina that prevents penetration and intercourse. In some cases, women who suffer from vaginismus also have arousal insufficiency, possibly the result of conditioned fears associated with _____ _____. (p. 434)

59. The medical term for painful coitus (sexual intercourse) is _____. It can occur in men but is far more common in women. (p. 434)

Causal factors in sexual dysfunction

60. Kaplan has concluded that couples with sexual problems are typically practicing _____ and _____ sexual techniques. (p. 434)

61. In addition to being repeatedly reminded of the risk of pregnancy, what two ideas may be part of a woman's early training about sex that subsequently exert a negative influence on her ability to fully enjoy sexual relations? (p. 435)

   a.

   b.

62. What may be the result of a young man having his first sexual experience under conditions where he is hurried and fears discovery? (p. 435)

63. Cooper (1969) reported that anxiety was a contributing factor in _____ percent of men with erectile difficulties. (p. 435)

64. Masters and Johnson (1975) have concluded that most sexual dysfunctions in males and females are due to crippling fears, attitudes, and inhibitions. These problems often are based on _____ and then exacerbated by later _____. Beck and Barlow play down the role of anxiety per se, instead emphasizing that it is the _____ frequently associated with anxiety in dysfunctional people that seem to interfere with sexual arousal. (p. 436)

65. As a result of the AIDS epidemic, the relatively carefree sexuality of the 1960s and 1970s has increasingly given way to concerns about "safe sex." One study of college-age women reported that the percentage of women reporting that their partners used condoms during sex increased from _____ percent in 1975 to ____ percent in 1989. (p. 437)

Sexual *dysfunctions: Treatment and outcomes*

66. Once the treatment of sexual dysfunctions was considered very difficult. However, a revolution in treating these difficulties has occurred and success rates approaching _____ percent are not unusual. (p. 437)

67. Masters and Johnson's approach to treating sexual dysfunction, described in their book *Human Sexual Inadequacy,* combines elements of traditional and behavioral therapy and emphasizes direct intervention aimed at _____. (pp. 437-438)

68. After Masters and Johnson's pioneering book, many approaches to treating sexual behavior dysfunction were developed. Most approaches are in general agreement about the major goals of treatment. Complete the following list of goals of sex therapy. (p. 438)
   a. Removing crippling _____, _____, and fears
   b. Fostering attitudes toward sexual behavior as a _____, _____, and _____ experience.

69. What do clinicians mean when they say that a particular sexual dysfunction is a "disorder of relationship"? (p. 438)

70. What range of successful outcomes has been reported by sex therapists and what variables affect the outcome? (p. 438)

◊ **CRITICAL THINKING ABOUT DIFFICULT TOPICS**

1. Freund and Blanchard's concept of erotic target location assumes that men are not born with a heterosexual orientation, but rather they "must learn which stimuli together constitute a female sex partner, who is their target stimulus" (p. 414). This model suggests that our biological motivations are quite diffuse and can be channeled in many different directions. Can you think of other examples? Consider cultural variations in dress, hairstyles, and personal ornamentation. Many of these have erotic significance, yet clearly the specific features are not genetically determined. More basically, consider the large cultural variations in food preferences. The need for food is biologically determined, but the precise foods that satisfy this biological motivation appear to be strongly influenced by learning. Can you explain how such an inherited motivational process can be so shaped by learning?

2. Your text notes that, although sexual advances to prepubertal children are viewed as a psychiatric disorder and diagnosed as pedophilia in DSM-IV, rape and incest (including advances directed at postpubertal children) are not. Your text interprets this difference as reflecting "the seriousness with which society views these offenses and its preference for treating coercive sex offenders as criminals rather than patients" (p. 416). On what basis would you decide whether sexual advances directed at postpubertal children should be seen as reflecting psychopathology or as simple criminal behavior? Would you make the same attribution for a biological father and a step-father? If not, why not? More generally, what are the defining features of any psychiatric disorder?

◊ CHAPTER 11 QUIZ

Circle the best of the four answers provided and check them according to answers provided at the back of this study guide. Be sure you understand why each answer is correct.

1. A form of paraphilia in which there usually is not a "victim" is: (p. 409)
   a. voyeurism.
   b. exhibitionism.
   c. sadism.
   d. transvestism.

2. Which of the following persons is most likely to engage in voyeurism? (p. 410)
   a. a married woman who is unhappy with her sexual relations
   b. a homosexual man who is "in between" lovers
   c. an adolescent male who is shy and feels inadequate in relations with women
   d. an elderly man who lives by himself

3. Most exhibitionists: (p. 410)
   a. are young adult males.
   b. are middle-aged married males.
   c. are also aggressive and assaultive.
   d. try to have sexual relations with their victims.

4. The most common sexual offense reported to the police is: (p. 411)
   a. exhibitionism.
   b. obscene phone calls.
   c. voyeurism.
   d. rape.

5. The most common adult outcome of boys with gender identity disorder appears to be: (p. 414)
   a. homosexuality.
   b. heterosexuality.
   c. homosexual transsexualism.
   d. heterosexual transsexualism.

6. In a probability sample of 3,000 persons in one city, Russell found that ____ percent of women and ____ percent of men reported forced sexual contact during childhood. (p. 417)
   a. 2, 1
   b. 7, 4
   c. 15, 2
   d. 25, 6

7. Kelly Michaels, an employee of Wee Care Day Nursery, was convicted in 1988 of pedophilia. Her conviction was overturned on appeal in 1993 due to concerns about: (p. 418)
   a. the bizzareness of the charges.
   b. the extreme rarity of pedophilia among women.
   c. falsification of evidence by parents.
   d. the manner in which child abuse "experts" elicited children's testimony.

8. In the "Sam Stone Study," Ceci found that _____ percent of children given a prior stereotype and asked leading questions during the initial interviews continued to give inaccurate testimony even when gently challenged, compared with only _____ percent among control children. (Highlight 11.3, pp. 420-421)
   a. 5, 1
   b. 14, 4.5
   c. 23, 8
   d. 44, 2.5

9. Girls outnumbered boys as victims of pedophilic practices _____ to _____. (p. 422)
   a. five to one
   b. ten to one
   c. two to one
   d. one hundred to one

10. Incest is almost certainly more common than is known because many victims: (p. 424)
    a. do not consider themselves victimized.
    b. have no desire to stop.
    c. are not educated.
    d. are unable to break from the familial pressure.

11. In Williams and Finkelhor's study, incestuous fathers tended to be _____ _____ than other fathers. (p. 424)
    a. more impulsive
    b. of lower intelligence
    c. more psychopathic
    d. less religious

12. Impairment of either the desire for sexual gratification or of the ability to achieve it is termed sexual: (p. 430)
    a. dysfunction.
    b. incompetence.
    c. perversion.
    d. variation.

13. According to the findings of Kinsey and his associates, about _____ of males become impotent by the age of 70. (p. 432)
    a. one-fourth
    b. one-half
    c. two-thirds
    d. three-fourths

14. More recent data suggest that about 50 percent of the cases of sexual dysfunction may involve _____ causes. (p. 432)
    a. drug-related
    b. organic
    c. psychological
    d. sociocultural

15. According to Masters and Johnson, sexual dysfunctions are usually disorders of: (p. 438)
    a. individuals as separate entities.
    b. the psyche and its conflicts.
    c. the relationships between individuals.
    d. the society and its sexual rules.

Chapter 12
The Schizophrenias

◊ OVERVIEW

The most severe derangement of human behavior possible may be seen in some cases of schizophrenia. Thus, this condition fascinates many people, including psychologists. Because schizophrenia involves disorders in thought, perception, affect, motor behavior, and social relationships, researchers have hoped that study of schizophrenics--where the processes have broken down--might lead to better understanding of unimpaired psychological functioning.

Several different types of schizophrenia are described in Chapter 12 and then the causal factors of the whole group are discussed. There are many different studies described, because the causes of schizophrenia have been more thoroughly researched than many of the other conditions studied so far. Finally, the treatment of schizophrenia--mainly with drugs--is described and evaluated. The chapter concludes with a short discussion of delusional disorders.

◊ LEARNING OBJECTIVES

After studying this chapter, you should be able to:

1. Review the history of the concept of schizophrenia and identify its major clinical features. (pp. 443-444, 448-451)

2. Illustrate the complexity of disentangling genetic and environmental influences in schizophrenia through the example of the Genain quadruplets. (pp. 445-448)

3. List the DSM-IV criteria for the diagnosis of schizophrenia. (Highlight 12.1, p. 450)

4. Compare and contrast the subtypes of schizophrenia. (pp. 452-459; Highlight 12.2, p. 453)

5. Summarize the biological, psychosocial, and sociocultural causal influences in schizophrenia. (pp. 459-474)

6. Evaluate the various biological and psychosocial treatments for schizophrenia. (pp. 474-475; Highlight 12.3, p. 476)

7. Describe the clinical features and subtypes of delusional disorders. (pp. 475-479; Highlight 12.4, p. 477; Highlight 12.5, p. 478)

8. Summarize the causal factors in and treatments for delusional disorders. (pp. 479-481)

9. Discuss the difficulty of conceptualizing schizophrenia. (pp. 481-482)

◊ **TERMS YOU SHOULD KNOW**

---

the schizophrenias (p. 443)

dementia praecox (p. 444)

process schizophrenia, poor premorbid schizophrenia, or *chronic schizophrenia* (equivalent terms) (p. 448)

reactive schizophrenia, good premorbid schizophrenia, or *acute schizophrenia* (equivalent terms) (p. 448)

negative symptom schizophrenia (p. 448)

positive symptom schizophrenia (p. 448)

cognitive slippage (p. 449)

delusion (p. 450)

breakdown of perceptual selectivity (p. 451)

hallucinations (p. 451)

anhedonia (p. 451)

blunting (of affect) (p. 451)

cosmic or *oceanic feelings* (p. 451)

reification (p. 452)

autism (p. 457)

undifferentiated type (of schizophrenia) (p. 452)

catatonic type (of schizophrenia) (p. 454)

catatonic stupor (p. 454)

echopraxia (p. 455)

echolalia (p. 455)

disorganized type (of schizophrenia) (p. 456)

word salad (p. 456)

paranoid type (of schizophrenia) (p. 457)

residual type (of schizophrenia) (p. 459)

schizoaffective disorder (p. 459)

schizophreniform disorder (p. 459)

index schizophrenic patients (in a genetic risk study) (p. 460)

polygenic (p. 460)

twin studies (p. 460)

concordance (p. 460)

adoption strategy (p. 462)

schizophrenic spectrum (p. 463)

studies of high-risk children (p. 464)

Israeli-NIMH High-Risk Study (p. 464)

dopamine hypothesis (p. 465)

chemical imbalance (p. 465)

smooth pursuit eye movement (SPEM) (p. 466)

computerized axial tomography (CAT) (p. 467)

magnetic resonance imaging (MRI) (p. 467)

hypofrontality (p. 467)

season of birth effect (p. 468)

diathesis-stress (p. 469)

schizophrenogenic mothers (p. 470)

marital schism (p. 471)

marital skew (p. 471)

double bind communication (p. 471)

amorphous style (of thinking) (p. 471)

fragmented style (of thinking) (p. 471)

expressed emotion (EE) (p. 472)

major tranquilizers (p. 474)

paranoia (p. 475)

delusional disorder (p. 475)

shared psychotic disorder (p. 475; Highlight 12.4, p. 477)

persecutory type (of delusional disorder) (p. 475)

jealous type (of delusional disorder) (p. 476)

erotomanic type (of delusional disorder) (p. 476)

somatic type (of delusional disorder) (p. 476)

grandiose type (of delusional disorder) (p. 476)

folie a deux (Highlight 12.4, p. 477)

ideas of persecution (p. 478)

delusions of grandeur (p. 478)

paranoid illumination (Highlight 12.5, p. 478; p. 480)

paranoid pseudo-community (Highlight 12.5, p. 478; p. 481)

◊ NAMES YOU SHOULD KNOW

Emil Kraepelin (p. 444)

Eugen Bleuler (p. 444)

David Rosenthal (pp. 445, 447)

Irving Gottesman (pp. 460, 462)

Kenneth Kendler (pp. 460, 461, 463, 465)

Paul Meehl (pp. 468, 469)

◊ CONCEPTS TO MASTER

1. The original term for the schizophrenias was *dementia praecox*. In light of our current views, the term *dementia praecox* is misleading because there is no convincing evidence that schizophrenia leads to permanent mental deterioration. Later, Bleuler introduced the term schizophrenia, which means split mind. He did not mean "split personality" by this term. What did he mean? (p. 444)

2. Briefly summarize the case study of the Genain quads, and explain why their schizophrenic breakdowns were probably due to both heredity and environment. (pp. 445-448)

3. Distinguish between process and reactive schizophrenia and between negative-symptom and positive-symptom schizophrenia, list some near-synonyms for each, and explain what is meant by paranoid and nonparanoid schizophrenia. (pp. 448-449)

4. Describe eight symptom domains that are relevant to the construct of schizophrenia. (pp. 449-451)

5. List the DSM-IV criteria for the diagnosis of schizophrenia. (Highlight 12.1, p. 450)

6. Give several reasons for the difficulty in defining schizophrenic behavior, and indicate how we should deal with this continuing problem. (pp. 451-452)

7. Describe four major subtypes of schizophrenia that have been identified, and list three additional schizophrenic patterns that appear in DSM-IV. (pp. 452-459)

8. Review the evidence from twin studies in support of a genetic contribution to schizophrenia and describe the confounding factors that make it more difficult to draw genetic etiologic conclusions from the classical twin study method. (pp. 460-461)

9. List the findings for 27 pairs of discordant MZ twins in the study by Torrey and colleagues and explain the implications of these findings. (pp. 461-462)

10. What was the design of Heston's adoption study, and what were his major findings and their interpretation? (p. 462)

11. Explain the basis for the following statement in your text: "In recent years, however, the dopamine hypothesis has proved inadequate as a general formulation of etiology." (pp. 465-466)

12. Describe some of the deficiencies in smooth pursuit eye movement that have been observed in schizophrenics and in some of their close relatives and discuss the implications of these findings. (p. 466)

13. Explain what is meant by *hypofrontality*, summarize the evidence in support of this concept, and note the authors' cautionary statement about these findings. (pp. 467-468)

14. Describe Walker's methodology and summarize her findings regarding early childhood deficits in emotional and facial expressions, motor skills, and neuromotor functioning among individuals who later developed schizophrenia. How do the authors of the text explain how such deficits might increase the risk of developing schizophrenia? (pp. 469-470)

15. Summarize the results of research concerning the possibility that some general sociocultural factors may contribute to the development of schizophrenia. (pp. 472-473)

16. What was the result of the Hogarty et al. review of treatments and outcomes in schizophrenia over the last century? To what did he attribute the recent decline in improvement rates? (Highlight 12.3, p. 476)

17. List and describe six types of delusional (paranoid) disorders that appear in DSM-IV, and explain why formal diagnoses of these kinds of abnormal behavior are rare. (pp. 475-477)

18. Describe the clinical symptoms that characterize delusional (paranoid) disorders, and evaluate the popular belief that paranoid individuals are dangerous. (pp. 477-479)

19. What is "paranoid illumination," and how does it lead to the establishment of a paranoid "pseudo-community"? (pp. 480-481)

20. Explain why the picture of treatments for delusional disorders is so bleak. (p. 481)

21 The authors believe that a reconceptualization of schizophrenia is badly needed. Summarize their reasons for this view, emphasizing especially their discussion of the heterogeneity and complexity of this phenomenon. (pp. 481-482)

◊ STUDY QUESTIONS

Introduction

1. The schizophrenias include the ultimate in _____, a term referring to a pervasive loss of contact with reality. The hallmark is a more or less sharp _____ _____. The component processes underlying this detachment from reality include peculiarities in _____, _____, perception, feeling, sense of self, and manner of _____. (p. 443)

2. Schizophrenia is a unitary process; all forms of schizophrenia represent different manifestations of the same disease. True or False (p. 443)

3. Currently, are delusional disorders considered manifestations of schizophrenia or as distinct from schizophrenia? (p. 443)

4. The term _____ was adopted by the German psychiatrist Emile Kraepelin to refer to a group of conditions that all seemed to have the feature of mental deterioration beginning early in life. (p. 444)

5. Schizophrenia is unknown in native or aboriginal groups. True or False (p. 444)

6. In the United States, the one-year prevalence rate of schizophrenia is estimated to be _____ percent, or at present approximately _____ million (aged 18 or older). (p. 444)

7. About _____ percent of new admissions to state and county mental hospitals are diagnosed as schizophrenic. Because schizophrenic individuals often require prolonged or repeated hospitalization, they have historically occupied about _____ of all available mental hospital beds in this country. (p. 444)

8. The median age (i.e., the age that has exactly half the cases below it and half the cases above it) of first admission to a psychiatric hospital with a diagnosis of schizophrenia is in the _____. (p. 444)

9. Complete the following list of reasons why schizophrenia is considered the most serious of all psychotic disorders. (p. 444)
   a. The schizophrenic disorders are complex.
   b. The schizophrenic disorders have a high rate of _____ (especially at the beginning of adult life).
   c. The schizophrenic disorders have a tendency to . . .

Clinical picture in schizophrenia

10. One of the major distinctions among the schizophrenias is the differentiation of process and reactive forms. Explain how these two forms differ with respect to early development and onset of symptoms, presence or absence of discrete stressors, presence or absence of emotional turmoil, and outcome. (p. 448)

11. A second distinction among the schizophrenias is between paranoid and nonparanoid symptom patterns. In general, paranoid schizophrenic individuals tend to be more _____ than process and to have more _____ courses and outcomes. However, a substantial number of people originally diagnosed as having paranoid forms of schizophrenic disorder later are diagnosed as having nonparanoid forms of schizophrenia. (p. 449)

12. The DSM-IV diagnostic criteria for schizophrenia are very behaviorally specific regarding the symptoms that must be present; the decrements of life functioning that must occur; the absence of symptoms of affective disorder, organic disorder, autistic disorder; and the duration of symptoms for at least six months. Complete the following list of the symptoms at least two of which must be present to qualify for a diagnosis of schizophrenia: (Highlight 12.1, p. 450)
   a. Delusions
   b. Prominent hallucinations
   c.
   d.
   e.

13. The text describes eight domains of disturbed behavior that are relevant to the construct of schizophrenia. These characteristics are listed in the following chart. Fill in the empty spaces by writing a short description of the characteristic or providing a clinical example chosen from the text to illustrate the characteristic as appropriate. (pp. 449-451)

Characteristics of Schizophrenia		
Characteristic	**Brief Description**	**Example**
Disturbance of language and communication		Patient says "I cannot be a nincompoop in a physical sense (unless Society would feed me chemicals for my picture in the nincompoop book)."
Disturbance in content of thought	Many types of delusions may be seen	

Disturbance in perception	Breakdown in perceptual selectivity occurs; hallucinations may be seen	
Inappropriate emotion	Anhedonia, emotional blunting; inappropriate strong affect	Patient can't find pleasure in almost any life events.
	Inappropriate strong affect	Patient laughs wildly upon news of a parent's death.
Confused sense of self		Patient feels tied up to universal powers.
Disrupted volition	A disruption of goal-directed activity occurs	
Retreat to an inner world (autism)		Young person develops fantasy world talking with imaginary people.
Disturbed motor behavior		Patient is in a stupor with rigid posture or shows ritualistic mannerisms with bizarre grimace."

Problems in defining schizophrenic behavior

14. Are the authors convinced that the DSM criteria since 1980 for diagnoses of schizophrenia have substantially improved validity? (pp. 451-452)

15. In pointing out the changing empirical foundations for the construct of schizophrenia, the authors of your text are not suggesting that it should be abandoned. Their intent is to ensure

that you avoid the common error of attributing to the _____ construct of "schizophrenia" a substantive existence--a _____. (p. 452)

Subtypes of schizophrenia

16. Match the following types of schizophrenia with the appropriate definition: (pp. 452-459; Highlight 12.2, p. 453)

a. Undifferentiated	__	Those persons who are in remission following a schizophrenic episode and show only mild signs of schizophrenia.
b. Paranoid type	__	A form of schizophrenia that occurs at an early age and includes blunting, inappropriate mannerisms, and bizarre behavior.
c. Catatonic type	__	A person in whom symptoms of schizophrenia have existed for six months or less.
d. Disorganized type	__	A person who shows absurd, illogical, changeable delusions and frequent hallucinations.
e. Residual type	__	A form of schizophrenia in which all the primary indications of schizophrenia are seen in a rapidly changing pattern.
f. Schizoaffective disorder	__	A person who shows some schizophrenic signs as well as obvious depression or elation.
g. Schizophreniform disorder	__	A type of schizophrenia characterized by alternating periods of extreme excitement and extreme withdrawal.

17. What has happened to the relative frequency of paranoid schizophrenia and undifferentiated schizophrenia in recent years? (p. 457)

18. Under what circumstances might a paranoid schizophrenic become violent? (p. 457)

19. At the present time, all new cases of schizophrenia would first receive a diagnoses of _____ until the symptoms have been established for six months. After six months, if symptoms persist, a formal schizophrenic diagnosis can be applied. (p. 459)

Causal factors in schizophrenia: Biological influences

20. Considering only the eight most adequately conducted twin studies in schizophrenia, the overall pairwise concordance rate for schizophrenia in MZ twins is _____ percent. The corresponding figure for DZ twin is _____ percent. Including the data of only the three most rigorous studies, these concordance figures become _____ and _____ percent, respectively. Thus, a reduction in shared genes from 100 percent to 50 percent is associated with a _____ to _____ decrease in the risk of developing schizophrenia. (p. 460)

21. If schizophrenia were *exclusively* a genetic disorder, what concordance rate for identical twins would be found? (p. 460)

22. In the most recent follow-up report of the Danish adoption studies by Kety and his colleagues, the diagnosis of "chronic schizophrenia" was _____ times more frequent among the biological relatives of schizophrenic adoptees (index cases or probands) than among the biological relatives of nonschizophrenic control adoptees. (p. 463)

23. In a reanalysis of the original Danish adoption data using DSM-III criteria, Kendler and Gruenberg found evidence for a genetic contribution to "schizophrenia spectrum" disorders, which consist of schizophrenia, _____ personality disorder, and _____ personality disorder. (p. 463)

24. More recently, Kendler, Gruenberg, and Kinney again showed a concentration of schizophrenia spectrum diagnoses among the biological relatives of the schizophrenic adoptees in the Danish adoption study, but this time the concept of schizophrenia spectrum was adjusted somewhat to include schizophrenia, _____ personality disorder, and _____ (but mainly schizophrenic symptoms). (p. 463)

25. How well have studies of high-risk children paid off? (p. 464)

26. Answer the following questions about the Israeli-NIMH High-Risk Study: (p. 464)

   a. Who were the index groups?

   b. In which group (Kibbutzim raised or home raised) did the majority of cases of schizophrenia occur?

27. Summarize the authors' overall conclusion regarding a genetic basis for schizophrenia based on evidence from high-risk research, family studies, twin studies, and adoption methods. (pp. 464-465)

28. The most attractive biochemical approach to schizophrenia has been the dopamine hypothesis, based on the observation that all of the _____ had the common property of _____. (p. 465)

29. According to the dopamine hypothesis, schizophrenia is the product of _____ _____ at certain synaptic sites. Variants of this view include hypotheses that a schizophrenic person has too many _____ or that these _____ have for some reason become _____. (p. 465)

30. Some findings indicate that persons who are merely "at risk" for schizophrenia often experience difficulties in _____, in _____, and in certain other indicators of cognitive functioning *before* a schizophrenic breakdown. (p. 466)

31. Research literature going back many decades documents an enormous variety of ways in which attentional and cognitive processes are disrupted among schizophrenic persons. The disjointed array of findings reported remains baffling in the absence of a _____ _____ within which the "pieces" of the schizophrenia puzzle can be put together. (pp. 466-467)

32. In some cases of schizophrenia, particularly those of chronic, negative symptom course, there is an abnormal enlargement of the brain's _____, as well as enlarged sulci. Both findings imply a loss of _____--possibly some type of _____ or degeneration. In a review of such findings, Bogerts concludes that the findings do not reflect progressive degeneration, but favor the hypothesis of some type of anomaly in _____ brain development. (p. 467)

33. In a review of neuroimaging studies, Gur and Pearlson conclude that the evidence implicates primarily three brain structures. These are the _____, the _____, and the _____. These authors also note, however, that few of these findings are _____ for schizophrenia. (p. 468)

34. In a thorough review of the "season of birth effect," Bradbury and Miller (p. 468) concluded that the evidence points to some type of _____ or early _____ pathogenic influence. Their best guess was that this influence was some type of _____ process or _____ complications (or both). (p. 468)

Causal factors in schizophrenia: Psychosocial influences

35. Based on interviews with at-risk children, Dworkin and colleagues found these youngsters to have more _____ deficits and _____ incompetence, which in turn were associated, respectively, with observed neuromotor and _____ dysfunctions. (p. 470)

36. Why was the concept of schizophrenogenic mothers largely abandoned in the 1970s? (p. 470)

37. What have several researchers (e.g., Mishler & Waxler; Liem) noted about the impact of schizophrenic children's behavior on their parents? (p. 471)

38. In a group of 14 families with schizophrenic offspring, Lidz and colleagues (1965) failed to find a single family that was reasonably well integrated. In 8 of the couples, there was a state of severe chronic discord where the continuation of the marriage was constantly threatened. This condition has been labeled _____. In the other six couples, a maladaptive equilibrium had been reached in which some family members collude to allow another member to behave abnormally. This condition is called _____. (p. 471)

39. Bateson (1959, 1960) coined the term double-bind to describe the conflicting and confusing nature of communications among members of schizophrenic families. Give an example of double-bind communication. (p. 471)

40. Singer and Wynne (1963, 1965) have described amorphous and fragmented communication patterns in schizophrenic families. Describe each of these patterns. (pp. 471-472)

41. In more recent work, Singer et al. (1978, 1979) have referred to high "communication defiance" in schizophrenic families. Were Goldstein and colleagues (1978) able to confirm a link between communication deviance and schizophrenia in their longitudinal study employing a variant of a high-risk strategy? (p. 472)

42. Relapse into schizophrenia following remission is often associated with a certain negative communication called expressed emotion (EE). What two components appear critical in the pathogenic effects of EE? (p. 472)
    a.
    b.

Schizophrenia: Treatment and outcomes

43. The chance that a schizophrenic patient admitted to a modern mental hospital and given chemotherapy will be discharged in a matter of weeks is _____ to _____ percent. However, the chance a patient will be readmitted during the first year after release is high. (p. 474)

291

44. The overall outcome of schizophrenia can be broken down into three groups. What percentage of schizophrenic patients fall into each of these groups? (p. 474)

_____ percent	a. Those patients who recover from the schizophrenia and remain symptom-free for five years.
_____ percent	b. Those patients who show partial recovery with some residual symptoms.
_____ percent	c. Those patients who remain largely or totally disabled for their entire life.

45. After attending a meeting of Schizophrenics Anonymous, Roger Brown concluded that there is something about schizophrenia that the antipsychotic drugs _____ or even always _____ on a long-term basis. (p. 475)

46. What forms of psychosocial intervention in schizophrenia can claim at least modest empirical validation? (p. 475)

Delusional (paranoid) disorder

47. DSM-IV requires that diagnoses of delusional disorder be specified by type on the basis of the predominant theme of the delusions. Complete the following list of the types of delusions that may be seen. (pp. 475-476)

Type of Delusion	Description
a. Persecutory type	a. The belief that one is being subjected to bad treatment. Often leads to lawsuits to seek redress.
b.	b.
c.	c. The belief that a famous person is in love with you or desires a sexual relationship with you.

d. Somatic type	d.
e.	e.

48. When *folie a deux* occurs, what is the most frequent familial relationship between the affected parties? (Highlight 12.4, p. 477)

49. Place the following stages in the development of paranoid thinking in their proper order: hostility, protective thinking, paranoid illumination, delusions, suspiciousness. (Highlight 12.5, p. 478)

    a. _____
    b. _____
    c. _____
    d. _____
    e. _____

50. Meissner (1978) regards feelings of frustration and brooding over fancied and real injustices to be an essential phase of personality development and a necessary component in the achievement of _____ and _____. (p. 480)

51. Grunebaum and Perlman (1973) have pointed to the naiveté of the preparanoid person in assessing the interpersonal world as a fertile source of hurtful interactions. "The ability to trust others realistically requires that the individual be able to tolerate minor and major _____ that are part of normal human relationships." (p. 480)

Unresolved issues

52. The authors believe that the understanding of schizophrenia will only increase if there is some sort of _____ that enables us to view the pertinent phenomena in a new and more productive light. (p. 481)

53. The authors predict that any major conceptual advance will entail not one but many _____, thereby emphasizing that the class of people who merit a diagnosis of schizophrenia is _____ not merely in manifest behavior, but also in the nature and development of the sources of their aberrant behavior. (p. 482)

◊ **CRITICAL THINKING ABOUT DIFFICULT TOPICS**

1. In the polygenic model proposed by Gottesman (cited in your text on page 460, but covered very briefly), there are three sources of liability for schizophrenia that combine *additively* to produce the total liability: specific genetic, nonspecific genetic, and nonspecific environmental. Specific genetic liability means that the increased risk is specific to schizophrenia. Nonspecific genetic liability means liability that could also apply to other disorders, but which increases the risk of schizophrenia (presumably in individuals with specific genetic liability). Similarly, nonspecific environmental liability means liability that increases the risk for many disorders, including schizophrenia. A stressful environment is an example of a nonspecific environmental source of liability, because stress increases the risk of anxiety, depression, ulcers, hypertension, etc., as well as of schizophrenia. Can you think of possible candidates for nonspecific genetic liability? Refer back to Question 3 of this section in Chapter 8 for a suggestion that inheritance of low IQ may make the world more stressful. What about inheritance of an anxiety-prone personality?

2. In his adoption study, Heston found that the adopted-away children of schizophrenic mothers were more likely (than controls) to be diagnosed as schizophrenic, but also as mentally retarded, neurotic (anxiety disorders), and psychopathic. Your text concludes that these findings suggest that "the genetic liability to schizophrenia is not specific to schizophrenia but also includes a liability for other forms of psychopathology" (p. 462). While it is true that what is inherited is broader than the DSM-IV diagnosis of schizophrenia, to try to include mental retardation, anxiety disorders, and psychopathy in the schizophrenia spectrum makes little sense. Can you think of other explanations? Consider two. First, it has been suggested that the fathers may have contributed genes increasing the risk of psychopathy. Second, as suggested in the preceding question, nonspecific genetic liability might involve low intelligence and anxiety-proneness. If you accept this argument, note how difficult it is to identify the forms of psychopathology that are *specifically* related to schizophrenia, because other genetic influences will affect the pathology seen among the relatives of schizophrenic index cases.

3. In Chapter 10 you learned that the mesocorticolimbic *dopamine* pathway is strongly involved in the brain reward system, also called the "pleasure pathway" (Highlight 10.5, pp. 364-365). In the present chapter, you have read that the vast majority of antipsychotic drugs exert their effect by essentially completely blocking dopaminergic activity (p. 465). Can you offer any explanation for why blocking reward/pleasure pathways would be therapeutic for a disorder characterized by anhedonia and disruption of (rewarded) goal-directed activity? If you have trouble doing so, you are in good company. This apparent contradiction is difficult to explain. Two possible approaches are to be found in the observations that (a) some factor other than dopamine causes schizophrenia, "the symptoms of which are then amplified by dopaminergic neural transmission" (p. 466) and (b) antipsychotic drugs are only partially effective in reducing negative symptoms (p. 448), of which anhedonia and disruption of goal-directed behavior are central components. Undoubtedly, you will have noticed that this perspective underscores the complexity of schizophrenia, since it is difficult to explain why blocking dopamine activity is beneficial in some respects but not others.

4. The authors of your text correctly emphasize the heterogeneity of schizophrenia and the need for a reconceptualization (pp. 481-482). How would you interpret their suggestion that such a conceptual advance will entail many "schizophrenias" (p. 482)? The most natural meaning of this term would be a number of different *categories* of schizophrenia that reflected qualitatively different causes? However, there is another possible meaning: that many different processes are involved in schizophrenia and that these interact and add together to create different clinical pictures. In this case, the differences are quantitative, and there may well be considerable overlap among the heterogeneous individuals with "many schizophrenias." Which meaning do you think is best supported by the findings reviewed in the present chapter? Note that the authors talk about "a host of moderating variables" and that "the schizophrenias result from interactions among variables that cross traditional disciplinary boundaries" (p. 482).

Circle the best of the four answers provided and check them according to answers provided at the back of this study guide. Be sure you understand why each answer is correct.

1. In the United States, the estimated incidence of schizophrenia is about _____ percent of the population. (p. 444)
   a. one   c. five
   b. three   d. seven

2. The median age of onset for schizophrenia is: (p. 444)
   a. below 15.   c. over 45.
   b. around 30.   d. older in females than males.

3. Hester Genain was never as well off psychologically as her sisters and moved in imperceptible steps toward psychosis. She could be viewed as a (an) _____ schizophrenic. (p. 448)
   a. acute   c. process
   b. residual   d. reactive

4. A schizophrenic's statement that he is "growing his father's hair" is an example of: (p. 449)
   a. anhedonia.   c. echolalia.
   b. autism.   d. cognitive slippage.

5. The new DSM criteria for the diagnosis of schizophrenia since 1980, according to the authors, have: (pp. 451-452)
   a. certainly increased diagnostic validity.
   b. increased the number of patients diagnosed as schizophrenic.
   c. probably decreased both diagnostic reliability and validity.
   d. increased diagnostic reliability.

6. The central feature of _____ schizophrenia is pronounced motor symptoms. (p. 454)
   a. undifferentiated   c. disorganized
   b. catatonic   d. paranoid

7. A person in whom symptoms of schizophrenia have existed for six months or less would be diagnosed as: (p. 459)
   a. undifferentiated type.   c. disorganized type.
   b. catatonic type.   d. schizophreniform disorder.

8. The results of twin studies of hereditary factors in the development of schizophrenia show: (p. 460)
   a. equal concordance rates for identical and fraternal twins.
   b. higher concordance rates for fraternal twins.
   c. higher concordance rates for identical twins.
   d. higher incidence of schizophrenia among twins than among others.

9. If schizophrenia were exclusively genetic, the concordance rate for identical twins would be _____ percent. (p. 460)
   a. 1   c. 50
   b. 25   d. 100

10. Monitoring over time children born to schizophrenic mothers is the research strategy known as: (p. 464)
    a. high-risk studies.   c. family studies.
    b. adoption studies.   d. twin studies.

11. Which of the following findings did not contribute to the demise of the dopamine hypothesis about the cause of schizophrenia? (pp. 465-466)
    a. Dopamine-blocking drugs also reduce psychotic symptoms for other disorders
    b. Dopamine-blocking drugs work almost immediately
    c. Dopamine-blocking drugs are an antidote for drug-induced "bad trips"
    d. Dopamine-stimulating drugs cause hallucinations

12. Because the brain normally occupies the skull fully, the enlarged ventricles of some schizophrenics imply a(an): (p. 467)
    a. decreased pressure on the brain.
    b. decrement in the brain mass.
    c. increased amount of spinal fluid.
    d. predisposition to hydrocephaly.

13. Which of the following was not a deficit found by Walker in her videotape study of preschizophrenic children? (p. 469)
    a. less positive emotion   c. cognitive slippage
    b. poor motor skills   d. neuromotor abnormalities

14. The concept that was never supported by robust research and that was largely abandoned by the 1970s was: (p. 470)
    a. schizophrenogenic mother.   c. expressed emotion.
    b. marital schism.   d. communication deviance.

15. What proportion of recovered schizophrenic patients remain symptom-free permanently? (p. 474)
    a. 10 percent
    b. 25 percent
    c. 50 percent
    d. 60 percent

◊ **OVERVIEW**

Most mental disorders do not involve any known brain pathology. Those that do are discussed in the first half of this chapter. The discussion of neuropsychological mental disorders begins with a description of the kinds of symptoms that may be seen as a result of brain damage, of the interaction of brain "hardware" and "software," of the general clinical features of neuropsychological disorders, and of the major neuropsychological syndromes. A newer and devastating organic syndrome caused by the HIV-1 virus is discussed, and the causal processes and effects of Alzheimer's disease are covered in depth. Finally, neuropsychological problems secondary to head injury are reviewed.

The second half of the chapter covers mental retardation and discusses the behavior that is characteristic of the different levels or degrees of mental retardation. The various causes of retardation are specified. The authors cover learning disorders, such as dyslexia, and talk about the lack of understanding and options available to the children suffering from them. Finally, issues regarding environmental influences on IQ test performance and the question of "culture-free" IQ tests are discussed.

◊ **LEARNING OBJECTIVES**

After studying this chapter, you should be able to:

1. Describe the general features and symptomatic consequences of neuropsychological mental disorders. (pp. 486-490)

2. List and characterize the major neuropsychological syndromes. (pp. 490-493)

3. Explain the relationship between AIDS and the neuropsychological problems in the form of AIDS dementia complex. (pp. 493-495)

4. Define Dementia of the Alzheimer's Type (DAT), describe its clinical features, and summarize what is known about its etiology and treatment. (pp. 495-502)

5. Compare and contrast Vascular Dementia (VAD) and DAT. (p. 502)

6. Outline the consequences of head injury for neuropsychological functioning. (pp. 502-506)

7. List the levels of mental retardation and describe the functioning associated with each level. (pp. 507-509)

8. Summarize the biological factors contributing to mental retardation and describe the subtypes of mental retardation based on specific biological etiologies. (pp. 509-514)

9. Explain what is meant by cultural-familial retardation and review evidence concerning its etiology. (pp. 514-516)

10. Describe problems of assessment of mental retardation and review various approaches to treatment and prevention of mental retardation. (pp. 516-519)

11. Define the term "specific learning disorders," describe the clinical features, and review attempts to explain the etiology of and to develop treatments for learning disorders. (pp. 519-522)

◊ TERMS YOU SHOULD KNOW

organic mental disorders (p. 486)

neuropsychological (p. 486)

diffuse brain damage (p. 486)

focal brain lesions (p. 486)

syndromes (p. 490)

delirium (p. 491)

dementia (p. 491)

amnestic syndrome (p. 492)

neuropsychological delusional syndrome (pp. 492-493)

neuropsychological mood syndrome (pp. 492-493)

neuropsychological personality syndrome (p. 493)

AIDS dementia complex (ADC) (p. 494)

AIDS-related complex (ARC) (p. 494)

Dementia of the Alzheimer's Type (DAT) (p. 495)

Alzheimer's disease (p. 495)

senile dementia (p. 495)

presenile dementia (p. 495)

senile plaques (p. 499)

vascular dementia (p. 502)

stroke (p. 502)

retrograde amnesia (p. 502)

intracranial hemorrhage (p. 503)

subdural hematoma (p. 503)

petechial hemorrhages (p. 503)

cerebral edema (p. 503)

punch drunk (p. 504)

mental retardation (p. 506)

mild mental retardation (educable) (p. 508)

moderate mental retardation (trainable) (p. 508)

severe mental retardation (dependent retarded) (pp. 508-509)

profound mental retardation (life support retarded) (p. 509)

fragile X (p. 509)

hypoxia (p. 510)

Down syndrome (p. 510)

Tay-Sach's disease (Highlight 13.4, p. 511)

Turner's syndrome (Highlight 13.4, p. 511)

Klinefelter's syndrome (Highlight 13.4, p. 511)

Niemann-Pick's disease (Highlight 13.4, p. 511)

Bilirubin encephalopathy (Highlight 13.4, p. 511)

rubella, congenital (Highlight 13.4, p. 511)

trisomy of chromosome 21 (p. 512)

phenylketonuria (PKU) (p. 513)

macrocephaly (p. 514)

microcephaly (p. 514)

hydrocephalus (p. 514)

cultural-familial retardation (pp. 514-515)

mainstreaming (p. 518)

◊ **CONCEPTS TO MASTER**

1. Define organic or neuropsychological mental disorders, and describe nine symptomatic consequences of these disorders that have mainly focal origins but commonly appear in the context of progressively diffuse damage. (pp. 486-487)

2. Compare and contrast the concepts of "hardware" and "software" as the authors apply them to the brain and mental processes. (pp. 487-488)

3. Describe the general functions attributed to the right and left hemispheres of the brain. (p. 489)

4. Define "syndrome" and describe four types of syndromes that are typical of persons with organic brain pathology. (pp. 490-493)

5. What is meant by the concept of dementia and what processes are most seriously disturbed? (p. 491)

6. Differentiate between senile and presenile dementias and describe two presenile types. (p. 495; Highlight 13.3, p. 496)

7. Describe the connection between Down syndrome and DAT and summarize the two etiological theories (by the Duke University group and by Potter et al.) involving apolipoprotein-E (ApoE). (p. 500)

8. Describe the differences and similarities between DAT and vascular dementia (VAD). (p. 502)

9. Describe the controversy regarding whether the large numbers of relatively mild closed-head brain concussions and contusions produce significant long-standing symptoms or impairments of various abilities. (p. 504)

10. Define mental retardation and describe its classification by DSM-IV. (pp. 506-507)

11. List and describe the behavior of four levels of mental retardation, and explain their distribution in the United States. (pp. 507-508)

12. List five biological conditions that may lead to mental retardation, and describe the various ways in which these factors cause mental retardation. (pp. 509-510)

13. Describe some of the physical characteristics of children born with Down syndrome. (pp. 510-511)

14. Describe the cause, diagnosis, and preventive treatment of phenylketonuria (PKU). (p. 513)

15. List three types of cranial anomalies and describe the diagnosis and treatment of each. (pp. 513-514)

16. How does the concept of cultural-familial mental retardation support a contribution of environmental factors to the etiology of mental retardation? (pp. 514-515)

17. Describe some of the forms of care for the mentally retarded that are alternatives to institutionalization according to Tyor and Bell. (p. 517)

18. Discuss the pros and cons of the "mainstreaming" approach to the education of retarded children. What is a reasonable conclusion about mainstreaming at this point? (p. 518)

19. Describe the Head Start program and discuss the strengths, weaknesses, frustrations, and potential benefits of this approach to preventing mental retardation. (p. 519)

20. What was implied by the term "minimal brain dysfunction" and why has this hypothesis fallen into disfavor? (p. 521)

◊ STUDY QUESTIONS

Brain disorders

1. When structural defects in the brain occur before birth or at a very early age, the typical result is _____, the severity of which depends on the severity of the defect. Such individuals fail to develop an optimal level of various skills that underlie the ability to independently cope with environmental demands. (p. 485)

2. Does it matter whether the brain damage occurs in early life before life skills have been developed or in adulthood after life skills have been mastered? (pp. 485-486)

Brain impairment and adult disorder

3. The destruction of brain tissue may involve only limited behavioral deficits or a wide range of psychological impairments, depending on four variables. Complete the following list: (p. 486)
   a.
   b.
   c. The individual's total life situation
   d.

4. Respond true or false to the following statements:
   a. Most neurologically impaired individuals develop psychiatric symptoms. True or False (p. 487)
   b. A person can have a breakdown in the brain's hardware without effects on the processing of software, or past and present experience. True or False (p. 488)
   c. Cell bodies and neural pathways in the brain have the power of regeneration but it is slow. True or False (p. 488)
   d. The amount of tissue damage to the brain does not predict impairment of function. True or False (p. 488)
   e. The location of damage may be of significance in predicting the impact of an injury because the parts of the human brain are specialized in their function. True or False (pp. 488-489)

5. The immense complexity of the brain makes it difficult to predict the effects of focal brain injury. In fact, all behavior is the product of neuronal activity in _____ _____. (Highlight 13.1, p. 489)

6. It is possible to make certain generalizations about the likely effects of damage to particular parts of the brain. Complete the following chart that summarize these. (p. 490)

Area of the Brain Damaged	Probable Clinical Picture
Frontal areas	either passivity and apathy or impulsiveness and distractibility
Right parietal area	
Left parietal area	
Temporal area	
Occipital area	

7. Psychiatric and personality disorders are classified on axes I and II of DSM-IV. Where are the neuropsychological mental disorders classified? (p. 490)

Neuropsychological symptom syndromes

The clusters of symptoms based on brain damage listed in the DSM-IV are grouped by the authors into four clusters: (1) delirium and dementia; (2) amnestic syndrome and hallucinosis; (3) organic delusional, mood, and anxiety syndromes; and (4) organic personality syndrome. Respond to each of the following questions about these symptom clusters:

8. Match the following: (p. 491)

a. Delirium	___ Caused by degenerative processes of old age, repeated strokes, infections, tumors, injuries, and dietary deficiencies.
b. Dementia	___ Caused by head injury, toxic or metabolic disturbances, insufficient blood to brain, withdrawal from alcohol or other drugs, and lack of oxygen to the brain.

9. Which of the following would a person with amnestic syndrome have the most problem remembering? (p. 492)
   a. The name of the doctor who just introduced him- or herself one second before.
   b. What he or she had for breakfast.
   c. Details of his or her childhood from 50 years ago.

10. Is overall cognitive functioning impaired in the amnestic syndrome as it is in dementia? (p. 492)

11. Are the most common forms of amnestic syndrome, those due to alcohol or barbiturate addiction, considered reversible? (p. 492)

12. Fill in the following chart which summarizes the most common causes of the following neuropsychological syndromes: (pp. 491-493)

Organic Syndrome	Common Etiological Factors
Delirium	head injury, toxic or metabolic disturbances, insufficient blood to brain, withdrawal from alcohol or other drugs, and lack of oxygen to the brain.
Dementia	
Amnestic syndrome	
Neuropsychological delusional syndrome	
Neuropsychological mood syndrome	
Neuropsychological personality syndrome	

Neuropsychological disorder with HIV-1 infection

13. Contrary to initial assumptions, the organic brain effects associated with AIDS patients was not due to opportunistic infections, but due to the presence of the _____ itself. (p. 494)

14. The clinical features of AIDS dementia complex (ADC) include psychomotor slowing, _____, _____, and perhaps _____. ADC progresses rapidly and the later phases include behavioral regression, _____, _____, _____, and marked _____. (p. 494)

15. Presently, the question of treatment for ADC is intimately tied to that involving _____ or _____ of the HIV-1 infection itself. Unfortunately, experience with AZT therapy in the more general AIDS context suggests that the hopeful effects reported by Sidtis, Gatsonis, and Price will probably prove temporary. It remains true, therefore, that _____ is the only certain defensive strategy. (p. 494)

Dementia of the Alzheimer's type

16. How common is Dementia of the Alzheimer's type: (p. 496)
    a. among persons over 65 years old?
    b. among persons over 85 years old?
    c. among nursing home residents?

17. Describe the onset of Alzheimer's disease. (p. 496)

18. Approximately _____ of all DAT patients show a course of simple deterioration, that is, they gradually lose mental capacities. Symptoms of psychopathology are brief and inconsistent over time. It is less frequent but not uncommon for Alzheimer's disease patients to develop a decidedly paranoid orientation, becoming markedly suspicious and developing jealousy delusions. (pp. 497-498)

19. The neurological degeneration that occurs in Alzheimer's disease includes degenerative changes in neurons (senile plaques and neurofibrillary tangles) and an abnormal appearance of small holes in neuronal tissues, called granulovacuoles, as a result of cell degeneration. While there is widespread destruction of neurons in DAT, among the earliest and most severely affected are a cluster of cell bodies located in the _____ and involved in the release of _____. This observation has given rise to the _____ depletion theory of DAT etiology. (p. 499)

20. Studies of the composition of the senile plaques in DAT reveal that their cores consist of a sticky protein substance, called _____, that also occurs in abnormal abundance in other parts of DAT patients' brains. This finding may turn out to be extremely important in leading to an understanding of DAT. (pp. 499-500)

21. Is it realistic to consider genetic factors as primary causes of early-onset DAT? Late-onset DAT? (p. 500)

22. Are there reports of Alzheimer's disease showing a familial transmission pattern? (p. 500)

23. What evidence is there that DAT is not determined solely by genetics? (p. 500)

24. There have been attempts to control at least some of the more troublesome behaviors associated with DAT such as _____, _____, inappropriate _____, and inadequate _____ skills using a _____ approach. (p. 501)

25. Some DAT patients respond to _____ or _____ medication to help with modulating their emotions and impulses. (p. 501)

26. Why has so much attention been given to the caregivers of those with DAT? (p. 501)

27. Why is the reluctance to hospitalize a DAT patient justifiable? On the other hand, why is hospitalization reasonable with the emergence of confusion, gross and argumentative demeanor, stuporous depression, inappropriate sexual behavior, etc.? (pp. 501-502)

Vascular dementia

28. A sudden interruption of the blood supply to parts of the brain is a _____. (p. 502)

29. When a series of small strokes occur, the condition is known as _____ dementia, the underlying cause of 10% of all dementia. (p. 502)

30. The characteristics between MID and DAT are similar, but the decline in MID is not so smooth because of (a) the discrete character of _____ and the processes they initiate; (b) variations over time in the volume of blood delivered by a _____; and (c) a tendency to be associated with more severe _____. (p. 502)

31. Few persons with head injury find their way into mental institutions because: (p. 502)

32. What causes people to experience retrograde amnesia after accidents? (p. 502)

33. Why is boxing potentially dangerous? (pp. 503-504)

34. Common aftereffects of moderate brain injury are chronic headaches, anxiety, irritability, dizziness, easy fatigability, and impaired memory and concentration. How common is epilepsy after a head injury? (p. 505)

35. List six factors in the following short example suggesting that the patient has an unfavorable prognosis. (pp. 505-506)

"An 18-year-old male who had several run-ins with the law during high school received a serious head injury in a motorcycle accident. He was in a coma for almost a month. The patient is currently suffering some paralysis and is very angry and depressed. He refuses to cooperate with his physical therapist. His parents, who live in a remote rural area where no rehabilitation facilities are available, will take him back home but are rather unenthusiastic about the prospect."

a.

b.

c.

d.

e.

f.

Mental retardation

36. The DSM-IV defines mental retardation as "significantly subaverage general intellectual functioning . . . that is accompanied by significant limitations in adaptive functioning in certain skill areas . . ." and manifested before age 18. The IQ cutoff for mental retardation used by DSM-IV is _____. (p. 506)

37. Is mental retardation associated with an increased risk of other disorders? Which ones? (p. 506)

38. Explain why the incidence of initial diagnoses of mental retardation increases markedly between ages 5 to 6, peaks at 15, and drops off sharply after that. (p. 507)

39. Diagnosed mental retardation in the U. S. is about 1 percent. What does this imply about the majority of persons with an IQ below 70? (pp. 506-507)

Levels of mental retardation

40. For most IQ tests the mean is _____ and the standard deviation is about _____ points. Thus, approximately _____ of the population score between IQ 85 and IQ 115. Assuming that IQ scores are normally distributed, if IQ 70 is used as the cutoff for mental retardation, about _____ percent of the population would fall in the mental retardation range (i.e., below 70). (p. 507)

41. Generally, IQ tests measure an individual's likely level of success in dealing with conventional _____. (p. 507)

42. Although an IQ test score lower than 70 tends to be the dominant consideration in the diagnosis of mental retardation, additional evidence is required. What additional evidence is required to make a diagnosis of mental retardation? (p. 507)

43. In 1992 the AAMR (American Association on Mental Retardation) adopted IQ _____ as the cutoff point for the diagnosis of mental retardation. (p. 507)

44. Of the mild, moderate, severe, and profound retardation levels, in which level do by far the *greatest* number of mentally retarded individuals fall? (p. 508)

45. Fill in the missing information in the following chart that summarizes the educational potential, level of care required, and the degree of physical deformities characteristic of each level of retardation: (pp. 508-509)

Level of Retardation	Description
Mild	Persons in this group are considered "educable." They can master simple academic and occupational skills and become self-supporting. Physically, these individuals are normal.
Moderate	Persons in this group are considered _____. Most can achieve partial independence in daily _____, acceptable behavior, and work within the family or sheltered workshop. Physically, these individuals usually appear _____ and ungainly.
Severe	Persons in this group are called "dependent retarded." They can develop limited levels of _____ and _____ skills. Physical handicaps are common.
Profound	Persons in this group are considered _____ retarded. They are capable of only the simplest tasks, and speech does not develop. They must remain in custodial care their whole lives. Serious physical deformities are common.

46. Which levels of retardation can be diagnosed readily in infancy? (p. 509)

47. The distribution of intelligence almost fits a perfect normal curve, but it is distorted by a frequency bulge in the lower IQ or mental retardation range. Why does this bulge at the lower end of the intelligence distribution occur? (p. 509)

Brain defects in mental retardation

48. Mental retardation is associated with known organic pathology in _____ percent of the cases. In cases with organic pathology, retardation is virtually always moderate and is often severe. Profound retardation is rare and never occurs in the absence of obvious organic damage. (p. 509)

49. The authors of the text list five biological conditions that may lead to mental retardation. They are presented below. Complete the requested information. (pp. 509-510)
   a. Genetic-chromosomal factors
   Mental retardation tends to run in families, but _____ and _____ also run in families. Exposure to social disadvantage may lead to retardation even in children who have inherited average intellectual potential. In some relatively infrequent types of mental retardation such as _____, genetic factors play a clear role.
   b. Infections and toxic agents
   Illnesses in a pregnant woman that can cause mental retardation of the offspring include _____, _____, and German measles. After birth, viral _____ in the newborn child may lead to mental retardation. Environmental toxins that may cause mental retardation in children are _____ and lead. Similarly, an excess of _____ taken by a pregnant woman may lead to congenital malformations.
   c. Prematurity and birth trauma
   Brain damage leading to mental retardation occurs in 1 birth out of _____.
   d. Ionizing radiation
   The list of sources of harmful radiation includes diagnostic x-rays, leakages at _____ _____, and nuclear weapons testing.
   e. Malnutrition
   The negative impact of malnutrition on mental development may, at least in some cases, be viewed as a special case of _____ deprivation.

Organic retardation syndromes

50. Complete the following list of seven disorders that are sometimes associated with mental retardation. (Highlight 13.4, p. 511)
   a. No. 18 trisomy syndrome
   b.
   c.
   d.
   e. Bilirubin encephalopathy
   f.

51. Down Syndrome is the most common condition that leads to moderate and severe mental retardation. It occurs in 1 in every _____ babies born in the United States. (p. 510)

52. What level of mental retardation is usually present in children with Down's syndrome? (p. 510)

53. How long do individuals with Down syndrome live, and how has this life expectancy changed in the past half century? (p. 511)

54. Is the intellectual defect in Down syndrome consistent across abilities? (p. 512)

55. Are these children unusually placid and affectionate? (pp. 511-512)

56. Down's syndrome is caused by an extra chromosome, number 21. (Normal children have 23 pairs of chromosomes--a total of 46. Down's syndrome children have 23 pairs also, but "pair" 21 has three chromosomes instead of the normal two--a total of 47.) Where does the extra chromosome come from? (p. 512)

57. The risk of having a child with Down's syndrome is high if the mother is age _____ or older or the father is age _____ or older. (p. 513)

58. In phenylketonuria (PKU), a baby lacks a liver enzyme needed to break down _____, an amino acid found in many foods. (p. 513)

59. A child with phenylketonuria (PKU) appears normal until _____ to _____ months of age. (p. 513)

60. What level of retardation is likely if PKU goes untreated? What is the median IQ of untreated PKU adults? (p. 513)

61. PKU can be identified by a simple test of the infant. Once found, how is PKU treated? (p. 513)

62. For a baby to inherit PKU, it appears that both parents must carry _____ genes. (p. 513)

63. How severely retarded are microcephalic children? (p. 514)

64. What are the causes of microcephaly? (p. 514)

65. What is the outcome for hydrocephalic children today? (p. 514)

Cultural-familial mental retardation

66. Most mental retardation is of the _____ type. (p. 515)

67. Children whose retardation is cultural-familial in origin are usually _____ retarded. (p. 515)

68. What proportion of mentally retarded children come from socially, economically, and culturally deprived homes? (p. 515)

The problem of assessing mental retardation

69. Complete the following list of the three factors that usually account for errors in measuring an individual's IQ: (p. 516)
    a. Errors were made in administering the test
    b.
    c.
    d. Limitations exist within the tests themselves

70. In the elaborated version of adaptive skills assessment recently proposed by the AAMR, many of the skills included _____ measured with existing techniques. (p. 516)

Treatment, outcomes, and prevention of mental retardation

71. Few retarded children are institutionalized today. Those likely to be institutionalized include two types. What are they? (pp. 516-517)

    a.

    b.

72. Are services for the mentally retarded adequate, and are all affected individuals being reached by specialized services? (p. 517)

73. List new techniques that have produced encouraging results in the education and training of the mentally retarded. (p. 517)
   a. computer-assisted instruction
   b.
   c. specifically targeted independence training in various everyday functions
   d.

74. Today, educational training procedures are often based on a behavioral approach. First, an assessment is carried out to determine which areas a person needs to improve. These areas are referred to as target areas. Typical target areas include personal grooming, social behavior, basic academic skills, and _____ for retarded adults. Within each area, the skills the individual needs to learn are broken down to their simplest components, and each component is taught separately. (p. 517)

75. What group of youngsters seem to benefit most from programs like "Sesame Street" and "The Electric Company"? (p. 519)

Specific learning disorders

76. Learning disorders are identified by the discrepancy between the _____ academic achievement and their _____ performance in one or more traditional school subjects. (p. 520)

77. Typically, these children have full-scale IQs that are consistent with at least _____ achievement at school. (p. 520)

78. The academic problems associated with learning disabilities cannot be attributed to the following common, alternative explanations for poor academic performance. Complete the list. (p. 520)
   a. obvious crippling emotional problems
   b. lack of _____
   c. lack of cooperativeness
   d. lack of _____ to please teachers and parents

79. Respond to the following statements: (pp. 520-521)
    a. There is mounting evidence that LD is due to a central nervous system dysfunction. True or False
    b. The idea that LD is genetically transmitted has been virtually abandoned. True or False
    c. Cognitive and psychosocial perspectives on causation exist, but not enough evidence exists to provide full discussion. True or False

80. Worden (1986) suggests we look at how people learn well and compare those strategies to the LD child. Complete the list of aspects of learning he suggests we look at: (pp. 521-522)
    a. Memory strategies
    b.
    c.
    d.

81. There are several reasons for a bleak outlook in treatment for learning disorders: (p. 522)
    a. We still do not have a firm grasp of what is wrong with LD children.
    b.
    c. Few positive results have been reported even for the most researched learning disorders such as reading disorders.
    d.

82. Recently, Ellis has offered a comprehensive intervention model to facilitate learning in LD, called _____ (ISI). Unfortunately, the model is too new to have been _____, but its knowledge-based and systematic character is a welcome addition to the analysis of the educational problems presented by LD children. (p. 522)

◊ CRITICAL THINKING ABOUT DIFFICULT TOPICS

1. The topic of mental retardation provides perhaps the clearest illustration of phenomena that do--and do not--fit the categorical approach to conceptualizing the phenomena of this course. Can you indicate which forms of mental retardation fit a categorical model and which do not? Down syndrome and PKU (pp. 510-513) largely are either present or absent and thus meet the demands for a categorical approach. With respect to the phenomena of interest, children with Down syndrome have more in common with each other than with those who do not have

Down syndrome. In contrast, cultural-familial retardation (pp. 514-516) applies to those who simply fall at the low end of the normal curve distribution of IQ (p. 507). When a cutoff of IQ 70 is applied to this continuous distribution, it is arbitrary to adopt a categorical view that someone with an IQ of 69 is retarded but that someone with an IQ of 71 is not. The person with IQ 69 has much more in common with someone whose IQ is 71 than with another "retarded" person with an IQ of 45. Similarly, the "normal" person with IQ 71 has more in common with the "retarded" person whose IQ is 69 than with another "normal" person whose IQ is 110. Thus, a categorical approach is completely inappropriate for cultural-familial mental retardation. Having examined this question, how well do you think the topics of the preceding chapters fit a categorical approach?

2. Your text states that "the original IQ tests were devised for the explicit purpose of predicting academic achievement among schoolchildren . . . what IQ tests measure is an individual's likely level of success in dealing with conventional academic materials" (p. 507). How narrowly would you interpret the last part of that statement? Is a person with low IQ only at a disadvantage in the classroom, or is the disadvantage broader than that? Note that in diagnosing mental retardation, a dual criterion is applied: in addition to IQ below 70, the person must show "significant limitations in adaptive functioning" (pp. 506, 507). Does this requirement imply that low IQ has consequences outside the classroom? Your text says that a majority of persons with IQ below 70 are not diagnosed as retarded because they meet adaptational demands at a minimally acceptable level (pp. 506-507), but that "a person with an IQ of 50 or below will inevitably exhibit gross deficiencies in overall adaptive behavior as well" (p. 507). What do these statements indicate about the relationship between IQ and adaptive functioning?

3. IQ tests assess many different types of intellectual abilities, yet we use the overall score as the index of intelligence. Can you justify this failure to attend to the profile of individual mental abilities for each person? How do you conceptualize IQ? Is it a unitary phenomenon--a single variable capturing the essence of one's intellectual abilities? Alternatively, could it be a collection of more or less unrelated abilities whose aggregate score is useful because they are to some extent interchangeable--i.e., we can use whatever abilities we have to achieve educational and social goals? For example, one person may perform well because of an excellent memory, whereas another person may achieve good performance as a result of good conceptual ability in spite of a poor memory.

4. Some people oppose the study of genetic influences on behavior and psychopathology because they are threatened by their perception that there is nothing that can be done about "genetic disorders." There is hardly a better example of a genetic disorder than PKU (p. 513), which is inherited as a simple Mendelian recessive disorder (i.e., the person receives a recessive gene for PKU from both parents) and it results in mental retardation in almost all affected individuals

who consume a normal diet (i.e., the gene is highly penetrant). Does the example of PKU support their fear that nothing can be done about genetic disorders? The treatment involves special diets that do not contain the amino acid phenylalanine. Under those dietary conditions, "intellectual functioning may range from borderline to normal" in spite of damage done by exposure to phenylalanine in utero and postnatally before diagnosis--i.e., the gene is no longer highly penetrant. This example illustrates that a disorder that may be highly genetic under one set of environmental conditions may not develop under another set of environmental conditions. What does it mean, then, to say that something is a genetic disorder?

5. A fair number of experts in assessment would subscribe to the following description of IQ tests and test scores. IQ tests were developed in an educational context to evaluate academic abilities. Intelligence as measured by these tests is permissive of good school performance, but many factors (e.g., lack of motivation, emotional disturbance) can interfere with that performance in individuals with good intelligence. One of the major applications is to determine whether poor academic performance is attributable to poor intellectual ability or to other factors. Intelligence has demonstrated construct validity and cannot be reduced to school grades. Thus, IQ tests do measure something we can call "intelligence" and intelligence probably predicts, at least to a significant degree, adaptive functioning outside of the classroom. However, there probably are aspects of intellectual functioning and control of adaptive behavior that are not assessed by IQ tests, which limits their predictive utility. "Intelligence" absolutely should *not* be viewed as directly reflecting "the quality of brain tissue" (p. 523) or genetic factors. Measured intelligence, like all behavior, reflects the complex outcome of many genetic and environmental factors. Intelligence tests *attempt* to test material to which almost all individuals in the culture have been exposed and, therefore, have had an opportunity to learn. If this assumption is met, then differences in performance on the test will largely reflect differences in the intellectual abilities the person has developed as a result of the combination of nature and nurture, and IQ scores will predict (albeit imperfectly) academic performance and some adaptive behaviors outside the classroom. When an individual's score is lowered due to environmental factors, there are two possible reasons with very different implications. In one case, specific information is required to which the person has not been exposed, but failure to learn this material has not affected the person's general academic or intellectual abilities. An example would be questions about different breeds of cattle, to which urban-reared individuals may not have been exposed. If there were many instances of this type of "culture bias," the IQ score is *truly biased* in the sense that it would underpredict--i.e., the person would function *better* in most contexts than predicted by the IQ score, because the test did not accurately assess intellectual abilities. In the second case, the person's intellectual ability itself has been affected adversely by the environment. The best example is cultural-familial retardation, in which a child "suffers from an inferior quality of interaction with the cultural environment and with other people" (p. 514). To the extent that this environmental disadvantage has truly adversely affected intellectual ability, the IQ score will as validly predict

academic performance and adaptive behaviors as for other individuals. If such adverse environmental factors are correlated with socioeconomic status, urban-rural backgrounds, or ethnicity, IQ scores will reflect these differences. The test is "culture-free" and unbiased in the sense that it accurately assesses current intellectual functioning and predicts equally well for all concerned, but it is not "culture-free" in the sense that there may be systematic differences in tested IQ as a function of sociocultural variables. How different is this view of IQ testing from that expressed by your text in the section on Unresolved Issues? Have the authors said the same thing in different words, or is their view different?

◊ **CHAPTER 13 QUIZ**

Circle the best of the four answers provided and check them according to answers provided at the back of this study guide. Be sure you understand why each answer is correct.

1. When structural defects in the brain occur before birth or at a very early age, the typical result is: (p. 485)
   a. mental retardation.
   b. delirium.
   c. dementia.
   d. amnesia.

2. In contrast to diffuse damage which results in dementia, focal lesions are _____ areas of abnormal change in brain structure. (p. 486)
   a. deep
   b. circumscribed
   c. large
   d. progressive

3. Computer hardware may be compared to the human _____, while software may be compared to psychosocial experience. (p. 488)
   a. psyche
   b. relationships
   c. mental experience
   d. brain

4. Some functions may be relearned after brain damage; however, there is usually _____ over a wide range of abilities. (p. 488)
   a. little damage
   b. unnoticed change
   c. loss of function
   d. increased metabolism

5. In DSM-IV, physical or medical disorders are coded on Axis: (p. 490)
   a. I.   c. III.
   b. II.   d. IV.

6. A rapid and widespread disorganization of complex mental processes caused by a generalized disturbance in brain metabolism is called: (p. 491)
   a. amnestic syndrome.   c. dementia.
   b. hallucinosis.   d. delirium.

7. Almost _____ percent of AIDS patients met DSM-IV criteria for dementia. (p. 494)
   a. 10   c. 40
   b. 20   d. 60

8. Outcome is particularly bleak for those with ADC because right now the only certain strategy is the _____ of the disease. (p. 494)
   a. prevention   c. mutation
   b. spread   d. destruction

9. One in _____ persons over age 65 in America are considered clinically demented. (p. 496)
   a. 1   c. 6
   b. 2   d. 10

10. Which of the following is the most common behavioral manifestation of Alzheimer's disease? (p. 497)
    a. simple deterioration   c. paranoid delusions
    b. jealousy delusions   d. psychopathological symptoms

11. DAT has been linked to _____, which is due to a trisomy involving chromosome 21. (p. 500)
    a. Huntington's chorea   c. MID
    b. Down syndrome   d. Tay-Sach's disease

12. Vascular dementia involves a(an): (p. 502)
    a. appearance of senile plaques.
    b. continuing recurrence of small strokes.
    c. increase in neurofibrillary tangles.
    d. loss of neurons in the basal forebrain.

13. If a head injury is sufficiently severe to result in unconsciousness, the person may experience retrograde amnesia or inability to recall: (p. 502)
    a. events immediately following the injury.
    b. events immediately preceding and following the injury.
    c. events immediately preceding the injury.
    d. names or faces of friends.

14. Any functional equivalent of mental retardation that has its onset after age 17 must be considered a _____ rather than retardation. (p. 506)
    a. pervasive developmental disorder   c. learning disorder
    b. dementia   d. organic syndrome

15. When we speak of levels of mental retardation we largely are referring to levels of: (p. 507)
    a. neuronal activity.   c. development.
    b. intelligence.   d. structural damage to the brain.

16. Which of the following degrees of retardation is by far the most common? (p. 508)
    a. Profound   c. Severe
    b. Moderate   d. Mild

17. About _____ percent of the cases of mental retardation occur with known brain pathology. (p. 509)
    a. 5   c. 25
    b. 15   d. 35

18. Ionizing radiation may harm a child by acting directly on the _____ or may damage the sex chromosomes of either parent. (p. 510)
    a. fertilized egg   c. brain tissue
    b. womb   d. unfertilized egg

19. Newer research points not only to organic causes of retardation but also to a lack of _____ (p. 514)
    a. specific enzymes.   c. normal environmental stimulation.
    b. education.   d. normal affection.

20. One reason the authors state that "mainstreaming" has not worked is: (p. 518)
    a. lack of funding.   c. no classroom space.
    b. teachers' attitudes.   d. classes that are too large.

21. Typically, a child with a learning disorder does not show overall poor performance but _____ difficulties. (p. 520)
    a. emotional
    b. specific
    c. physical
    d. family

22. There are several theories regarding brain function in learning disorders. One theory hypothesizes some type of defect or imbalance in the brain's normal _____ (p. 521)
    a. circulation.
    b. electrical stimulation.
    c. laterality.
    d. attentional capacity.

◊ OVERVIEW

Many of the mental disorders described in previous chapters do not develop until early or middle adulthood. In dealing with children, there are some problems that are unique to childhood, such as hyperactivity, and other problems, such as withdrawal, that may be forerunners of serious adult problems with depression or schizoid behavior. The types of problems seen in children are described in this chapter, as well as the treatments typically used for each one. In each instance, there is an attempt to indicate the long-range outcome for the problem. It is important to place emphasis on the treatment of children and adolescents, because successful treatment at these stages prevents the occurrence of more serious pathology and spares years of suffering.

◊ LEARNING OBJECTIVES

After studying this chapter, you should be able to:

1. List special features of childhood disorders that make them different from adult disorders and discuss general issues in the classification of childhood and adolescent disorders. (pp. 528-530)

2. Describe the clinical features, list several of the multiple causes, and summarize approaches to treatment of attention-deficit hyperactivity disorder. (pp. 531-533)

3. Describe the clinical features, longitudinal data, causal factors, and treatment of conduct disorder and oppositional defiant disorder. (pp. 533-538)

4. Discuss delinquency as a major societal problem, summarize the many causal factors involved in delinquency, and describe different ways that society deals with delinquency. (pp. 538-543)

5. Describe the clinical features, causal factors, and treatment of the anxiety disorders of childhood. (pp. 543-545)

6. Describe the clinical features, causal factors, and treatment of childhood depression. (pp. 545-548)

7. Summarize what is known about the symptom disorders of functional enuresis, functional encopresis, sleepwalking, and tics as they occur in children and adolescents. (pp. 548-551)

8. Describe the clinical features, causal factors, and treatment of autism. (pp. 551-555)

9. List and explain six special factors that must be considered in relation to treatment for children. (pp. 556-558)

10. Outline the findings regarding the prevalence of child abuse, list the deficits seen among abused children, discuss potential causal factors in child abuse, and summarize efforts to prevent child abuse. (pp. 558-561)

11. Describe the need for mental health services for children and review the history of ineffectual efforts to increase the available resources. (pp. 561-562)

12. Discuss the evidence regarding the transmission of psychopathology from parents to children. (pp. 562-563)

◊ **TERMS YOU SHOULD KNOW**

developmental psychopathology (p. 527)

categorical strategy (of classification) (p. 530)

dimensional strategy (of classification) (p. 530)

presenting symptoms (p. 530)

Child Behavior Checklist (CBCL) (p. 530)

internalizing (p. 530)

externalizing (p. 530)

attention-deficit hyperactivity disorder (or hyperactivity) (p. 531)

Ritalin (Highlight 14.2, p. 534)

conduct disorder (p. 534)

juvenile delinquency (pp. 534, 538)

early-onset conduct disorder (p. 536)

adolescent-onset conduct disorder (p. 536)

deviant peer groups (p. 536)

cohesive family model (p. 537)

coercive hypothesis (p. 537)

status offenses (p. 538)

"continuous" delinquents (p. 538)

adolescence limited delinquency (p. 538)

"run from's" (Highlight 14.3, p. 539)

"run to's" (Highlight 14.3, p. 539)

social rejects (p. 542)

recidivism rate (p. 543)

separation anxiety disorder (p. 543)

overanxious disorder (p. 544)

in vivo methods (p. 545)

anaclitic depression (p. 545)

functional enuresis (p. 548)

functional encopresis (p. 549)

somnambulism (sleepwalking) (p. 549)

NREM sleep (p. 550)

tics (p. 551)

Tourette's syndrome (p. 551)

pervasive developmental disorder (p. 551)

autistic disorder (p. 552)

echolalia (p. 552)

self-stimulation (p. 553)

emotional refrigerators (p. 554)

treatment contracts (p. 555)

change agents (p. 555, 557)

mature minors (p. 556)

emancipated minors (p. 556)

mental health child advocacy (p. 562)

Children's Defense Fund (p. 562)

◊ NAMES YOU SHOULD KNOW

Russell Barkley (p. 531; Highlight 14.2, p. 534)

Stephen Hinshaw (pp. 532, 535, 536)

Jan Loney (p. 532)

William Pelham (pp. 532, 533)

Terrie Moffitt (pp. 535, 536, 538)

Benjamin Lahey (pp. 535, 563)

John Coie (p. 536)

Gerald Patterson (pp. 536, 537)

Michael Rutter (pp. 537, 554, 555)

◊ **CONCEPTS TO MASTER**

1. List and explain several special vulnerabilities of childhood. (p. 528)

2. Describe children's responses in the aftermath of a disaster, indicate both characteristics of the disaster and characteristics of children that make the situation more upsetting, and outline Vogel and Venberg's four-phase model for managing children's adjustment difficulties in a disaster. (Highlight 14.1, p. 529)

3. Explain three reasons why early childhood diagnostic systems were inadequate, and compare and contrast two kinds of systems that have been used. (pp. 529-530)

4. Explain the structure of the Child Behavior Checklist (CBCL) developed by Achenbach and his colleagues. (p. 530)

5. Define *hyperactivity*, and describe its clinical picture. (pp. 531-532)

6. Compare and contrast the short-term effects of pharmacological and behavioral treatments of ADHD. (pp. 532-533)

7. Summarize the long-term outcomes of individuals diagnosed as ADHD in childhood. (p. 533)

8. Summarize and discuss the controversy surrounding the use of drug therapy for ADHD. (Highlight 14.2, p. 534)

9. Define conduct disorder and oppositional defiant disorder, describe their clinical picture, and indicate the relationships among oppositional defiant disorder, early-onset conduct disorder, and adolescent-onset conduct disorder. (pp. 535-536)

10. Discuss the contributions of social rejection (peer, teacher, parent) and deviant peer associations to the development of antisocial behavior. (p. 536)

11. Describe the family patterns that contribute to childhood conduct disorders and pathways by which they do this. (pp. 536-537)

12. Summarize the assumptions and major features of Patterson's cohesive family model treatment strategy. (p. 537)

13. Define *delinquency*, describe the seriousness of crimes committed by delinquents, and indicate how gender affects the probability of different types of crime. (p. 538)

14. Compare and contrast Moffitt's subtypes of delinquents. (p. 538)

15. Describe and evaluate several systems that have been used to deal with delinquency. (pp. 542-543)

16. List several general characteristics of anxiety disorders in childhood and adolescence, and describe two subclassifications noted by DSM-IV. (pp. 543-544)

17. Explain four causal factors that have been emphasized in explanations of childhood anxiety disorders, and summarize what is known about their treatment. (pp. 544-545)

18. Explain why therapeutic intervention with children is a more complicated process than providing psychotherapy for adults and compare the procedures employed in family therapy and play therapy. (Highlight 14.4, p. 546)

19. Discuss the symptoms associated with childhood depression and their relationship to adult depression. (p. 545)

20. Summarize the biological and environmental factors that appear to contribute to the development of childhood depression. (pp. 545, 547)

21. Define functional enuresis, summarize its clinical features, and discuss etiological factors. (pp. 548-549)

22. Conditioning procedures have proven successful in the treatment of enuresis. Describe how this treatment is conducted. (p. 549)

23. Explain why autistic disorder is classified as a pervasive developmental disorder, and describe its clinical picture. (pp. 552-553)

24. Summarize what is known about the causes and treatments of autistic disorders, giving special attention to educational and behavioral therapy. (pp. 554-555)

25. List and explain six special factors that must be considered in relation to treatment for children. (pp. 556-558)

26. Describe the study by Wolf and colleagues of families at high-risk for child abuse. What has been learned so far? (p. 561)

27. Define *advocacy* and evaluate the success of several governmental agencies and private groups that have tried to provide this function for children. (p. 562)

28. Discuss the evidence regarding the transmission of psychopathology from parents to children. (pp. 562-563)

◊ **STUDY QUESTIONS**

Introduction

1. Recent multisite studies in several countries have provided estimates of childhood disorder that range from _____ to _____ percent. In most studies, maladjustment is _____ among boys than among girls. (p. 527)

Maladaptive behavior in different life periods

2. Some of the emotional disturbances of childhood may be relatively _____, _____, and _____ compared with those of later life. (p. 528)

3. Young children do not have as complex and realistic a view of themselves and their _____. As a result, they often have more difficulty coping with stress. They have a limited perspective and explain events with unrealistic concepts. On the other hand, children typically recover _____ from their hurts. (p. 528)

Classification of childhood and adolescent disorders

4. Kraepelin's (1883) classic text on classification did not include childhood disorders. In 1952, a classification system for childhood was made available but it was inadequate. The authors list several reasons for the inadequacy of early childhood diagnostic systems. Complete the following list of these reasons: (p. 528-529)

   a. In the past, the same categories used to classify adults were used for children.
   b. Children's symptoms are highly influenced by the family's _____ or _____ of the behavior.
   c. Symptoms were not considered with respect to a child's _____.

5. The general goals and methods employed by categorical and dimensional approaches are different, and it is unlikely that they will ever totally agree in their classification of children, although there will be overlap. Place a C next to the choices on the following chart that characterize the categorical approach to classification of childhood disorders. Place a D next to the choices that characterize the dimensional approach to the classification of childhood disorders. (p. 530)

   a. Follows the disease model of psychopathology clinical study
   b. Based on the idea that behaviors are continuous and are found even among normals
   c. Uses classes or types as the basis for classification
   d. Strives for broad coverage and includes even very rare conditions
   e. Can require the presence of relatively few symptoms to arrive at a diagnosis
   f. Involves the application of sophisticated statistical methods, such as factor analysis

Attention-deficit hyperactivity disorder

6. Attention deficit-hyperactivity disorder, often called hyperactivity, is characterized by maladaptive behavior that interferes with effective task-oriented behavior in children. Hyperactivity is the most frequent reason children are referred to mental health and pediatric facilities. It is estimated that between ____ and ____ percent of elementary school-aged children manifest the symptoms of hyperactivity. The disorder is 6 to 9 times more common in boys than girls. It occurs with greatest frequency before age _____, although some residual effects may persist into adolescence or adulthood. (p. 531)

7. Describe the clinical picture in hyperactivity in the following areas: (pp. 531)

    a. Muscular activity
    b. Attention
    c. Impulse control
    d. Intelligence
    e. Parental relationships

8. Complete the following summary of current thinking regarding the possible causes of hyperactivity: (pp. 532)

    a. Biological basis: likely, but genetic basis has not been established.
    b. Diet:

    c. Parental personality problems: There are no clearly established psychological causes, but some evidence points to parental personality problems, particularly diagnoses of personality disorder or hysteria.

9. Cerebral stimulants, such as amphetamines, have a _____ effect on hyperactive children--just the opposite of what one might expect of a stimulant drug. (p. 532)

10. Some authorities consider stimulants the first drug of choice for treating ADHD. Although the drugs do not _____ hyperactivity, they have reduced the behavioral symptoms in about _____ to _____ of the cases in which medication appears warranted. For example, it has been found that medication reduced the problems of _____ but not the impulsivity in hyperactive children. (pp. 532-533)

11. Carson and Bunner concluded that studies of achievement over long periods of time _____ _____ that medication has beneficial effects. _____ has been expressed about the effects of the drugs, particularly when used in heavy dosages over time. (p. 533)

12. An effective approach to treating hyperactive children involves behavior therapy techniques. What techniques does a behavioral therapy involve? (p. 533)

13. The use of behavioral treatment methods for hyperactivity has reportedly been _____ _____, at least for _____ gains. (p. 533)

14. In a recent study, Pelham and colleagues (1993) found that both behavior modification and medication therapy significantly reduced ADHD. _____, however, appeared to be the more effective element in the treatment. (p. 533)

15. In their follow-up at ages 16 to 23 years of boys who had been hyperactive at ages 6 to 12 years, Gittleman and colleagues concluded that the "most striking finding is the degree to which the syndrome consisting of _____, _____, and _____ persisted." (p. 533)

16. What criticism has been made about the way children are selected to receive drugs? (Highlight 14.2, p. 534)

17. What criticism has been made about the purposes for which drugs are used in children? (Highlight 14.2, p. 534)

18. What do we know about the long-range side effects of drug therapy on children? (Highlight 14.2, p. 534)

Conduct disorders

19. The authors conclude that the terms *conduct disorder, a predelinquent pattern,* and early stages in the development of an _____ are difficult, if not impossible, to distinguish. (p. 535)

20. The essential symptomatic behavior in conduct disorders involves a persistent and repetitive _____ and a disregard for the _____.
Complete the following more detailed list of the characteristics of conduct disordered children: (p. 535)

a. overt or covert hostility   f.
b.   g. destructiveness
c.   h. lying
d. physical and verbal aggressiveness i.
e.   j. temper tantrums

21. An important precursor of the antisocial behavior seen in children with conduct disorder is often what is now called _____ disorder, which usually begins by the age of _____ years, whereas full-blown conduct disorder does not typically begin until the age of _____. (p. 535).

22. Only about _____ percent of children with oppositional defiant disorder go on to develop conduct disorder within a three-year period. The risk factors for both include _____ _____, socioeconomic disadvantage, and _____ behavior in the parents. (p. 535)

23. Evidence has accumulated that a genetic predisposition leading to low _____, mild _____ problems, and _____ temperament sets the stage for early-onset conduct disorder. (p. 535)

24. Although only about _____ to _____ percent of cases of early-onset conduct disorder go on to develop adult antisocial personality disorder, over 80 percent of boys with early-onset conduct disorder do continue to have multiple problems of _____ dysfunction. By contrast, most adolescents who develop conduct disorder in adolescence do not go on to become adult psychopaths or antisocial personalities. (p. 536)

25. Foster home or institutional placement for conduct disorders is ineffective unless the changed environment offers a _____, _____, and _____--yet _____ and _____--setting. (p. 537)

26. Fareta (1981) reported that many conduct disordered children grew up to be adults who have _____. Stattin and Magnusson (1989) found that high ratings of childhood aggressiveness (at ages 10-13) for boys predicted later commitment of _____ and _____. This relationship was not found for girls. (p. 537)

27. How is behavior therapy used to assist the parents of conduct disordered children? (pp. 537-538)

28. Parents often have difficulty carrying out treatment plans that are part of behavior therapy. If so, other techniques, such as _____ or _____ can be employed to ensure that the parent is sufficiently assertive to follow through on the program. (p. 545)

Delinquent behavior

29. Delinquency is a legal term that refers to acts committed by individuals under the age of 16-18, depending on the state, that call for some punishment or corrective action. One out of every 15 teenagers have been arrested. In 1988, juveniles accounted for 1 out of every _____ arrests for robbery and crimes against property, and 1 out of every 6 rapes. (p. 538)

30. The form of juvenile delinquency differs between male and female adolescents. (p. 538)

   a. For what crimes are girls commonly arrested?

   b. For what crimes are boys most often arrested?

31. According to the Uniform Crime Reports, are juvenile criminals dangerous and violent? (p. 538)

32. What is the average age of a runaway child? (Highlight 14.3, p. 539)

33. Is it common for parents of a runaway child to fail to call the police? (Highlight 14.3, p. 539)

34. Of runaways reported to the police, _____ percent are eventually located. (Highlight 14.3, p. 539)

Causal factors in delinquency

35. The authors highlight four causal factors in delinquency: personal pathology, pathogenic family patterns, undesirable peer relationships, general socio-cultural factors, and special stress. Fill in the missing information on the following chart that summarizes the research on the causal factors of juvenile delinquency. (pp. 539-542)

345

Causal Factors in Juvenile Delinquency

Personal Pathology	
Genetic determinants	Schulsinger (1980) found adopted sociopathic criminals more often had sociopathic fathers than non-sociopathic criminals.
Brain damage	Less than _____ percent of delinquents have been found to have brain damage that could lead to lowered inhibitory controls and violent behavior.
Learning disability	Lombardo and Lombardo concluded that there is no evidence linking learning disabilities with delinquency. However, there is a clear relationship between low intelligence and delinquency.
Psychological disorders	A small percentage of delinquent acts are associated with _____. Delinquent acts associated with psychotic behavior often involve prolonged emotional turmoil, culminating in an outburst of _____ _____.
Psychopathic traits	Many habitual delinquents appear to share traits typical of psychopathic persons, such as _____ _____ _____.
Drug abuse	Many delinquents acts--particularly _____, _____, and _____--are committed in order to obtain money to buy expensive drugs, such as heroin.

Pathogenic Family Patterns	
Parental absence or family conflict	Delinquency seems to be more common in homes broken by _____ or _____ than in homes broken by death of a parent.
Parental rejection and faulty discipline	When the father rejects a boy, it is difficult for a boy to _____ with him or use him as a _____ for his own development. Bandura and Walters studied boys whose fathers rejected them, used inconsistent discipline, and were physically punitive. The end result was a _____, _____, _____ youth who lacked normal _____ and tended to act out aggressive impulses.
parental models	Psychopathic behaviors found in the fathers of delinquents of _____ include _____ _____. Psychopathic parents may contribute to the delinquency of girls by _____ _____ _____.
Limited parental relationships outside the family	Children's oppositional behavior (negativism) is greater when parents have few friendly contacts outside the home.

Undesirable Peer Relationships	
Delinquency as a shared experience	About _____ of delinquent acts involved one or two other persons, and most of the remainder involved three or four other persons.

General Sociocultural Factors	
Alienation and rebellion	Alienation from family and from the broader society allows teenagers to become captives of their _____.
Social rejection	Social rejects have discovered that they are not _____ in our society.
Gang cultures	What type of feelings does belonging to a gang give a delinquent? _____ _____ _____

Dealing with delinquency

36. Behavior therapy techniques--based on the assumption that delinquent behavior is _____, _____, and _____ according to the same principles as other learned behavior--have shown promise in the rehabilitation of juvenile offenders who require institutionalization. (p. 542)

37. The overall recidivism rate for juvenile offenders depends heavily on the type of _____ _____ and the particular _____ _____. (p. 543)

Anxiety disorders of childhood and adolescence

38. Separation anxiety disorder is the most common of the childhood anxiety disorders, reportedly occurring with a prevalence of ____ percent of children in a population health study. (p. 543)

39. Separation anxiety disorder is characterized by unrealistic fears, oversensitivity, self-consciousness, nightmares, and chronic anxiety. They lack self-confidence, are apprehensive _____, and tend to be immature for their age. (p.543)

40. Overanxious disorder is characterized by excessive worry and persistent fear; however, the fears are usually not specific and are not due to a _____. (p. 544)

41. One study found overanxious disorder in _____ percent of a sample of children in a large epidemiological study in Canada. (p. 544)

42. The authors list four general causal factors of anxiety disorders: (p. 544)
    a. Unusual sensitivity, easy conditionability, and a build-up of _____.
    b. Undermining of self-adequacy and security by early _____, _____, or
       _____.
    c. Modeling by an overanxious parent who sensitizes the child to _____ and
       _____ in the outside world.
    d. Detached or indifferent parents who fail to provide adequate _____.

43. The anxiety disorders of childhood may continue into adolescence and adulthood but this is not usually the case. As they grow up and have wider interactions in school and in peer-group activities, they often benefit from such corrective experiences as making _____ and _____ at given tasks. (p. 545)

44. Psychopharmacological treatment of anxiety disorders in children and adolescents is becoming more common today. However, one factor contributing to caution in using medications is that anxiety is often found to coexist with other conditions, particularly _____. Often there is not the diagnostic clarity required for cautious use of antianxiety medication. (p. 545)

45. Behavior therapy procedures employed in structured group experiences at school can often speed up favorable outcomes. Included here are _____ training, help with mastering essential competencies, and desensitization. Desensitization must be explicitly tailored to _____, and _____ methods (using graded life situations) may be more effective than the use of imagined situations. (p. 545)

Childhood depression

46. In a large-scale study of normal children in an elementary school system, Lefkowitz and Tesiny found the overall prevalence rate of depressive symptoms to be _____ percent. (p. 545)

47. Currently, childhood depression is classified using the _____ categories in the DSM-IV _____ diagnostic system. (p. 545)

48. Explain why pharmacological treatment for childhood depression appears unattractive at present. (p. 547)

49. Psychotherapy for childhood depression generally follows the model used with _____
    _____. (p. 547)

50. The term functional enuresis refers to the habitual involuntary discharge of urine after the age of expected continence, which is age ___, that is not _____ caused. (p. 548)

51. Estimates of the prevalence of enuresis reported in DSM-IV are ___ percent for boys and ___ percent for girls at age 5, and ___ percent for boys and ___ percent for girls at age 10. In an extensive epidemiological study conducted in Holland, Verhulst et al. determined that, between the ages of 5 and 8, the rates of enuresis among boys are _____ to _____ times higher than the rates among girls. (p. 548)

52. Although enuresis may result from a variety of organic conditions, the authors emphasize three psychosocial factors. Complete the requested information in the following list of causes of enuresis: (pp. 548-549)

Causal Factor	Description
1. Faulty learning	Results in a failure to acquire the _____ reflex of bladder emptying.
2. _____	Associated with or stems from emotional problems.
3. Disturbed family interactions	Particularly situations that lead to sustained _____ or _____, or both. Also, regression when a new _____ arrives.
4. Stressful events	Child may _____ in response to stressful event.

53. Explain why pharmacological treatment for functional enuresis appears unattractive at present. (p. 549)

54. What happens to the incidence of enuresis as the child gets older if it is untreated? (p. 549)

55. In a recent review of the treatment of bedwetting, Houts, Berman, and Abramson concluded that treated children were _____ at follow-up than nontreated children and that psychological treatment was _____ effective than were physical treatments. (p. 549)

Other symptom disorders: Functional encopresis

56. Encopresis refers to the absence of appropriate bowel control after age ____. (p. 549)

57. Respond TRUE or FALSE to the following statements about encopresis: (p. 549)
    a. One third of encopretic children are enuretic.   True or False
    b. Six times more boys than girls are encopretic. True or False
    c. A common time for encopresis is after school. True or False
    d. Most children know they need to have a bowel movement. True or False
    e. Many encopretic children suffer from constipation. True or False

Other symptom disorders: Sleepwalking (somnambulism)

58. Sleepwalking involves repeated episodes in which a person leaves his or her bed and walks around without _____ or _____. (p. 549)

59. The onset of a sleeping disorder is usually between _____ and _____ years of age. A Swedish study reported that _____ percent of children experience sleepwalking episodes. (p. 549)

60. During sleepwalking, the eyes are _____ and obstacles are _____. Episodes usually last from ____ to ____ minutes. (p. 550)

61. Causes of sleepwalking are not fully understood, but it takes place during _____ sleep and appears related to some _____ situation that has just occurred or is expected to occur. (p. 550)

62. Does a fully described and evaluated treatment program exist for sleepwalking? (p. 550)

63. The use of conditioning treatments such as pairing awakening with the nightmare that triggered sleepwalking in Bobby is similar to that used to treat _____. (Highlight 14.5, p. 550)

Other symptom disorders: Tics

64. A tic is a persistent muscle twitch, usually limited to a _____. (p. 551)

65. Tics occur most frequently between the ages of ___ and ___. (p. 551)

66. An extreme tic disorder involving multiple motor and vocal patterns is called _____ syndrome. About one-third of individuals with this syndrome manifest _____, which is a complex vocal tic that involves the uttering of obscenities. Most cases of this syndrome have an onset before age ___. Evidence suggests an organic basis for it. (p. 551)

Pervasive developmental disorder: Autism

67. Autism afflicts some 80,000 American children and is ___ or ___ times more frequent among boys than girls. Autism is usually diagnosed before _____ months of age and may be suspected in the _____ of life. (pp. 551-552)

68. Complete the following chart summarizing the clinical picture in autistic disorders by writing a brief description of autistic children's behavior in each area: (pp. 552-553)

Area of Behavior	Characteristics
Interactions with parents	Mothers remember them as never being cuddly. They do not evidence any need for affection or contact.
Use of speech	Speech is absent or severely restricted. Echolalic repetition of a few words may be observed. There are suggestions that some autistic children do comprehend language, but they do not use it to express themselves.
Self-stimulation	
Interactions with objects	
Cognitive/intellectual deficits	Compared to other children, impairment is seen. While most investigators have viewed autistic children as retarded, Koegel and Mentis (1985) have raised the possibility that the deficits result from motivational differences; they found that autistic children can perform tasks at higher levels if motivation for a task is found.

69. Circle YES, NO, or MAYBE as appropriate to indicate whether each of the following factors is currently thought to be an important cause of autism: (p. 554)

Brain pathology	YES	NO	MAYBE
Genetic basis	YES	NO	MAYBE
Chromosome abnormalities	YES	NO	MAYBE
Defect in perceptual/cognitive functions	YES	NO	MAYBE
Personality characteristics of parents	YES	NO	MAYBE

70. It appears reasonable to suppose that autism begins with an _____ in brain functioning, regardless of what other causal factors may later become involved. (p. 554)

71. Bartak et al. (1973), at the Maudsley Hospital, compared three different approaches to treating autism: an approach emphasizing formal schooling, a structured form of play therapy, and free play therapy. Which approach was found to be most successful? (p. 554-555)

72. Some of the most impressive results in the treatment of autism have been obtained with parents as therapists to treat their own autistic children. YES or NO (p. 555)

73. What is the prognosis for autism in children who show symptoms before age 2? (p. 555)

74. One particular problem with treating autistic children is that they have difficulty _____ _____ to situations outside of the one in which they learn a new behavior. (p. 555)

75. How many children who receive treatment attain even a marginal adjustment in adulthood? (p. 555)

Special factors associated with treatment for children and adolescents

76. In what ways do children have difficulty seeking assistance for emotional problems? (p. 556)

77. What does it mean to say a child from a pathogenic home is at a "double disadvantage"? (pp. 556-557)

78. What is meant by the expression, "using parents as change agents"? (p. 557)

79. Give some reasons that placement of a child in a foster home often works out less than ideally for the child. (p. 557)

Child abuse

80. An astounding statistic is that the number of children reported as abused and neglected rose _____ percent from 1980 to 1988. (p. 559)

81. List some of the effects that child abuse may have: (p. 559)
    a. Impaired cognitive ability
    b.
    c. Feel that outcomes of events are beyond their own control
    d.
    e.
    f. Demonstrate less interpersonal sensitivity
    g.
    h. When abused children reach adulthood, they are likely to abuse their own children

82. What common factors have been found among families with abusing parents? (p. 560)

83. Describe the various approaches to prevention of child abuse that are available: (p. 560)

    a.

    b.

    c.

    d.

84. In 1970, the National Institute of Mental Health estimated that fewer than _____ percent of disturbed children in the United States were receiving any kind of help, and only half of those receiving help were receiving adequate treatment. (p. 561)

85. One approach to meeting children's mental health needs is advocacy. Twice in recent years the federal government has established a National Center for Child Advocacy. What happened both times? (p. 562)

Unresolved issues on transmission of pathology

86. The evidence appears clear that children of disturbed parents are more vulnerable to developing psychological problems themselves, but the actual _____ for the transmission of pathology from parent to child remain _____. (p. 562)

◊ CRITICAL THINKING ABOUT DIFFICULT TOPICS

1. In the chapter on substance abuse, you saw that long-term substitution of methadone for opium is sometimes used for treatment, even though methadone and heroin are similar drugs. There do not appear to be obvious, dire, negative consequences of long-term methadone consumption. In the present chapter, you have seen that long-term use of cerebral stimulants such as the amphetamines or Ritalin are viewed by many as the treatment of choice (pp. 532-533). Again, there do not appear to be obvious, dire, negative consequences of long-term Ritalin consumption. Some psychiatrists will see the use of Ritalin as a medication that corrects a "chemical imbalance" and would have no misgivings about very long-term use of the drug. Others have expressed alarm about "the possibility of adverse long-range effects resulting from sustained use during early growth and development . . ." (Highlight 14.2, p. 534). What is your own evaluation of this argument? Note that both methadone and Ritalin share many properties of street drugs of abuse (heroine in the case of methadone, amphetamines in the case of Ritalin). Is it okay to take the same drug prescribed as "medicine" under medical supervision but not to take it purchased as a street drug without medical supervision? If so, why--i.e., what important differences do you see between the two? At least some drugs, such as alcohol and the phenothiazines (used to treat schizophrenia), have

adverse effects on the brain when used in large doses for long periods of time. Does the concept of correcting a chemical imbalance imply that there should be no adverse effects, since the brain's neurochemistry is being adjusted to a more normal state? How would you resolve these competing views?

◊ CHAPTER 14 QUIZ

Circle the best of the four answers provided and check them according to answers provided at the back of this study guide. Be sure you understand why each answer is correct.

1. In recent multisite studies in several countries, estimates of childhood disorders ranged from ___ to ___ percent. (p. 527)
   a. 5, 8   c. 17, 22
   b. 8, 12   d. 21, 26

2. Compared to a categorical system for classifying childhood and adolescent disorders, a dimensional strategy: (p. 530)
   a. assesses fewer behaviors for each category.
   b. has more diagnostic categories.
   c. ignores presenting symptoms in favor of case studies.
   d. requires more symptoms to make a diagnosis.

3. A researcher gathers his or her symptomatic information through teachers', parents', or clinicians' observations or through a child's _____. (p. 530)
   a. presenting symptoms   c. peer reputation
   b. school record   d. statistical profile

4. Which of these would not fit under Achenbach's internalizing dimension? (p. 530)
   a. anxiety   c. depression
   b. social withdrawal   d. aggression

5. Which of the following is not a usual characteristic of children with ADHD? (p. 531)
   a. low frustration tolerance
   b. lower in intelligence
   c. great difficulties in getting along with their parents
   d. higher in anxiety

6. In a recent study, Pelham and colleagues (1993) concluded that in the treatment of children with ADHD: (p. 533)
   a. only medication was effective.
   b. only behavior modification was effective.
   c. both medication and behavior modification were effective, but the latter was better.
   d. both medication and behavior modification were effective, but the former was better.

7. In their follow-up at ages 16 to 23 years of boys who had been hyperactive at ages 6 to 12 years, Gittleman and colleagues found three symptoms that persisted into adolescence and young adulthood. Which of the following was *not* one of them? (p. 533)
   a. impulsivity   c. inattention
   b. lower intelligence   d. hyperactivity

8. In 1988, about one teenager out of every _____ in the nation was arrested. (p. 538)
   a. 5   c. 25
   b. 15   d. 35

9. Many habitual delinquents share the traits typical of the _____ personality. (p. 540)
   a. antisocial   c. narcissistic
   b. obsessive-compulsive   d. passive-aggressive

10. Haney and Gold found that most delinquent acts were committed: (p. 542)
    a. alone, without any help.
    b. in association with one or two other persons.
    c. with three or four other persons.
    d. with five or six other persons.

11. Alienation from family and the broader society causes juveniles to become more vulnerable to: (p. 542)
    a. incest and related sexual crimes.
    b. negative influences of TV and other media.
    c. peer pressures to engage in delinquent acts.
    d. solitary acts of violence.

12. Children diagnosed as suffering from anxiety disorders usually attempt to cope with their fears by: (p. 543)
    a. becoming overly dependent on others.
    b. denying the existence of fearful things.
    c. developing compulsive behaviors.
    d. indulging in "guardian angel" fantasies.

13. Typically, children with anxiety disorders: (p. 545)
    a. become adolescents with maladaptive avoidance behavior.
    b. become adults with idiosyncratic thinking and behavior.
    c. become suicidal when they reach 30.
    d. have experiences that reduce their fears and insecurity.

14. Which of the following is *not* one of the reasons for suggesting caution in the use of antidepressant medication to treat childhood depression? (p. 547)
    a. Some studies have failed to show them to be more effective than a placebo.
    b. Many undesirable side effects have been seen when these drugs are used with children.
    c. Antidepressants may precipitate mania in some children with latent bipolar disorder.
    d. Several deaths through accidental overdose have been reported.

15. Kales and associates have shown that sleepwalking takes place in: (p. 550)
    a. REM sleep.   c. stage 4 sleep.
    b. NREM sleep.   d. stage 1 sleep.

16. All of the following are true of infantile autism except: (pp. 551-552)
    a. it afflicts about 4 children in 10,000.
    b. it is usually identified before the child is 30 months old.
    c. it occurs much more frequently in boys than in girls.
    d. most cases are found in the upper classes.

17. Autism has been associated with: (p. 554)
    a. parental education.   c. genetic factors.
    b. racial origin.   d. a cold and unresponsive mother.

18. The drug(s) used most often in autism is/are _____, but the effects have not been very impressive. (p. 554)
    a. haloperidol   c. barbiturates
    b. caffeine   d. anti-anxiety

19. One of the major factors that needs to be taken into account when studying or treating children is: (p. 556)
    a. child advocacy programs are always available.
    b. children are dependent on those around them.
    c. drug therapy is usually warranted.
    d. children are small adults.

Chapter 15
Clinical Assessment

◊ OVERVIEW

The clinical assessment process is described in this chapter. Clinical assessment includes the use of psychological tests but also depends on data from other sources, such as observation and interview. Psychological tests have a mystique in our society and have recently come under serious public scrutiny. Questions regarding the validity of tests as predictors of academic performance have been raised. Also, concerns have been voiced publicly that tests may invade privacy and reveal things about an individual that he or she did not realize were being revealed. Chapter 16 describes what the different types of tests are, how they are constructed, and what types of information can be obtained from them. The chapter concludes with a discussion of how assessment information is put together with data obtained by other members of the clinical team.

◊ LEARNING OBJECTIVES

After studying this chapter, you should be able to:

1. Describe the nature and purpose of clinical assessment, the types of information sought, and the different types of data of interest. (pp. 567-570)

2. Explain what is meant by rapport between the clinician and client and outline the components of a relationship that leads to good rapport. (p. 570)

3. Summarize the various approaches to assessment of physical problems. (pp. 570-574; Highlight 15.1, p. 573)

4. Discriminate between structured and unstructured interviews for the assessment of psychosocial functioning and evaluate the relative merits of the two. (pp. 574-575)

5. Describe the various approaches to the clinical observation of behavior and identify the advantages of each. (pp. 575-579)

6. List the features of psychological tests and describe the major intelligence and personality tests. (pp. 579-589)

7. Describe how psychological assessment is used in the legal system, which tests are commonly used, and why these tests are appropriate. (pp. 589-590)

8. Outline the issues involved in the use of psychological tests for personnel selection and personnel screening. (pp. 590-592)

9. Summarize the process of integrating assessment data into a model for use in planning or changing treatment. (pp. 594-597)

10. Discuss the controversy over the use of computerized assessment. (pp. 596-597)

◊ TERMS YOU SHOULD KNOW

---

clinical assessment (p. 567)

dynamic formulation (p. 569)

rapport (p. 570)

electroencephalogram (EEG) (p. 571)

dysrhythmia (p. 571)

computerized axial tomography (CAT scan) (p. 571)

positron emission tomography (PET scan) (p. 571)

magnetic resonance imaging (p. 572)

neuropsychological assessment (p. 572)

Halstead-Reitan battery (Highlight 15.1, p. 573)

Halstead Category Test (Highlight 15.1, p. 573)

Tactual Performance Test (Highlight 15.1, p. 573)

Rhythm Test (Highlight 15.1, p. 573)

Speech Sounds Perception Test (Highlight 15.1, p. 573)

Finger Oscillation Task (Highlight 15.1, p. 573)

Luria-Nebraska battery (p. 573)

mental status exam (p. 574)

"operational" assessment approach (p. 574)

direct observation (p. 575)

self-monitoring (p. 575)

rating scales (pp. 575-576)

D-Tree (Highlight 15.2, p. 576)

Brief Psychiatric Rating Scale (BPRS) (p. 577)

Hamilton Rating Scale for depression (HRSD) (p. 578)

role playing (p. 579)

psychological tests (p. 579)

Wechsler Intelligence Scale for Children-Revised (WISC-R) (p. 579)

Stanford-Binet Intelligence Scale (p. 579)

Wechsler Adult Intelligence Scale-Revised (WAIS-R) (p. 579)

general information (p. 579)

picture completion (p. 579)

personality tests (pp. 579-580)

projective tests (p. 580)

Rorschach Test (p. 580)

Exner Comprehensive Rorschach System (p. 581)

Thematic Apperception Test (TAT) (p. 581)

sentence completion tests (p. 582)

objective tests (pp. 582-583)

Minnesota Multiphasic Personality Inventory (MMPI) (p. 583)

MMPI-2 (pp. 583, 584)

"Minnesota normals" (p. 583)

empirical keying (p. 583)

clinical scales (p. 583)

validity scales (p. 583)

diagnostic standard (p. 584)

descriptive diagnosis (p. 584)

content interpretation (p. 584)

MMPI-2 clinical scales: (Highlight 15.3, p. 585)

hypochondriasis	*paranoia*
depression	*psychasthenia*
hysteria	*schizophrenia*
psychopathic deviate	*hypomania*
masculinity-femininity	*social introversion*

MMPI-2 special scales: (Highlight 15.3, p. 585)
    anxiety   *ego-strength*
    repression   *MacAndrew addiction scale*

factor analysis (p. 588)

computer-based MMPI interpretation (p. 589)

actuarial procedures (p. 589)

faking good (p. 590)

Woodworth Personal Data Sheet (p. 591)

personnel selection (p. 591)

personnel screening (p. 591)

◊ NAMES YOU SHOULD KNOW

Robert Carson (pp. 575, 579, 589, 597)

Gordon Paul (p. 578)

James Butcher (pp. 583, 584, 589, 590, 592, 596)

Joseph Matarazzo (pp. 596-597)

◊ CONCEPTS TO MASTER

1. Explain the difference between diagnosis and clinical assessment, and list several components that must be integrated into the dynamic formulation. (pp. 567-569)

2. Outline the three basic components that are essential to establishing rapport between the clinician and the client. (p. 570)

3. Compare and contrast four important neurological procedures, explaining especially what makes each one valuable. (pp. 571-572)

4. List, describe, and explain the purpose of the five tests included in the Halstead-Reitan battery. (Highlight 15.1, p. 573)

5. Describe the characteristics of a good assessment interview, and list some advantages and disadvantages of the interview method. (pp. 574-575)

6. List and describe several examples of computerized diagnostic interviews and enumerate the strengths and weaknesses of this approach. (p. 575)

7. Explain what is meant by the decision tree approach to classification and evaluate the effectiveness of the D-Tree computer program designed to provide DSM-IV diagnosis using the decision tree approach. (Highlight 15.2, pp. 576-577)

8. Explain the kind of data gathered by psychological tests, and list two types that are commonly used. (p. 579)

9. List and describe three intelligence tests used by clinicians and explain how this information can be used in assessment. (p. 579)

10. Explain the assumptions behind the use of projective tests, and describe the use of the Rorschach Test and the Thematic Apperception Test (TAT) in clinical assessment. (pp. 580-582)

11. Define *objective tests* and describe the Minnesota Multiphasic Personality Inventory (MMPI) and its uses in clinical assessment. (pp. 582-584, 588); Highlight 15.3, pp. 585-588)

12. Define the concept of *empirical keying* and summarize the steps involved in this approach in developing the MMPI. (p. 583)

13. Describe the changes made on the new MMPI-2, and discuss the benefits and effects the changes will have. (pp. 584, 588)

14. Explain what is meant by the actuarial approach used to interpret the MMPI and discuss the limitations of this approach. (p. 589)

15. List three tests that are widely used in court testimony and explain why these rather than other tests are accepted as evidence. (pp. 589-590)

16. Cite some general objectives of personnel screening, and describe the use of some psychological tests to accomplish these goals. (pp. 590-591)

17. List and explain three questions which must be addressed before implementing a psychological assessment program for pre-employment screening. (pp. 591-592)

18. Summarize the psychological case study of Esteban, noting the various types of clinical assessment that were used to build the dynamic formulation. (pp. 592-594)

19. Explain the functions of a staff conference in integrating the assessment data and making decisions about the client. (pp. 594-596)

20. Describe the controversy over computerized psychological assessment including the debate over Matarazzo's criticisms. (p. 596)

21. Describe four possible reasons for the underutilization of computer-based assessment procedures. (p. 597)

Introduction

1. The goal of clinical assessment is to identify and understand the _____ and _____ of the problem. (p. 567)

2. Data from clinical assessment is used for two purposes. First, it serves as a basis for treatment decisions. A less obvious but equally important function is that of establishing a _____ against which to evaluate progress made during and following treatment. (p. 568)

The information sought in assessment

3. Although there has been a trend against overdependence on labeling, adequate classification is needed for three reasons: (1) for _____, (2) for treatment decisions, and (3) to establish the range of diagnostic problems represented among the patient population in order to know which treatment facilities need to be available. (p. 568)

4. For clinical purposes, knowledge about an individual's _____, _____ _____, personality characteristics, and environmental pressures and resources is more important than a formal diagnosis. (p. 569)

5. The material gained through assessment is integrated into a consistent and meaningful picture, often called the _____, that should lead to an explanation of why the person is engaging in maladaptive behavior and to hypotheses about the person's future behavior as well. (p. 569)

Varying types of assessment data

6. What assessment techniques would be favored by the following? (pp. 570-571)

   a. Biologically oriented clinician

   b. Psychoanalytically oriented clinician

   c. Behaviorally oriented clinician

   d. Humanistically oriented clinician

Assessment of the physical organism

7. Medical examinations are necessary in some situations to rule out physical abnormalities or to determine the extent to which physical problems are involved. The two types of medical examinations that may be performed include the general _____ examination and the _____ examination. (pp. 570-571)

8. Neurological tests identify abnormalities in the brain's physical properties. In contrast, neuropsychological assessment identifies gross impairments in _____ and varied psychological _____. (p. 572)

9. The Halstead-Reitan battery consists of a standard set of tests that have been preselected so as to sample in a systematic and comprehensive manner a _____ _____ known to be adversely affected by various types of brain injury. (p. 573)

10. The Halstead-Reitan is a highly regarded neuropsychological test. However, if time is at a premium, the _____ could be used. (p. 573)

11. Match the following subtests of the Halstead-Reitan neuropsychology battery with the correct description of its purpose: (Highlight 15.1, p. 573)

Subtest	Purpose
__ Halstead category test	a. Determines if an individual can identify spoken words
__ Tactual performance test	b. Measures a patient's ability to learn and remember
__ Rhythm test	c. Gives clues to the extent and location of brain damage
__ Speech sounds perception	d. Measures attention and sustained test concentration
__ Finger oscillation test	e. Measures motor speed, response to the unfamiliar, and the learning of tactile and kinesthetic cues

Psychosocial assessment

12. Psychosocial assessment attempts to provide a realistic picture of the individual in interaction with the _____. (p. 574)

Psychosocial assessment: Assessment interviews

13. There appears to be widespread _____ among clinicians in the accuracy of their own assessment methods and judgments. In order to minimize sources of error and increase reliability, an assessment interview should be carefully structured in terms of goals, comprehensive _____ review, other content to be explored, and the type of relationship the interviewer attempts to establish with the subject. The reliability of the assessment interview may also be enhanced by the use of _____ that help to focus inquiry and quantify the interview data. (p. 574)

14. The clinical interview has been criticized as an unreliable source of information on which to base clinical decisions. What type of evidence is used to demonstrate that interviews are unreliable? (p. 574)

15. Give an example of a structured interview for children that has been developed for computer administration. (p. 575)

Psychosocial assessment: Clinical observation of behavior

16. The main purpose of direct observation is to find out more about the person's psychological functioning through the objective description of behavior in various contexts. Ideally, such observations would occur in the individual's _____, but they are typically confined to _____ or _____ settings. In addition, many clinicians ask their patients to report their own behavior, thoughts, and feelings as they occur in various natural settings--a procedure called _____. (p. 575)

17. As in the case of interviews, the use of _____ in clinical observation and self-reports helps not only to organize information but also to encourage reliability and objectivity. (p. 575)

18. What is the most widely used rating scale for recording observations in clinical practice and psychiatric research? What is a similar rating scale designed specifically for depression? (p. 577)

19. Paul and his colleagues developed a comprehensive behavioral assessment program that they have used experimentally in a number of hospitals. How have they used the observational rating scales? (p. 578)

20. Jones, Reid, and Patterson (1975) have developed a method of coding and quantifying observations of the _____ at _____ and at _____. This method provides the clinician with information about the stimuli that are controlling the child's interactions. (p. 578)

21. Often it is not feasible to observe a subject's behavior in everyday situations. Describe how observational data are obtained in the following: (pp. 578-579)
    a. When a patient is institutionalized and family observations are desired
    b. When a person has a phobia for snakes
    c. During role playing

Psychosocial assessment: Psychological tests (intelligence and personality tests)

22. Psychological tests are standardized sets of procedures to obtain samples of a subject's behavior that can be compared to the behavior of other individuals, usually through the use of established test _____ or test score _____. (p. 579)

23. Among the characteristics about which the clinician can draw inferences from psychological tests are coping patterns, motive patterns, personality characteristics, role behaviors, values, levels of depression or anxiety, and _____. (p. 579)

24. Individual intelligence tests such as the WISC-R or the WAIS-R require two to three hours to administer, score, and interpret; in many clinical situations, there is not sufficient time or funding to use these tests in every assessment situation. (p.579)

    a. In what type of cases would an individual intelligence test be indicated?

    b. In which cases would an individual intelligence test be unnecessary?

25. Match the following psychological tests with the appropriate description of each test's purpose: (pp. 577-583)

Psychological Test	Purpose
___ Rorschach Test	a. Rating scale based on standardized interview
___ Thematic Apperception Test	b. Intelligence scale for children
___ Minnesota Multiphasic Personality Inventory (MMPI)	c. Intelligence scale for adults
___ WAIS-R	d. Projective test using inkblots
___ WISC-R	e. Projective test using pictures
___ Brief Psychiatric Rating Scale (BPRS)	f. Structured personality test
___ Sentence Completion Test	g. Test that pinpoints topics that should be explored

26. The Rorschach has been criticized because it can be _____ as a result of the subjective nature of test data interpretations. In addition, current treatments generally require _____ descriptions rather than descriptions of deep-seated personality dynamics. (pp. 580-581)

27. The TAT has been criticized for its dated pictures, lengthy administration, and the fact that interpretation is often _____ and limits the _____ and _____ of the test. (p. 583)

28. Objective tests are _____--that is, they typically use questionnaires, self-report inventories, or rating scales in which questions are carefully phrased and alternative responses are specified as choices. They are more amenable to objectively based _____ than projective tests. One virtue of such _____ is that of precision, which in turn enhances the _____ reliability of test outcomes. (p. 583)

29. Place a 1, 2, or 3 in front of the following steps to indicate the sequence in which the step appeared during the construction of the MMPI. (p. 583)

____ Scales are constructed.

____ Items analyses are performed.

____ Items are administered to large groups of normal subjects and psychiatric patients.

30. As used in the MMPI, what is the purpose of a validity scale? (p. 583)

31. How is the MMPI used as a diagnostic standard? (p. 584)

32. What criticisms have been made of the MMPI? (p. 584)

33. List the following changes made for the MMPI-2 having to do with: (p. 584)

a. Language:

b. Questions (items) on the test:

c. Normative data:

34. Complete the chart below that compares the overall strengths and weaknesses of projective and objective tests. (pp. 580-589)

Test	Strengths	Weaknesses
Projective		Interpretations are subjective, unreliable, and difficult to validate, require trained staff to administer and score
Objective	Cost effective, reliable, objective, administered and scored by computer	

35. The potential for job failure or for psychological maladjustment under stress is so great in some high-stress occupations that measures need to be taken in the hiring process to evaluate applicants for emotional _____. (p. 591)

36. The use of personality tests in personnel screening has a long tradition. The first formal use of a standardized personality scale took place in _____ to screen out draftees who were psychologically unfit for military service. (p. 591)

37. Place the following words in the correct blanks: Personnel selection, personnel screening. (p. 591)

   a. Screening out is called _____. This type of selection is done to alert employers to possible maladjustment that would impact adversely upon the way in which the individual would function in a critical job.
   b. Screening in is called _____. This type of selection is done when the employer believes that certain personality characteristics are desirable for a particular job.

38. Before personality tests are used in personnel screening, the psychologist needs to consider three issues: (a) how much weight should the test be given, (b) determine if the job is critical enough to justify the invasion of privacy involved in the use of psychological testing, and (c) _____. (pp. 591-592)

Integration of assessment data

39. In a clinic or hospital setting, assessment data is usually evaluated in a _____ attended by members of the interdisciplinary team who are concerned with the decision to be made regarding treatment. (p. 594)

Unresolved issues

40. Concerns have been raised by Matarazzo (1986) that the widespread use of computer-based assessment procedures is not sufficiently supported by the research and that there is substantial overselling of invalidated measures. Butcher and Fowler (1986) replied that there are already controls in place, specifically the APA guidelines for _____ _____. (p. 596)

41. Is it appropriate for practitioners to employ computer-based interpretations as their final report on a client according to APA guidelines? (p. 596)

42. The authors suggest that computer-based assessment procedures are actually underutilized. Complete the following list of reasons why this may be so: (p. 597)

   a. Practitioners trained prior to the microcomputer age may not have the time to become familiar with these machines and may be uncomfortable with them.

   b.

   c. Some clinicians view the booklets and answer sheets as contrary to the image and style of warm and personal engagement they hope to convey to clients.

   d.

◊ CRITICAL THINKING ABOUT DIFFICULT TOPICS

1. In discussing computerized assessment, the text says there is no substitute for expert clinical judgment (p. 575). Although the text does not discuss the topic explicitly, this issue is a specific instance of the broader and controversial topic of actuarial versus clinical prediction. By and large, clinicians have believed that their expertise allowed them to make accurate predictions, but research results have found their predictions to be inferior to those based on actuarial data. To illustrate this point, imagine yourself in charge of college admissions with five times more applicants than you have openings. How would you go about deciding which applicants to admit. Past evidence has shown that the actuarial approach of using a combination of SAT or ACT scores and high school grades predicts college GPA reasonably well. Do you think you could use your "expert clinical judgment" to improve on these predictions? If so, what variables would you take into account? What errors might you introduce in doing so? What is the reliability and validity of the predictors you would use in the manner in which you would use them?

2. Read the statements regarding the characteristics of assessments used for court testimony (pp. 589-590) and then review the material on the Rorschach (pp. 580-581) to see whether you could make a case for its use in the legal system. In particular, attend to the question of the evidence for its validity, which is critical if it is to be used in the legal system.

◊ CHAPTER 15 QUIZ

Circle the best of the four answers provided and check them according to answers provided at the back of this study guide. Be sure you understand why each answer is correct.

1. In assessing a client's social context, all of the following are pertinent *except:* (p.569)
   a. environmental demands.
   b. interpersonal skills.
   c. sources of emotional support.
   d. special stressors.

2. A neurological diagnostic aid that reveals how an organ is functioning by measuring metabolic processes is the: (p. 571)
   a. PET scan.
   b. CAT scan.
   c. EEG.
   d. angiogram.

3. Which of the following is the *most highly regarded* six-hour neuropsychological test? (p. 573)
   a. Halstead-Reitan
   b. Luria-Nebraska
   c. Stanford-Binet
   d. Wechsler Adult Intelligence Scale

4. Clinical interviews have been criticized as unreliable and evidence of this unreliability includes the finding that different clinicians often arrive at different formal diagnoses. For this reason, recent versions of the DSM have emphasized an approach that: (p. 574)
   a. employs a hierarchical structure.
   b. employs multidimensional assessments.
   c. requires confirmation by convergent information.
   d. employs "operational" assessment.

5. A rating scale specifically targeted for depression that has almost become the standard for selecting clinically depressed research subjects is the: (p. 578)
   a. Beck Depression Inventory.
   b. Schedule for Rating Depressive Temperament.
   c. Leeds Depression Rating Scale.
   d. Hamilton Rating Scale for Depression.

6. Two general categories of psychological tests used in clinical practice are: (p. 579)
   a. intelligence and personality.
   b. philosophy and religion.
   c. speech perception and reaction time.
   d. tactual performance and auditory perception.

7. An instrument used to measure the present level of intellectual functioning in adults is the: (p. 579)
   a. WISC-R.   c. TAT.
   b. WAIS-R.   d. MMPI.

8. Personality tests are often grouped into two categories: (p. 579-580)
   a. behavioral and psychodynamic.
   b. conscious and unconscious.
   c. projective and objective.
   d. verbal and performance.

9. The aim of a projective test is to: (p. 580)
   a. predict a patient's future behavior.
   b. compare a patient's responses to those of persons who are known to have mental disorders.
   c. assess the way a patient perceives ambiguous stimuli.
   d. assess the role of organic factors in a patient's thinking.

10. Which of the following is a structured personality test? (pp. 582-583)
    a. MMPI   c. Sentence Completion Test
    b. Rorschach   d. TAT

11. A clinical researcher devises a new psychological test that assesses neuroticism. She is concerned with the possibility that some individuals might not answer the questions in a straightforward, accurate way. To determine whether an individual is honest, she should: (p. 583)
    a. factor analyze the responses.
    b. make use of actuarial interpretation.
    c. construct a validity scale.
    d. test the instrument on a group of college students.

12. Behaviorists have criticized the MMPI for being too: (p. 584)
    a. action-oriented.   c. objective.
    b. "mentalistic."   d. superficial.

13. Advantages of computer scoring include all of the following *except:* (p. 589)
   a. sophisticated scoring may be done efficiently.
   b. less chance for error in scoring (reliable).
   c. the computer integrates the descriptions it picks up.
   d. it can give large amounts of information such as probable diagnosis.

14. Which of the following personality tests would *most likely* be used for personnel screening for a dangerous job? (p. 591)
   a. California Psychological Inventory
   b. MMPI
   c. 16 PF
   d. Strong Vocational Inventory

15. The APA guidelines on computer-based assessment assume that computerized test results will be used as: (p. 600)
   a. a last resort only.
   b. final recommendations.
   c. the sole basis for diagnosis.
   d. working hypotheses.

<blockquote>
Chapter 16
Biologically Based Therapies
</blockquote>

◊ OVERVIEW

Many states have passed laws during the past few years allowing or requiring pharmacies to post prices for the most frequently used prescription drugs in order to help consumers comparison shop. When such signs were posted, it surprised quite a few people to learn that several of the most frequently used drugs are chemicals that alter the emotional state and not drugs for "physical disease." Because of this widespread use of psychoactive drugs, an informed person should have some understanding of what such drugs can really accomplish and the tradeoffs involved in using them.

Chapter 16 presents details about the major types of drugs used for mental disorders: antianxiety, antipsychotic, antidepressant, and antimania, discussing their major effects, side effects, modes of action, and effectiveness. Other biological treatments, such as electric shock and psychosurgery, are also described briefly.

◊ LEARNING OBJECTIVES

After studying this chapter, you should be able to:

1. Describe early attempts at biological intervention, including coma and convulsive therapies and psychosurgery, and indicate which are currently believed to be effective. (pp. 601-608)

2. Summarize the major pharmacological treatments currently in use (antipsychotics, antidepressants, antianxiety drugs, lithium, and stimulants), discussing their major effects, side effects, modes of action, and effectiveness. (pp. 608-618; Highlight 16.2, p. 615; Highlight 16.3, pp. 619-620)

3. Discuss the advantages of combining biological and psychological forms of treatment. (pp. 618, 621)

4. Outline the issues associated with the widespread use of "personality-altering" drugs such as Prozac. (p. 621)

◊ TERMS YOU SHOULD KNOW

insulin coma therapy (p. 603)

electroconvulsive therapy (ECT) (pp. 603-604)

bilateral ECT (pp. 603-604)

unilateral ECT (pp. 603-604)

psychosurgery (p. 606)

neurosurgery (p. 606)

prefrontal lobotomy (p. 606)

cingulotomy (pp. 606-607)

capsulotomy (p. 607)

pharmacology (p. 608)

psychotropic drugs (pp. 608-609)

antipsychotic drugs (major tranquilizers) (p. 609)

reserpine (p. 609)

chlorpromazine (Thorazine) (pp. 609-610)

haloperidol (Haldol) (p. 610; Highlight 16.3, pp. 619-620)

tardive dyskinesia (p. 610)

target dosing (p. 611)

◊ NAMES YOU SHOULD KNOW

Timothy Crow (p. 610)

Gerard Hogarty (p. 611)

Herbert Meltzer (p. 612)

Frederick Goodwin (pp. 612, 613)

Gerald Klerman (p. 613)

◊ CONCEPTS TO MASTER

1. Briefly summarize the early history of attempts at biological intervention, and explain why medical treatment for physical diseases is far more advanced than medical treatment for behavior disorders. (pp. 601-602)

2. Describe the use of insulin coma therapy, and explain why it has largely disappeared. (pp. 602-603)

3. Describe the discovery and use of electroconvulsive therapy (ECT) and its positive and negative effects on the patient. (pp. 603-606)

4. Explain the controversy about using ECT and the reasons for its continued use. (pp. 604-606)

5. Describe prefrontal lobotomy and its effects on the patient. (p. 606)

6. Compare the psychosurgery of today with its earlier forerunners, and describe the current debate over "brain-disabling" therapies. (pp. 606-608)

7. List several antipsychotic compounds, and describe their effects and side effects in the treatment of behavior disorders. (pp. 609-612)

8. List several antidepressant compounds, and describe their effects and side effects in the treatment of mental disorders. (pp. 612-614)

9. List several antianxiety compounds, and describe their effects and side effects in the treatment of maladaptive behavior. (pp. 614-616)

10. What was the evaluation by the Institute of Medicine of the safety of the benzodiazepines (e.g. Valium, Librium, Dalmane) as sleeping medication? (Highlight 16.2, p. 615)

11. Describe the use of lithium in the treatment of bipolar mood disorders, and list its effects and side effects. (pp. 616-617)

12. List some of the drugs that have been used in treating maladaptive behavior in children and describe the benefits of amphetamines and Ritalin in treating children who are distractible and/or hyperactive. (pp. 617-618)

13. Evaluate the overall advantages and disadvantages of using pharmacological therapy for treating behavior disorders. (p. 618)

14. Discuss the controversy over the effects and popularity of the drug Prozac. (p. 621)

◊ STUDY QUESTIONS

Early attempts at biological intervention

1. List several treatments in the history of medicine that involve substantial disruption of biological processes (and suffering to the patient). (pp. 601-602)

Coma and convulsive therapies

2. Insulin coma therapy is no longer practiced. Why was it abandoned? (p. 603)

3. Electroconvulsive therapy (ECT) is much more widely used than insulin therapy, mostly because of its effectiveness in alleviating depressive episodes. Describe what happens during ECT. (pp. 603-604)

4. After awakening several minutes after ECT, the patient has _____ for the period immediately preceding the therapy. With repeated treatments, usually administered three times weekly, the patient gradually becomes _____. (p. 604)

5. Provide the following information about unilateral ECT: (p. 604)

   a. What is unilateral ECT?

   b. Is it widely employed?

6. Memory impairment resulting from ECT can remain for some months or possibly years. The damage created by electroshock is difficult to estimate in precise terms, but it is possible that it destroys a varying number of _____ causing such side effects as memory loss or impairment. (p. 605)

7. In 1985, the National Institute of Mental Health sponsored a Consensus Development Conference on electroconvulsive therapy.

   a. The panel recognized a number of potential risks associated with the use of ECT. What were the risks and are they still a problem? (p. 605)

   b. With present techniques, the death rate from ECT is ____ per 10,000 patients. (p. 605)

   c. Complete the following information about the kinds of cases where the panel concluded that ECT might be beneficial. (p. 605)
      • Some types of depression, particularly _____ and _____ depression, but ECT is not effective for another type of depression, _____ disorder.
      • Some types of manic disorders, particularly _____ mania.
      • The evidence for effectiveness with schizophrenia is _____.

   d. The panel concluded that relapse rates following ECT were high unless the treatment was followed up by _____.

Psychosurgery

8. After extended initial enthusiasm, physicians began to recognize that the results of psychosurgery could be very undesirable. What are some of the undesirable results that were found? (p. 606)

9. The advent of _____ caused an immediate decrease in the widespread use of psychosurgery, especially prefrontal lobotomy. (p. 606)

10. In the mid-1970s, the United States Congress initiated a special investigation into the effects of psychosurgery. They concluded that some modern psychosurgery resulted in surprisingly beneficial effects but also warned that such benefits were often achieved at the expense of the loss of certain _____. (p. 606)

Emergence of pharmacological methods

11. Pharmacology is the science of _____. (p. 608)

Types of drugs used in therapy

12. Fill in the missing information in the following chart that summarizes the four types of drugs commonly used for mental disorders: (pp. 608-617)

Class of Drugs	Biological Effect	Behavioral Effect	Example
Antipsychotics		Reduce the intensity of schizophrenic symptoms (including delusions and hallucinations) and have a calming effect	Thorazine
Antidepressant-tricyclics	Increase concentration of biogenic amines at synapses		
Antianxiety-benzodiazepines	Selectively diminish generalized anxiety		
Lithium			Resolve 70-80% of manic episodes and may also be useful in depression of bipolar type

389

13. The following is a schematic diagram of the antipsychotic class of drugs that illustrates the two general types of antipsychotics, official clinical names for these drugs, and the trade names under which they are sold in the drugstore (by prescription only). Fill in the missing trade names. (pp. 609-612; Highlight 16.3, pp. 619-620)

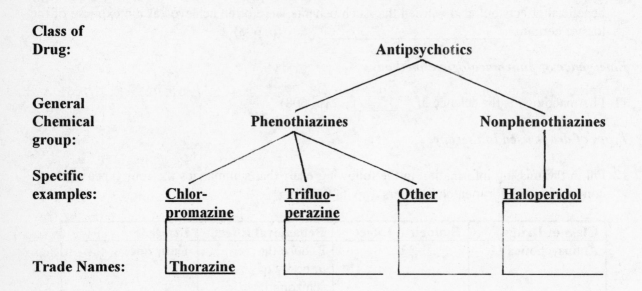

14. Compared to anything we have known before, the effects of the antipsychotic compounds in the treatment of schizophrenia are remarkable. At the same time, there are many treatment-resistant patients. Which types of patients and which types of symptoms tend not to respond to antipsychotic drugs? (p. 610)

15. Over the past ten years, a great deal of research has been undertaken to determine how drugs operate to alleviate depression. However, little progress has been made in identifying _____ or other _____ that relate to success by a given treatment method. (pp. 613-614)

16. The following is a schematic diagram of the antidepressant class of drugs that illustrates the three general types of antidepressants, the official chemical names for these drugs, and the trade names under which they are sold in the drugstore (by prescription only). Fill in the missing information in the blanks. (pp. 612-614; Highlight 16.3, pp. 619-620)

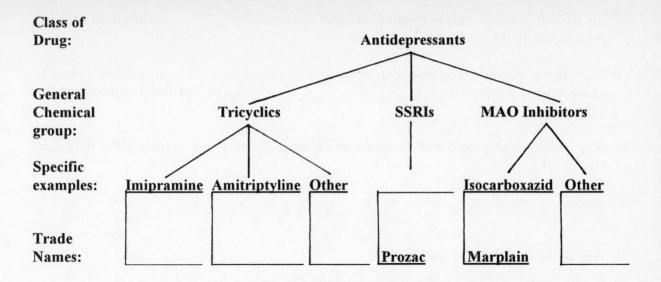

Class of Drug: Antidepressants

General Chemical group: Tricyclics · SSRIs · MAO Inhibitors

Specific examples: Imipramine · Amitriptyline · Other · Isocarboxazid · Other

Trade Names: Prozac · Marplain

17. The following is a schematic diagram of the antianxiety class of drugs that illustrates the two general types of antianxiety drugs, the official chemical names for the drugs, and the trade names under which they are sold in the drugstore (by prescription only). Fill in the missing information in the blanks: (pp. 614-616; Highlight 16.3, pp. 619-620)

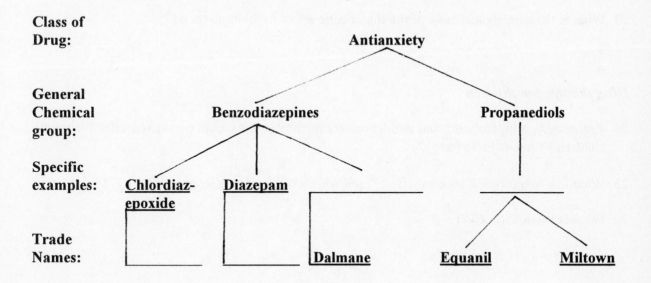

Class of Drug: Antianxiety

General Chemical group: Benzodiazepines · Propanediols

Specific examples: Chlordiaz-epoxide · Diazepam

Trade Names: Dalmane · Equanil · Miltown

391

18. All antianxiety drugs have the serious potential of inducing _____ when used unwisely or in excess. (p. 615)

19. The range of application of antianxiety compounds is quite broad. They are used in all manner of conditions in which _____ and _____ may be significant components. (p. 615)

20. Why should older people who complain of insomnia not be given sleeping pills? (Highlight 16.2, p. 615)

21. Why is lithium difficult to use? (p. 616)

22. Although lithium was slow to catch on in the United States, there can be no doubt at this point concerning its remarkable effectiveness in promptly resolving about _____ percent of all manic states. (p. 617)

23. What is the biochemical basis of the therapeutic effect of lithium? (p. 617)

Drug therapy for children

24. Antianxiety, antipsychotic, and antidepressant medications have all been used effectively with children. True or False (p. 617)

25. What is a "paradoxical reversal effect," and what would cause it to occur? (p. 617)

26. What is Ritalin? (p. 617)

27. All in all, pharmacological therapy has outmoded more drastic forms of treatment and has led to a much more favorable hospital climate for patients and staff alike. However, there are a number of limitations in the use of psychotropic drugs in addition to their undesirable side effects. Complete the following list of limitations: (p. 618)
   a. It is difficult to match drug and dosage to the _____.
   b. It is sometimes necessary to change medications in _____.
   c. The use of medications in isolation from other treatment methods for psychological disorders is usually inappropriate and ineffective, since drugs themselves do not _____ disorders.

Unresolved issues

28. As a result of the very positive effects of Prozac on subjective well-being, patients are often understandably reluctant to give up the drug. This reluctance is reminiscent of the serious problems the overuse of _____ eventually produced during the 1970s and 1980s. (p. 621)

29. In his book *Listening to Prozac*, Kramer addresses the disturbing questions raised by the availability of a prescription drug that seems not only to ameliorate depression but in addition, for many persons, to alter their _____. (p. 621)

◊ CRITICAL THINKING ABOUT DIFFICULT TOPICS

1. In prefrontal lobotomy the frontal lobes of the brain are severed from the deeper centers underlying them. One could hardly imagine a treatment more likely to produce disastrous negative effects, and eventually these negative effects were documented. However, "as is often the case with newly developed therapeutic techniques, initial reports of results tended to be enthusiastic, downplaying complications (including a 1-4 percent death rate) and undesirable side effects" (p. 606). This enthusiasm lasted so long that Moniz, the person who introduced prefrontal lobotomies in 1935, was awarded the Nobel Prize in Medicine in 1949. If such a "treatment" as prefrontal lobotomy is seen in uncontrolled clinical trials as highly successful and if "clinical wisdom" endorsed it for two decades, what does this tell you about all new forms of treatment that are touted as highly promising? How do you think the field of

medicine should deal with this problem? Is it possible to avoid false claims while not failing to take advantage of new and effective treatments? How can you as a consumer attempt to deal with it--or can you?

2. In this section for Chapter 14 you were asked to think about the concept of correcting a "chemical imbalance" through the use of drugs. This term seems to imply that the brain has too little of a given neurotransmitter and that pharmacological treatment can directly increase the amount of that neurotransmitter. However, as you have seen with the drugs of abuse, it is common for the brain to adapt to the presence of drugs (called tolerance) in an effort to oppose or negate their effects. To illustrate that something similar may happen with "medications," consider the following statements from the present chapter:

   a. Tardive dyskinesia caused by the antipsychotic drugs, which have the property of blocking dopamine receptors, "is believed to be due to an imbalance in dopamine and acetylcholine activity in the brain, secondary to alteration in receptor sensitivity by antipsychotics and other drugs commonly used in combination to control their side effects" (p. 610). What this means is that blocking dopamine receptors causes a compensatory increase in dopamine receptor sensitivity. The same may be true for cholinergic receptors when antiparkinsonian drugs are used to reduce the Parkinsonian symptoms produced by the antidopaminergic effects of the antipsychotics.

   b. "Although the immediate short-term effects of tricyclics are to increase the availability of norepinephrine and serotonin in the synapses, the long-term effects of these drugs . . . are to produce functional decreases in available norepinephrine and serotonin . . . It is also known that when the tricyclics are taken for several weeks they act to decrease the number and sensitivity of certain types of receptors and to increase the responsiveness of others" (pp. 612-613).

   c. "Because of their potential for producing dependence, withdrawal from [all of the antianxiety] drugs can be extremely difficult . . ." (p. 615).

   Thus, you can see that, in three very different classes of psychotropic medications, the brain reacts to their presence in complex ways. From this perspective, what does it mean to correct a chemical imbalance by administering drugs? Do these examples (e.g., tardive dyskinesia with antipsychotics, physical dependence with antianxiety drugs) cause you to think adverse effects of long-term consumption may have a significant probability?

3. In his book *Listening to Prozac*, Kramer expresses surprise and concern that an antidepressant drug that should ameliorate symptoms of depression should also alter the person's personality (p. 621). Is this surprising to you? The field of behavioral neurochemistry is concerned with the effects of neurotransmitters on behavior. Investigators in that field automatically assume that manipulating the functioning of a major neurotransmitter will have major effects on behavior. Similarly, temperament theorists have long assumed that there is a biological contribution to temperament. Thus, there is good reason to expect that psychotropic drugs

would affect behaviors that we think of as related to temperament. When the author of this Study Guide asked a distinguished psychiatrist what was surprising about the effects of Prozac, he was told, 'psychiatrists are so caught up in the disease model that they expect "medicines" to treat only "diseases" and not to affect other behavior.' In adopting that perspective, psychiatrists are blinding themselves to a basic scientific understanding of brain-behavior relationships. Can you try to conceptualize how psychotropic drugs have the primary effect of manipulating brain-behavior relationships while, at the same time, affecting symptomatology of behavior disorders? To do so, you will need to get beyond a simple-minded disease model and think in terms of the biopsychosocial model embraced by the text--in which there is a biological contribution to almost all aspects of behavior.

◊ CHAPTER 16 QUIZ

Circle the best of the four answers provided and check them according to answers provided at the back of this study guide. Be sure you understand why each answer is correct.

1. Electroconvulsive therapy (ECT) was developed as a result of speculation by Von Meduna, a Hungarian physician, that: (p. 603)
   a. electricians who were severely shocked often became epileptic.
   b. epileptics rarely developed schizophrenia.
   c. schizophrenics often had seizures.
   d. survivors of lightening strikes seldom became schizophrenic.

2. Psychiatrists often employ an unnecessarily damaging, inefficient form of ECT. Which of the following treatments is still effective, but without as many distressing side effects as the damaging, outdated method? (p. 604)
   a. ECT accompanied by muscle stimulants   c. unilateral ECT
   b. bilateral ECT   d. cerebellar ECT

3. Criticisms of the use of ECT for depression include all of the following except: (p. 605)
   a. it is ineffective.
   b. benefits may be short-lived.
   c. it causes demonstrable brain damage.
   d. it is sometimes used with patients for whom evidence of effectiveness is not convincing.

4. The 1985 NIMH Consensus Panel concluded that relapse rates following electroconvulsive therapy (ECT) were high unless the treatments were followed by: (p. 605)
   a. changes in the patient's psychosocial environment.
   b. maintenance doses of antidepressant medication.
   c. regular psychodynamic therapy sessions.
   d. sedative and muscle relaxant medication.

5. Which of the following caused an *almost* immediate halt in the widespread use of psychosurgical procedures in this country? (p. 606)
   a. a 1951 law banning all such operations
   b. the advent of electroconvulsive therapy (ECT)
   c. the advent of the major antipsychotic drugs
   d. the unusually high mortality rate

6. A modern psychosurgical technique known as "cingulotomy" is used to remove the subjective experience of: (p. 606)
   a. depression.
   b. guilt.
   c. mania.
   d. pain.

7. Antipsychotic, antidepressant, antianxiety, and lithium compounds are all referred to as _____ drugs. (pp. 608-609)
   a. hallucinogenic
   b. mind-expanding
   c. narcotic
   d. psychotropic

8. The unique quality of antipsychotic drugs is their ability to: (p. 609)
   a. calm patients down.
   b. put patients to sleep.
   c. reduce patients' anxiety.
   d. reduce the intensity of delusions and hallucinations.

9. Which of the following is a trade name for a major antipsychotic drug? (p. 610)
   a. Haldol
   b. Valium
   c. Dyserl
   d. Synaquon

10. Virtually all of the antipsychotic drugs accomplish the same biochemical effect, which is: (p. 610)
   a. blocking dopamine receptors.
   b. blocking the production of noradrenalin.
   c. stimulating the production of endorphins.
   d. stimulating the production of glutamic acid.

11. Pharmacological treatment of depression with tricyclics is believed to: (p. 612)
   a. reduce central nervous system arousal.
   b. reduce intracranial pressure by absorbing cerebral spinal fluid.
   c. increase the availability of lithium in the central nervous system for absorption.
   d. increase the concentration of serotonin and norepinephrine at synaptic sites.

12. One of the most commonly used tricyclic drugs in the treatment of depression is: (p. 613)
   a. methylphenidate (Ritalin).   c. chlordiazepoxide (Librium).
   b. imipramine (Tofranil).   d. haloperidol (Haldol).

13. Lithium compounds are used in the treatment of: (p. 616)
   a. anxiety.
   b. hyperactivity and specific learning disabilities.
   c. bipolar mood disorders.
   d. hallucinations and delusions.

14. The side effects of lithium include all the following *except: (p. 616)*
   a. lethargy.   c. decreased motor coordination.
   b. memory impairment.   d. gastrointestinal difficulties.

15. In the case of Osherhoff v. Chestnut Lodge, Osherhoff received a settlement out of court because Chestnut Lodge: (p. 618)
   a. put him on a wait list for 6 months, during which he continued to suffer major depression.
   b. had not administered drug therapy.
   c. had administered the wrong drug therapy.
   d. had provided psychotherapy by a minimally trained psychotherapist.

Chapter 17
Psychologically Based Therapies

◊ OVERVIEW

This chapter describes in some detail what mental health professionals do about all the types of problems discussed in the earlier chapters. There are a wide variety of techniques available, and often completely different approaches have been developed for the same problem behavior. These various approaches to treatment are all outgrowths of the different models of psychopathology described earlier. This material is confusing at first because of the natural tendency to feel that one approach might be right and the others wrong. In reality, no general approach to psychotherapy has proved capable of handling the wide range of problems seen clinically. Consequently, the inclination to identify strongly with one approach or another is decreasing. Today, many therapists are familiar with a variety of techniques chosen from several therapeutic approaches and use them depending on the type of problems the client is having. Some therapists, however, prefer to use only one type of treatment. In this case, they try to develop a professional reputation as a specialized therapist so that only clients appropriate to their chosen orientation are referred to them.

◊ LEARNING OBJECTIVES

After studying this chapter, you should be able to:

1. Provide a general overview of (a) the assumptions underlying psychotherapy, (b) the varied types of individuals who receive psychotherapy, (c) the various categories of providers of psychotherapeutic services and their specialized training, (d) the critical elements of the therapeutic relationship, and (e) the various types of therapy interventions. (pp. 625-631)

2. List and describe the basic techniques of psychoanalysis, summarize recent developments, and evaluate the effectiveness of the psychodynamic approach to the treatment of maladaptive behavior. (pp. 631-636)

399

3. List and describe the basic techniques of the behavior therapies, summarize recent developments, and evaluate the effectiveness of the behavior therapies in the treatment of maladaptive behavior. (pp. 636-644)

4. List and describe the basic techniques of the cognitive-behavior therapies, summarize recent developments, and evaluate the effectiveness of the cognitive-behavior therapies in the treatment of maladaptive behavior. (pp. 644-650)

5. List and describe the basic techniques of the humanistic-experiential therapies, summarize recent developments, and evaluate the effectiveness of the humanistic-experiential therapies in the treatment of maladaptive behavior. (pp. 650-654)

6. Describe the basic techniques of couples counseling and family therapy, summarize recent developments, and evaluate the effectiveness of these in the treatment of maladaptive relationships. (pp. 654-658)

7. Summarize the reasons for interest in integrating quite disparate forms of treatment (psychodynamic vs. cognitive-behavioral, psychosocial vs. biological) and the difficulties attendant upon attempting to do so. (pp. 658-659)

8. Discuss the many difficulties associated with attempting to evaluate the effectiveness of psychotherapy. (pp. 659-663)

9. Explain what is meant by negative or deteriorative effects in psychotherapy and outline the problems associated with trying to eliminate these effects. (pp. 663-664)

◊ TERMS YOU SHOULD KNOW

psychotherapy (p. 625)

"YAVIS" phenomenon (p. 627)

clergy (p. 627)

clinical psychologist (p. 627)

psychiatrist (p. 627)

psychiatric social worker (p. 627)

counseling psychologist (Highlight 17.1, p. 628)

school psychologist (Highlight 17.1, p. 628)

psychoanalyst (Highlight 17.1, p. 628)

psychiatric nurse (Highlight 17.1, p. 628)

occupational therapist (Highlight 17.1, p. 628)

pastoral counselor (Highlight 17.1, p. 628)

paraprofessional (Highlight 17.1, p. 628)

community mental health worker (Highlight 17.1, p. 628)

alcohol or drug-abuse counselor (Highlight 17.1, p. 628)

interdisciplinary team (Highlight 17.1, p. 628)

therapeutic relationship (p. 628)

expectation (of receiving help) (p. 629)

causal primacy (p. 631)

psychodynamic therapy (p. 631)

Classical psychoanalysis (p. 631)

psychoanalytically oriented therapy (p. 631)

free association (p. 632)

manifest content (p. 632)

analysis of dreams (p. 632)

latent content (p. 632)

resistance (p. 632)

analysis of resistance (p. 632)

transference (p. 632)

analysis of transference (pp. 632-633)

transference neurosis (p. 634)

counter-transference (p. 634)

hypnosis (Highlight 17.3, p. 633)

induction (Highlight 17.3, p. 633)

age regression (Highlight 17.3, p. 633)

dream induction (Highlight 17.3, p. 633)

post-hypnotic suggestion (Highlight 17.3, p. 633)

time-limited dynamic psychotherapy (p. 635)

interpersonal psychotherapy (IPT) for depression (p. 635)

behavior therapy (p. 636)

behavior therapists (p. 636)

extinction (p. 636)

implosive therapy (p. 637)

flooding (or *in vivo procedures*) (p. 637)

systematic desensitization (pp. 638-639)

anxiety hierarchy (p. 639)

aversion therapy (pp. 639-640)

differential reinforcement of other responses (DRO) (p. 640)

modeling (pp. 640-641)

response shaping (p. 641)

token economies (pp. 641-642)

behavioral contracting (p. 642)

assertiveness therapy (pp. 642-643)

biofeedback (pp. 643-644)

cognitive-behavior therapy (pp. 644-645)

rational-emotive therapy (RET) (pp. 645-646)

stress-inoculation therapy (p. 646)

cognitive preparation (p. 646)

skill acquisition and rehearsal (p. 646)

cognitive-behavior therapy for depression (p. 647)

selectively perceive (p. 647)

overgeneralize (p. 647)

magnify significance (p. 647)

absolutistic thinking (p. 647)

humanistic-experiential therapies (p. 650)

◊ NAMES YOU SHOULD KNOW

Gordon Paul (pp. 641, 642)

Aaron Beck (pp. 645, 647-649)

Donald Meichenbaum (pp. 645, 646)

Albert Ellis (p. 645)

◊ CONCEPTS TO MASTER

1. List and explain several reasons why people enter psychotherapy, and describe three types of mental health professionals who are trained in the identification and treatment of mental disorders. (pp. 626-627)

2. Outline the major features of the therapeutic relationship that promote better outcomes in psychotherapy. Note that these are "common" or "nonspecific" factors in the sense that they have little to do with specific techniques or specific theoretical approaches. (pp. 628-629)

3. The patient's "expectation of receiving help" is also important to the outcome of therapy and may operate to some degree as a placebo does in medicine. Explain this statement. (p. 629)

4. Describe five general types of therapy, and explain the "continuous loop" perspective. (Highlight 17.2, p. 630; p. 631)

5. List the four basic techniques of psychoanalysis and explain how they are used in psychodynamic therapy. (pp. 632, 634).

6. Summarize the changes in psychodynamic therapy that have taken place since Freud and evaluate the effectiveness of the psychodynamic approach to the treatment of maladaptive behavior. (pp. 634-636)

7. Explain the principle of extinction, and describe several therapeutic techniques that make use of this phenomenon. (pp. 636-638)

8. Explain the learning principles underlying systematic desensitization, and list three steps in its application to maladaptive behavior. (pp. 638-639)

9. Define *aversion therapy,* and give several examples of its use to treat behavioral disorders. (pp. 639-640)

10. Define *modeling,* and explain how it can be used in the treatment of mental disorders. (pp. 640-641)

11. Explain what is meant by systematic use of positive reinforcement, and describe three general techniques based on this plan. (pp. 641-642)

12. Describe *assertiveness therapy* and explain the learning principles that are involved in its use. (pp. 642-643)

13. List three steps in the biofeedback approach to therapy, and describe several of its applications to maladaptive behaviors. (pp. 643-644)

14. List and explain three advantages that behavior therapy has over other psychotherapies, and indicate why it cannot be a cure-all. (p. 644)

15. Define *cognitive-behavior therapy*, and describe several techniques used by rational-emotive therapists to treat mental disorders. (pp. 645-646)

16. Why does Ellis believe that many of us behave irrationally and feel unnecessarily that we are failures? How have Arnhoff and Glass (1982) criticized this viewpoint? (pp. 645-646)

17. Describe the three stages of stress-inoculation therapy. (pp. 646-647)

18. Describe Beck's cognitive-behavior therapies and explain the theory on which they are based. (pp. 647, 649; Highlight 17.4, p. 648)

19. Compare the outcomes of cognitive-behavior therapy with other psychotherapies, and describe some trends in its use. (pp. 649-650)

20. Describe Carl Rogers' client-centered therapy, and indicate the impact it has had on the field. (pp. 650-652)

21. "Pure" client-centered therapy is rarely used today, but it has been influential. How are the humanistic therapies of today similar to client-centered therapy, and how are they different? (p. 652)

22. List several important concepts that underlie existential psychotherapy, and describe its application to maladaptive behavior. (p. 652)

23. Explain the main goals of Gestalt therapy, and describe several techniques used by Perls and others to treat mental disorders. (p. 653)

24. List some criticisms of the humanistic-experiential therapies, and point out some of their positive contributions to the field. (p. 654)

25. Describe several foci and techniques of couples counseling, and indicate some of its difficulties and outcomes. (pp. 654-656)

26. Describe two types of family therapy, and give some examples of their use to treat maladaptive behavior. (pp. 656-657)

27. List Kendall's four reasons for the current interest in integrating behavior therapy with other methods, and explain three problems that he sees in achieving this goal. (p. 658)

28. List five sources of information used to evaluate the effectiveness of psychological treatment, and describe the limitations of each. (p. 659)

29. Discuss the effectiveness of psychotherapy compared with treatment delivered by nonprofessionals and compared with no treatment at all. (p. 660)

30. List the personal characteristics of a psychotherapist that are relevant to the outcome of psychotherapy and indicate how important they are. (p. 661)

31. Describe the controversy centering around possible conflicts between the role of the therapist and the values of society. (p. 662)

32. Define negative or deteriorative effects in psychotherapy and discuss this problem both generally and in the special case of therapist-client sexual entanglements. (pp. 663-664)

◊ STUDY QUESTIONS

Introduction

1. Psychotherapy is based on the assumption that even in cases where physical pathology is present, changes in _____, evaluations, _____, and coping strategies will have to occur if maximum benefit is to be realized. The belief that individuals can _____ is the underlying assumption of all psychotherapy approaches. (p. 625)

2. There are seven general goals of psychotherapy. Following are four of the goals; fill in the missing three: (p. 625)
   a. Changing maladaptive behavior
   b. Changing environmental conditions that may be causing or maintaining the maladaptive behavior
   c. Improving interpersonal skills
   d. Resolving conflicts among motives
   e.
   f.
   g.

3. It has been estimated that there are several _____ "therapeutic" approaches in existence, ranging from psychoanalysis to Zen meditation. (p. 626)

Who receives psychotherapy

4. Describe the most obvious clients for psychotherapy. (p. 626)

5. What types of individuals are likely to be reluctant or resistant clients? (p. 626)

6. Clients who do the best in psychotherapy are often "YAVIS" types. Explain what is meant by "YAVIS" and why such patients do best in psychotherapy. (pp. 626-627)

7. Fill in the blank spaces in the following chart that summarizes the training and special duties of the professionals on the mental health team: (p. 627)

Professional	Training	Special Duties
Psychiatrist	MD degree plus three-year residency of hospital	
Clinical psychologist		
Psychiatric social worker	BA in social sciences, MSW in social work	Family evaluation

The therapeutic relationship

8. Describe the client's major contribution to the therapeutic relationship. (p. 628)

9. Motivation to _____ is probably the most crucial element in determining the success or failure of psychotherapy. (p. 628)

10. Almost as important as the preceding is a client's _____ of receiving help--often sufficient in itself to bring out some improvement. (p. 629)

11. To at least some extent, effective therapy depends on a good _____ between client and therapist. Hence, a therapist's own _____ is necessarily a factor of some importance in determining therapeutic outcomes. (p. 629)

A perspective on therapeutic pluralism

12. The authors discuss a continuous loop of relationships among (a) the client conceived as a system of integrated cognitions and affects; (b) his/her abnormal behavior which is assumed to be the product of (a); and (c) the reactions of the person's environment to that output, in turn feeding back information to the person's cognition-affect-physiologic system. Respond to the following two questions about this continuous loop: (p. 631; see also Highlight 17.2, p. 630)

a. What is causal primacy, and how important is it?

b. In order to effect positive overall therapeutic outcome, where in the loop should the therapist intervene?

Psychodynamic therapy

13. Psychodynamic therapy is a treatment approach that focuses on individual personality dynamics from a _____ perspective. As developed by Freud, classic psychoanalysis is an intensive, long-term procedure for uncovering repressed memories, thoughts, fears, and conflicts presumably stemming from problems in early _____ _____--and helping the individual come to terms with them in light of adult reality. (p. 631)

14. There are four basic techniques of psychoanalysis: free association, dream interpretation, analysis of resistance, and analysis of transference. Briefly explain how the analyst uses each technique: (pp. 632, 634)

Technique	How it is Used
Free association	
Analysis of dreams	
Analysis of resistance	
Analysis of transference	

15. How do most modern analysts like Mann and Strupp differ in emphasis from strict Freudian psychoanalysis? (pp. 634-635)

16. Indicate whether each of the following statements represents a valid criticism of psychodynamic therapy. Circle the correct response: (p. 635)
   a. It's time consuming and expensive.   True or False
   b. It's based on a questionable theory of human nature.   True or False
   c. It neglects the patient's current problems.   True or False
   d. There is inadequate proof of its effectiveness.   True or False

17. For whom is psychodynamic therapy the treatment of choice? (p. 636)

The use of hypnosis in therapy

18. Describe how a hypnotic trance is induced. (Highlight 17.3, p. 633)

19. Hypnosis may be used to accomplish the following outcomes. Briefly describe what each one is: (Highlight 17.3, p. 633)

   a. Recall of buried memories
   b. Age regression
   c. Dream induction
   d. Posthypnotic suggestion

20. Is there any evidence that hypnosis differs from the response in subjects who are only responding to the demand characteristics of the procedure? (Highlight 17.3, p. 633)

21. How might drugs sometimes be used to produce phenomena similar to those in a hypnotic trance? (Highlight 17.3, p. 633)

Behavior therapy

22. The behavioristic perspective views the maladjusted person as one who has (a) failed to acquire _____, or (b) learned faulty _____ or _____ patterns that are being maintained by some kind of reinforcement, or (c) both. Instead of exploring past traumatic events or inner conflicts, behavior therapists manipulate environmental _____ to alter maladaptive behavior. (p. 636)

23. The extinction technique is based on the observation that learned behavior patterns weaken over time if not _____. It works best on behavior that is being reinforced _____ by others. (p. 636)

24. Implosive therapy and flooding techniques rely on the principle of _____. (p. 637)

25. With implosion, the therapist removes problematic behavior by deliberately trying to _____ anxiety rather than to minimize it. (p. 637)

26. In extinction therapies, what technique can be used with patients who are not able to realistically imagine scenes? (pp. 637-638)

27. What unfavorable results have been reported from flooding therapy? (p. 638)

28. Systematic desensitization is designed to eliminate behaviors that are being _____ reinforced but can be used for other types of problems. (p. 638)

29. Systematic desensitization consists of three steps. What are they? (p. 639)

30. Aversion therapy involves modification of behavior by _____, which can be of two types. What are these types? (p. 639)

31. Why has the use of electric shock as an aversive stimulus decreased recently? (p. 640)

32. What method is often used instead of electric shock by clinicians such as Lovaas? (p. 640)

33. Modeling involves learning skills through _____. (p. 640)

34. Modeling may be used in clinical situations, such as _____ in a profoundly retarded child or being more effective in _____ for a shy, withdrawn adolescent. (pp. 640-641)

35. Briefly describe each of the following techniques: (pp. 641-642)

a. Response shaping

b. Token economy

36. What are the goals of a token economy program? (p. 642)

37. A behavioral contract often specifies a client's _____ as well as the responsibilities of the other person to provide tangible rewards in return. (p. 642)

38. Briefly list some of the ways a behavioral contract can facilitate therapy. (p. 642)

a.

b.

c.

d.

e.

f.

39. Assertiveness training is used both as an alternative to _____ in desensitization therapy and as a means of teaching more effective coping techniques. (p. 642)

40. Assertiveness training works because each act of intentional assertion inhibits the _____ associated with the situation. (p. 643)

41. Biofeedback consists of three steps. What are they? (p. 643)

a.

b.

c.

42. Is there unequivocal data supporting the effectiveness of biofeedback with conditions such as migraine headaches and Raynaud's disease? (p. 643)

43. What control or comparison group is essential in evaluating the effectiveness of biofeedback? When such comparisons are made, how effective is biofeedback found to be? (p. 644)

44. Respond true or false to the following statements about behavior therapy. (p. 644)

a. The treatment is precise.   True or False

b. Behavior therapy is particularly successful in the treatment of childhood autism, schizophrenia, and severe depression.   True or False

c. Behavior therapy techniques are important in the treatment of sexual dysfunction.   True or False

Cognitive-behavior therapy

45. How have behavioral therapists recently changed their thinking so that many are now labeled "cognitive-behavioral therapists"? (pp. 644-645)

46. At present, there are several alternative approaches to cognitive-behavioral therapy, but two main themes seem to characterize them all. Complete the following: (p. 645)
a. The conviction that cognitive processes influence affect, motivation, and behavior
b.

47. The chart below summarizes three different cognitive-behavioral therapies.   Fill in the requested information:

Therapeutic Approach	Description
Rational-emotive therapy	a. This approach was developed by _____. Today, it is one of the most widely used therapeutic approaches. (p. 645)
	b. To eliminate irrational beliefs, the RET therapist disputes these false beliefs through _____ _____ and also uses _____ _____ techniques to bring about changed thoughts and behaviors. (p. 646)
Stress-inoculation therapy	a. Stress-inoculation training usually involves three stages. Briefly describe what happens at each of the stages: (pp. 646-647) Cognitive preparation Skill acquisition and rehearsal Application and practice
Beck's Cognitive-behavior therapies	a. This therapy was originally developed for the treatment of _____. (p. 647)
	b. A basic assumption of this approach is that problems like depression result from a person's negative views about himself or herself, the world, and the future. Such behavior typically includes features such as the following. Briefly describe each one: (p. 647)

	Selective perception
	Overgeneralization
	Magnification
	Absolutistic thinking
	c. Describe how Beck's approach to changing irrational thinking differs from Ellis' RET. (p. 647)
	d. Cognitive restructuring may involve other techniques as well. Briefly describe each one: (p. 647) Schedule of daily activities Discovery of dysfunctional assumptions or depressogenic schemas

48. Do data on RET indicate that it is effective for severe anxiety disorders and depression? (p. 649)

49. Stress-inoculation therapy has been successfully used with a number of clinical problems, especially _____, _____, _____ behavior, and mild forms of _____. (p. 649)

50. How do Beck's type of cognitive-behavioral treatments for depression compare with drug treatment? (p. 649)

51. Many empirical studies in the past decade have compared cognitive-behavioral method with other treatment approaches for a variety of other clinical disorders. The most dramatic recent results have been in the treatment of _____ disorder and _____ disorder. (p. 649)

52. These approaches have developed in reaction to behavioral and psychodynamic therapies which are believed to fail to take into account either the _____ or the _____ of human beings. (p. 650)

53. Humanistic-experiential therapies are based on a major assumption. What is it? (p. 650)

54. How do behavioral therapists differ from humanistic therapists with respect to responsibility for the direction and success of therapy? (p. 650)

55. The chart below summarizes the major approaches to psychotherapy that are humanistic-experientially oriented. Fill in the requested information: (pp. 651-655)

Therapeutic Approach	Description
Client-centered therapy	a. This therapy was originated by _____ in the 1940s as an alternative to psychoanalysis. In this therapy, the psychoanalytic view of humans as irrational and the idea that the proper role of the therapist is to be the director of therapy are rejected. (p. 650)
	b. The primary role of client-centered therapy is to remove "incongruence." What is incongruence, and how does it come about? (p. 650)
	c. How does the client-centered therapist remove incongruence? (p. 650)
Existential therapy	a. Existential therapists do not follow any rigidly prescribed procedures, but they all emphasize the _____ of each individual. (p. 652)

	b. In contrast to the behavioral therapist and the psychoanalyst, the existential therapist _____ his or her feelings and values with the client. (p. 652)
	c. For what types of clients is this therapy indicated? (p. 652)
Gestalt therapy	a. This therapy was originated by _____ as a means of teaching clients to recognize the _____ _____ and emotions they had been _____ from awareness. (p. 653)
	b. The main goal of Gestalt therapy is to increase an individual's _____ and _____. (p. 653)
	c. Gestalt therapy sessions focus on the more obvious elements of a person's behavior; thus the sessions are often called _____ training. (p. 653)
	d. What is "taking care of unfinished business"? (p. 653)

56. What format is most often employed in group therapy? (Highlight 17.5, p. 651)

57. Complete the following list of the three major criticisms that have been made of humanistic-experiential therapies. (Ironically, the points of criticisms are seen by proponents of humanistic-experiential therapies as the strengths of their approach.) (p. 654)
a. Lack of a highly systematized model of human behavior
b.
c.

58. These therapeutic techniques focus on relationships rather than individuals and emphasize the role of faulty communication in causing maladaptive behavior. The following chart summarizes the major forms of interpersonal therapy. Fill in the missing information:

Therapeutic Approach	Description
Couples counseling	a. Can improvements in marital relationships usually be accomplished by undertaking therapy with one member but not the other? (p. 654)
	b. How do happily married couples differ from unhappily married couples? (p. 655)
	c. How are videotapes useful in couple counseling? (p. 655)
	d. How effective are marital therapies at resolving crises according to Cookery (1980)? (p. 656)
Family therapy	a. How did family therapy originate? (p. 656)
	b. Who does the family therapist view as the "patient" to be directly involved in therapy if lasting improvement is to be achieved? (p. 656)

	c. The most widely used approach to family therapy is _____ developed by Satir. This therapy emphasizes improving family communication and interactions. (p. 656)
	d. Another approach is called "structural family therapy" and was developed by _____. This therapy assumes that if the family context changes, then the individual members will change. Thus, an important goal is to change the family organization so that family members will behave _____ in accordance with the changed requirements of the new family context. (p. 657)
	e. Structural therapy has been used successfully with anorexia, _____, childhood _____ disorders, and _____ addiction. (p. 657)
	f. Which approach to family therapy has been found to be most effective by Gurman, Kniskern, and Pinsof (1986) and by Shadish and colleagues (1993)? (p. 658)

Integration of therapy approaches

59. What have psychodynamic therapists had to acknowledge about behavioral techniques? (p. 658)

60. What have behavioral therapists had to acknowledge about relationship factors? (p. 658)

61. Kendall has summarized the reasons there is interest in integrating the approaches to psychotherapy, but he has also noted the obstacles to integration. Summarize these arguments in the following chart: (p. 658)

Reason for Integration of Therapeutic Approaches	Obstacles to Integration of Therapeutic Approaches
a.	a.
b.	b.
c.	c.
d.	

Evaluation of success in psychotherapy

62. The chart below lists some of the sources of information that can be used to gauge the outcome of psychotherapy and also note the bias inherent in each source. Fill in the missing information: (p. 659)

Source	Bias
Therapist	Wants to see him/herself as competent and successful
Patient	
	May be more objective than ratings by those directly involved in the therapy.

63. Changes in preselected and specifically denoted _____ appear to be the safest measures of outcome. (p. 660)

64. Some forms of psychopathology, such as _____ and _____ episodes and some instances of _____, appear to run a fairly brief course that is not influenced one way or another by psychotherapy. (p. 660)

65. Most researchers today would agree that psychotherapy is more effective than _____ _____. (p. 660)

66. Underline the correct phrase: The largest proportion of the gain in treatment occurs (in the beginning, in the middle, close to the end) of psychotherapy according to Howard et al. (1986). (p. 660)

67. How important are the personal characteristics of the therapist providing therapy versus the physician prescribing drug treatment? Is this difference a distinct advantage for biological treatments? (p. 661)

Unresolved issues

68. In perhaps _____ percent of client-therapist relationships, the client ends up worse off than before treatment. (p. 663)

69. What therapist styles can be dangerous to client functioning, particularly when it is unmodulated by warmth and empathy? (p. 663)

70. Even with a treatable problem and a skilled therapist, negative events, such as _____, in a client's life outside therapy can obviously interfere with therapeutic progress. (p. 663)

71. Discuss the following points in reference to sexual relationships between therapist and clients: (pp. 663-664)

   a. Are such relationships ethical for the therapist to participate in under certain circumstances?

   b. Are sexual relationships between therapists and clients common?

72. The authors suggest a "trial" interview. What is this? (p. 664)

73. Why don't all therapists practice a multifaceted, multitargeted approach to every case? (p. 664)

◊ CRITICAL THINKING ABOUT DIFFICULT TOPICS

Consider the following statements from the text and keep them in mind in attempting to answer the questions that follow.

- "Most of us have experienced a time or situation when we were dramatically helped by 'talking things over' with a relative or friend. Or perhaps we made a drastic change in our customary behavior after a particular event led to new understanding. . . . formal psychotherapy as practiced by a mental health professional shares many aspects in common with this type of familiar experience." (p. 625)

- "Individuals who seem to have the best prognosis for personality change, according to repeated research outcomes, . . . are Young, Attractive, Verbal, Intelligent, and Successful. Ironically, those who tend to do best in psychotherapy are those who seem objectively to need it least." (p. 627)

- "Motivation to change is probably the most crucial element in determining the success or failure of psychotherapy . . . . Almost as important is a client's expectation of receiving help . . . Just as a placebo pill often lessens pain for someone who believes it will do so, a person who expects to be helped by psychotherapy is likely to be helped, almost regardless of the particular methods used by a therapist." (pp. 628-629).

- "... even under the best of circumstances there is always the possibility that improvement will be attributed to the particular form of treatment used, when it is in fact a product of other events in a client's life or even of 'spontaneous' change." (p. 660)

- "In view of the many ways that people can help each other, it is not surprising that often considerable improvement occurs without professional therapeutic intervention. Relevant here is the observation that treatment offered by professional therapists has not, in general, been clearly demonstrated to be superior in outcome to nonprofessionally administered therapies." (p. 660)

- "Take, for example, a therapist himself or herself as a variable, including such attributes as ... interpersonal skill, familiarity with the subcultural background of a client, faith in the treatment, and perhaps even personal attractiveness or charisma as experienced by the client. We have solid reason ... to believe that such things may be of crucial significance in determining the outcome of any psychosocial treatment effort." (p. 661)

1. The text offers the rather modest summary statement that "Most researchers today would agree that psychotherapy is more effective than no treatment" (p. 660). How many of the quotations above suggest that a significant portion of this effectiveness has little or nothing to do with the treatment provided, but rather have to do with the client's characteristics (e.g., abilities, motivations, and expectancies) and response to the fact of being treated? If so, how do we know that the specific procedures in psychotherapy are at all effective?

2. Each of the approaches to psychotherapy (e.g., systematic desensitization, client-centered, cognitive-behavioral therapy for depression) reviewed in this chapter asserts that specific aspects of that approach are important to the outcome of therapy. On the other hand, many components are seen in any form of psychotherapy and thus are "common factors" that have nothing to do with specific procedures for that particular form of therapy. It has been argued that these common factors account for most of the success in psychotherapy. How many of the quotations above refer to these nonspecific or common factors? How can we know that a form of therapy is effective because of its specific features?

3. The text does not discuss the topic of the "attention-placebo" control group--perhaps because this is a complex topic. In such a control group the client meets with a therapist for a short time (e.g., fifteen minutes) on a regular basis. The client believes this interaction is treatment and, indeed, the therapist expresses interest in and support for the client, but nothing resembling formal psychotherapy is attempted. On the whole, this type of control group shows a significantly better outcome than do untreated clients. Thus, like psychotherapy, attention-placebo is more effective than no treatment. What does this finding imply for the design of studies on the effectiveness of specific forms of psychotherapy? If Brand X psychotherapy is

not better than attention-placebo, what would you conclude about the importance of its specific techniques?

4. A closely related issue in the psychotherapy literature concerns whether therapy involves technical skills. The implication of such skills is that only a trained person could deliver them effectively and that therapy provided by such trained individuals would be more effective than therapy offered by others. How many of the quotations above challenge the notion that the effectiveness of psychotherapy is attributable to technical skills acquired during training?

5. Read carefully the discussion on page 659 of the limitations of all sources of evaluation of the outcome of psychotherapy. In view of these limitations and the quotations above, how can we ever determine whether psychotherapy is effective? Can we argue that the sources of error are random and equal across groups in controlled clinical trials, making it possible to compare treatments with no treatment and with each other?

6. It is not uncommon to hear a psychotherapist assert, "I know from my own experience that psychotherapy works and that I have helped many patients." Develop a response to the therapist indicating that such a response reflects a failure in his or her education. That is, explain why it is extremely difficult to know why an individual client improves and why it is necessary to evaluate the effectiveness of therapy with controlled clinical trials involving random assignment of clients to groups (to control for client factors) and to include an attention-placebo control group (to control for common or nonspecific factors).

7. Your text focuses on the NIMH-sponsored multisite study of the treatment of depression (p. 661-662), which is an important study because of the unusually large sample size (number of clients treated for depression). In the original report by Elkin et al., for all patients taken together there were *no* significant differences among the treatments. Across many outcome measures, the rank order from least to most improvement was placebo plus clinical management (PLA-CM), cognitive-behavior therapy, interpersonal therapy, and imipramine plus clinical management, but these differences generally were not statistically significant. By way of explanation, the authors made the following comment:

> "The main reason for the general lack of significant findings seems to be due, not to lack of improvement in the psychotherapy groups, but rather to the very good performance of the PLA-CM condition. This is in contrast to the finding of fairly poor performance of waiting-list or delayed-treatment groups used as controls in other studies of brief psychotherapies for depression. . . . PLA-CM . . . is not a no-treatment condition or even an 'inactive' placebo condition. Patients were seen once a week for 20 to 30 minutes by a well-trained and experienced psychiatrist, who not only administered the [placebo] medication and reviewed symptoms, side effects, and general functioning, but also offered support and encouragement" (Elkin et al., p. 978).

This comment underscores the magnitude of the attention-placebo effect mentioned above in question 3. Note that the attention-placebo effects are psychological and that, under normal conditions of drug administration, the client experiences both this attention-placebo and the biological effects of the drug. As a result, the apparent benefit of the drug actually includes the psychological factors associated with the attention-placebo. What does this observation imply about the purely biological effects of psychotropic drugs? As indicated above, the additional effect of the antidepressant was usually not significant when compared with PLA-CM for all patients taken together, indicating a modest biological effect. When clients were subdivided on the basis of severity of depression, the effect of the antidepressant compared with PLA-CM was significant for the more severely depressed but not for the less severely depressed patients. Thus, biological treatments are effective with more severely depressed clients, but psychological factors are more important in the response to treatment of less severely depressed clients. On the basis of this argument, how do you think antidepressant drugs should be prescribed?

◊ CHAPTER 17 QUIZ

Circle the best of the four answers provided and check them according to answers provided at the back of this study guide. Be sure you understand why each answer is correct.

1. Individuals who seek therapy because they feel overwhelmed by sudden highly stressful situations typically respond best to: (p. 626)
   a. existential approaches that reduce alienation.
   b. long-term psychodynamic analysis.
   c. short-term, directive, crisis-oriented treatment.
   d. therapies that employ confrontational methods.

2. Which type of patient may make substantial gains in personal growth in psychotherapy? (pp. 626-627)
   a. those with physical problems who were referred by a physician
   b. those who have experienced long-term psychological distress
   c. severely disturbed psychotic individuals
   d. those described in terms of the so-called YAVIS pattern

3. The member of the mental health team who has specialization in personality theory, psychological assessment, and psychotherapy is a: (p. 627)
   a. psychiatrist.
   b. clinical psychologist.
   c. psychiatric social worker.
   d. pastoral counselor.

4. The patient's major contribution to the therapeutic relationship is his/her: (p. 628)
   a. motivation.
   b. financial incentive for therapist.
   c. expectation of receiving help.
   d. suggestibility.

5. Which of the following is *not* a general type or class of therapy intervention according to the principal client subsystem targeted for therapeutic attention? (p. 630)
   a. Type A
   b. Type B
   c. Type C
   d. Type E

6. A son of a critical father comes to therapy one day and with no provocation is extremely hostile in his remarks to the therapist. The therapist might consider that _____ is occurring. (p. 632)
   a. free association
   b. countertransference
   c. transference
   d. positive transference

7. Contemporary psychodynamic treatment differs from Freudian psychoanalysis by placing more emphasis on: (p. 635)
   a. early repressed sexuality.
   b. current ego functioning.
   c. long-term treatment.
   d. childhood events.

8. Both implosive therapy and flooding focus on: (pp. 636-637)
   a. bombarding maladaptive behavior with aversive stimuli.
   b. exploding inner conflicts.
   c. extinguishing the conditioned avoidance of anxiety-arousing stimuli.
   d. inundating a person with positive reinforcement.

9. All of the following are steps in Wolpe's approach to systematic desensitization *except:* (p. 639)
   a. asking the client to imagine anxiety-producing situations while relaxing.
   b. constructing a hierarchy of anxiety-producing situations.
   c. placing the client in anxiety-producing life situations.
   d. training the client to relax.

10. Aversion therapy reduces maladaptive behavior by following it with: (pp. 639-640)
    a. a request for the client to avert his or her eyes from the stimulus.
    b. negative reinforcement.
    c. punishment.
    d. stimuli diverting the client's attention.

11. Which of the following statements regarding biofeedback is true? (pp. 643-644)
    a. Biofeedback is a more elaborate means of teaching relaxation.
    b. Biofeedback is more effective than relaxation training.
    c. The effects of biofeedback are often generalized outside the laboratory.
    d. Recent well-controlled studies of biofeedback have shown a treatment effect for migraine patients.

12. According to Aaron Beck (1979), individuals maintain false beliefs even in the face of contradictory evidence because: (p. 647)
    a. they are reinforced for doing so.
    b. of biologically-based drives to do so.
    c. of a strong regressive pull to be a "child" or a "parent" rather than an ``adult."
    d. they engage in selective perception and overgeneralization.

13. Not only was Carl Rogers rated as one of the most influential psychotherapists of his time, but he was also a pioneer in: (p. 652)
    a. advocating health insurance for mental illness.
    b. carrying out empirical research on psychotherapy.
    c. initiating, broad spectrum mental health program.
    d. reorganizing mental hospital procedures.

14. The rate of improvement in treatment offered by professional therapists compared to nonprofessionally administered therapies: (p. 660)
    a. is about twice as high.   c. is about the same.
    b. is about 50% higher.   d. is actually worse.

15. In a national survey of psychologists by Pope and Vetter, ____% of the respondents reported assessing or treating at least one client who have been sexually intimate with a prior therapist. (p. 663)
    a. 11   c. 50
    b. 26   d. 77

Chapter 18
Contemporary Issues in Abnormal Psychology

◊ OVERVIEW

Previous chapters have catalogued the many forms of mental disorders and have briefly described various treatment programs, most of which focus either directly on the patient or involve only immediate family members. Chapter 18 is different. Here "primary prevention" is emphasized, which includes programs and research at the level of the broader society in order to prevent maladaptive behavior in the first place. The chapter discusses how the U.S. government is involved both nationally and internationally in improving mental health. The chapter also addresses controversial legal issues. Many people were shocked when John Hinckley was found not guilty of shooting President Ronald Reagan, especially since we all saw him do the shooting on television. The chapter attempts to describe the maze of laws pertaining to the insanity defense and other pertinent legal issues.

◊ LEARNING OBJECTIVES

After studying this chapter, you should be able to:

1. Define primary prevention, review the role of risk and protective factors in the etiology of clinical disorders, explain how primary prevention includes biological, psychosocial, and sociocultural efforts, and describe several types of primary prevention programs that illustrate primary prevention strategies. (pp. 668-674)

2. Define secondary prevention and describe and illustrate several types of secondary prevention. (pp. 675-678)

3. Define tertiary prevention and describe and illustrate several types of tertiary prevention. (pp. 678-681)

4. Outline the procedures involved in civil commitment and the safeguards for due process in involuntary commitment. (pp. 681-683; Highlight 18.2, p. 682)

5. Discuss the problems of assessing and predicting "dangerousness" and explain the obligations of the clinician under the "duty-to-warn" legal doctrine. (pp. 683-687)

6. Review the various legal rulings relevant to the insanity defense and discuss the problems associated with this concept. (pp. 687-689)

7. Trace the history of deinstitutionalization of chronic mental patients and summarize the current responses to this phenomenon. (pp. 689-693)

8. List and describe the various U.S. government, professional, voluntary, private industrial, and international organizations involved in mental health efforts. (pp. 693-696)

9. Discuss the problems associated with the interface between the law and mental health. (pp. 698-700)

◊ **TERMS YOU SHOULD KNOW**

---

primary prevention (p. 668)

secondary prevention (pp. 668, 674)

tertiary prevention (pp. 668, 678)

risk factors (pp. 668, 669)

protective factors (pp. 668, 669)

epidemiological studies (p. 669)

crisis intervention (p. 674)

short-term crisis therapy (p. 674)

hot line (pp. 674, 676)

consultation and education (of intermediaries) (p. 676)

therapeutic community (p. 678)

milieu therapy (p. 678)

social learning program (p. 679)

aftercare programs (p. 680)

halfway house (p. 680)

forensic psychology (p. 681)

civil commitment procedures (p. 681)

voluntary hospitalization (p. 681)

involuntary commitment (p. 681)

right to treatment (Highlight 18.2, p. 682)

freedom from custodial confinement (Highlight 18.2, p. 682)

right to compensation for work (Highlight 18.2, p. 682)

right to live in a community (Highlight 18.2, p. 682)

right to less restrictive treatment (Highlight 18.2, p. 682)

right to legal counsel (Highlight 18.2, p. 682)

right to refuse treatment (Highlight 18.2, p. 682)

hold order (p. 683)

dangerousness (pp. 683, 684)

false negative (p. 685)

"overcontrolled" hostile person (p. 685)

duty-to-warn doctrine (p. 686)

insanity defense (p. 687)

M'Naughten rule (p. 688)

irresistible impulse (p. 688)

Durham rule (p. 688)

substantial capacity (p. 688)

guilty but mentally ill (p. 689)

deinstitutionalization (p. 689, 690)

National Institute of Mental Health (NIMH) (p. 693)

National Institute on Alcohol Abuse and Alcoholism (NIAAA) (pp. 693-694)

National Institute on Drug Abuse (NIDA) (pp. 693-694)

National Association for Mental Health (NAMH) (p. 694)

National Association for Retarded Citizens (NARC) (p. 695)

employee assistance programs (p. 695)

World Health Organization (WHO) (p. 696)

1. Define *primary prevention* and summarize the basic observations of the NIMH panel of experts regarding the relationship between risk and protective factors, on the one hand, and disorders, on the other hand. (pp. 668-669)

2. Describe six types of primary prevention programs that illustrate primary prevention strategies. (pp. 671-674)

3. Define *secondary prevention* and describe the two types that differ in the immediacy and duration of services. (p. 674)

4. Define *crisis intervention* and indicate what type of personnel are involved. (p. 674)

5. Explain how mental health professionals are able to reach a larger group through the process of consultation and the education of intermediaries. (p. 676)

6. Describe the three types of secondary prevention services that have been shown to be effective in dealing with the psychological problems related to air disasters. (pp. 677-678)

7. List and explain three general therapeutic principles that guide the milieu approach to treatment, and compare the relative effectiveness of three treatment approaches. (p. 678)

8. Define *tertiary prevention* and describe several aftercare programs that perform this function. (pp. 678, 680-681)

9. List four conditions that must be met before involuntary commitment to a mental institution can occur, and describe the legal process that follows, including the stringent safeguards to ensure due process. (pp. 681-683)

10. Describe the findings regarding violence and mental disorder, and discuss the following three problems associated with predicting dangerousness: the ambiguity of the concept of "dangerous," the role of situational circumstances, and the pressure to err on the conservative side. (pp. 683-685)

11. Describe some methods for assessing a patient's potential for dangerousness, and explain the implications of the Tarasoff decision on a therapist's duty to warn persons that a patient is planning to harm. (pp. 685-687)

12. Explain what is meant by the insanity defense in criminal cases, and describe five established precedents defining this plea. (p. 688)

13. Discuss variations from state to state in law regarding the insanity defense, note problems with the basic concept, and explain the role of "guilty but mentally ill" in this context. (pp. 688-689)

14. Define *deinstitutionalization*, briefly summarize its history, and describe the current facilities that partially serve the chronically mental ill. (pp. 689-693)

15. List and describe four major functions of the National Institute of Mental Health (NIMH). (p. 693)

16. List several professional organizations in the mental health field, and explain three key functions that they perform. (p. 694)

17. Describe some of the major functions of the National Association for Mental Health (NAMH). (p. 694)

18. List and describe six areas of job design and conditions of work in which serious problems may exist. (p. 695)

19. Describe the functions of WHO and the World Federation for Mental Health. (p. 696)

20. Describe several opportunities that individuals have to contribute to the advancement of mental health, and list some basic facts that should help them to succeed in those endeavors. (pp. 697-698)

21. Summarize the problems encountered with mental health professionals' attempt to offer "expert" testimony in the courts regarding the insanity defense, malingering, conversion disorders, and dissociative identity disorder. (pp. 698-699)

◊ STUDY QUESTIONS

Introduction

1. Why are funds targeted for prevention programs likely to be cut during periods of economic conservatism and restraint? (p. 667)

Primary prevention

2. Primary prevention involves research into the conditions that foster mental disorders. It also involves the eradication of negative conditions and institution of circumstances that foster mental health. Fill in the missing information on the following chart that illustrates various primary prevention measures:

Form of Primary Prevention	Example
Biological (pp. 669-670)	Biologically based primary prevention begins with help in _____ and includes both _____ and _____ care. Many of the goals of health psychology can also be viewed as primary prevention. To the extent that physical illness always produces some sort of _____ _____ that can result in problems such as depression, good health is primary prevention with respect to good mental health.
Psychosocial (p. 670)	The first requirement for psychosocial health is that a person develop the skills needed for effective _____ _____, for expressing _____ constructively, and for satisfying _____ with others. The second requirement is that a person acquire an accurate _____ on which to build his or her identity. Third, psychosocial well-being also requires _____ for the types of problems a person is likely to encounter during given life stages.
Sociocultural (p. 670-671)	Sociocultural prevention is focused on making the _____ as "nourishing" as possible. Examples of sociocultural prevention include a broad spectrum of social measures ranging from public _____ and _____ to economic planning and social legislation directed at ensuring adequate health care for all citizens.

Secondary prevention

3. Crisis intervention is an attempt at secondary prevention that aims at delivering prompt treatment. Complete the list of ways by which prompt services are given. (p. 674)
   a.
   b. Telephone hot line

4. The sole concern of *short-term* crisis therapy is the current problem with which the individual or family is having difficulty. How long does such therapy last? (p. 674)

5. Explain why both face to face and telephone hot line crisis intervention are discouraging for the therapist. (p. 676)

6. What does "consultation and education of intermediaries" mean? (p. 676)

Tertiary prevention

7. Describe the following aspects of a therapeutic community: (p. 678)

    a. Staff expectations

    b. Do-it-yourself attitude

    c. Group cohesiveness

8. A persistent danger with hospitalization is that the hospital will become a permanent refuge. To keep the focus on returning patients to the community and on preventing a return to the institution, hospital staffs try to establish _____ with patients' families and communities and to maintain a _____ attitude. Between ___ and ___ percent of psychotic patients treated this way can be discharged within a few weeks or at most a few months. (p. 679)

9. Paul and Lentz (1977) performed an evaluation of the relative effectiveness of three treatment approaches for chronic hospitalized patients: milieu therapy, social-learning treatment program, and traditional mental hospital treatment. Respond to the following questions about this study: (p. 679)

a. Briefly describe each of the three treatments that were compared:

Milieu therapy

Social-learning treatment

Traditional mental hospital treatment

b. Describe how the study was carried out.

c. Who were the subjects?

10. The results of the Paul and Lentz study were quite impressive. Both milieu therapy and social learning therapy produced significant improvement in overall functioning and resulted in more successful hospital releases than the traditional hospital care. However, the _____ _____ was clearly superior to the more diffuse program of _____. The relative improvement rates for the different treatments were that ___ percent of the social-learning program, ___ percent of the milieu therapy group, and less than ___ percent of the traditional treatment group remained continuously in the community. (p. 679)

11. Many studies have found that as many as ___ percent of schizophrenic patients have been rehospitalized within one year of their discharge. Aftercare programs reduce the rehospitalization. Describe the following aftercare programs: (pp. 680-681)

a. Halfway houses or community-based treatment facilities

b. Day hospitals

12. Does adequate aftercare reduce the chances of rehospitalization, according to Glasscote? (p. 680)

13. Penk, Charles, and Van Hoose showed that _____ in a day treatment center resulted in as much improvement as full inpatient psychiatric treatment at a lower cost. (p. 681)

14. One of the chief problems of community-based treatment facilities is that of gaining the _____ and _____ of community residents. (p. 681)

The commitment process

15. In most cases, people are sent to state mental hospitals voluntarily. However, there are four conditions on which a person can be formally committed. Complete the following list of them: (pp. 681-682)
    a. Dangerous to himself or herself
    b.
    c. Unable to make responsible decisions about hospitalization
    d.

16. Commitment is a civil court proceeding that varies slightly from state to state. In a typical procedure, a court order must be obtained for commitment. If there is imminent danger, however, the law allows emergency hospitalization without a formal commitment hearing. In such cases a physician must sign a statement. The person can then be picked up—usually by the police—and detained under a _____, usually not to exceed 72 hours. (p. 683)

Assessment of "dangerousness"

17. What did Monahan conclude regarding the possible association between mental disorder and violence? (p. 683)

18. In his review of the literature on violence and mental disorder, Monahan cited two well-established findings: (p. 683)
    a. The increased risk of violence in mental disorder appears to be limited to persons who are _____ symptoms.
    b. Approximately ___ percent of all currently disordered persons show no propensity toward violence.

19. Violent acts are particularly difficult to predict. Complete the following list of critical dilemmas involved in prediction of dangerousness among psychiatric patients: (p. 684)
    a. Some people are capable of uncontrolled violence and hence are potentially dangerous if left unsupervised in the community.
    b. Mental health professionals must exhibit some degree of trust in the people they rehabilitate.
    c.

20. Violent acts are difficult to predict because they are determined as much by _____ circumstances as they are by the personality traits of the individual. Mental health professionals typically err on the conservative side when assessing violence proneness. (p. 685)

21. The two major sources of personality information for the prediction of dangerousness are data from _____ and the individual's _____. (p. 685)

22. Using demographic data on family background, history of violence, friendships, and substance use, Klassen and O'Connor were able to identify ___ percent of the people who later became violent. (pp. 685-686)

23. When does a clinician have a "duty-to-warn" or "duty to protect"? (pp. 686-687)

24. Does the "duty to protect" doctrine extend to suicidal cases? (pp. 686-687)

The insanity defense

25. How frequently is the insanity plea used? (p. 688)

26. How does the time served by the criminal sent to a psychiatric hospital compare to time served by criminals sent to prison? (p. 688)

27. The established precedents that define the insanity defense are listed below. Briefly describe each one. (p. 688)

    a. The M'Naughten Rule

    b. The irresistible impulse

    c. The Durham Rule

    d. Diminished capacity

Deinstitutionalization

28. Since 1955, what has happened to the number of persons hospitalized in state and county mental hospitals? What accounts for the changes? (p. 690)

29. Complete the list below of five unforeseen problems that have arisen in the effort to deinstitutionalize the mentally ill? (pp. 690-691)

    a. Many residents of mental institutions had no families or homes to go to.
    b.
    c.

    d. Many patients had not been carefully selected for discharge and were ill-prepared for community living.
    e. Many of those who were discharged were not followed-up sufficiently to ensure successful adaptation.

30. Recently, Rossi estimated that ___ percent of homeless individuals suffer from chronic mental disorder and about ___ percent have severe addiction problems. (p. 692)

31. Deinstitutionalization notwithstanding, some ___ percent of all the dollars spent on mental health care are spent for hospitalization. (p. 692)

32. As a result of the need for alternative care facilities following deinstitutionalization and of financial incentives provided by Medicare, _____ persons make up 51 percent of the nursing home population at present. (p. 693)

Organized efforts for mental health

33. The extent of mental disorders was brought to public attention during World War II. How? (p. 693)

34. What type of activities does the NIMH do? (p. 693)

35. Does the federal government directly supervise: (p. 694)
    a. local community services?
    b. state mental hospitals?
    c. What happened to these programs in the 1980s compared to the 1960s and 1970s?

36. What is the role of voluntary groups in regard to mental health needs? (p. 694)

37. Private industries also have a role in mental health services. Many companies have introduced numerous psychological services, often referred to as _____.
    In contrast, employers have been slower to deal with issues of _____ and work _____ as means of maximizing worker mental health. (p. 695)

38. It has been estimated that over _____ million people worldwide are affected by mental disorders. (p. 696)

39. An important contribution of WHO is its _____, which enables clinicians and researchers in different countries to use a uniform set of diagnostic categories. (p. 696)

40. To some people in our society, social planning seems contrary to the American way of life and the ideal of individual freedom. How do the authors respond to this view? (p. 697)

41. List some constructive courses of action open to each citizen to work for improved health in society. (p. 697)

42. Indicate whether each of the following is true or false by circling the appropriate response: (p. 698)
    a. From time to time, everyone has serious difficulty coping with problems.   True or False
    b. During such a crisis, professional assistance may be needed.   True or False
    c. Such difficulties can happen to anyone if the stress is severe.   True or False
    d. Early detection and treatment is important to prevent chronic conditions.   True or False

Unresolved issues

43. One of the major problems in the interface between the law and mental health, as illustrated most clearly in the case of the insanity defense, the law tends to frame its issues relating to mental states of parties to a trial in ways not ultimately resolvable by any _____ assessment methods known or available to mental health professionals. (p. 698)

◊ **CRITICAL THINKING ABOUT DIFFICULT TOPICS**

1. Your text discusses the difficulty of predicting dangerousness and tells you that approximately 90% of all currently disordered patients are not violent (p. 683) and that Classen and O'Connor were able to identify (as dangerous) 76% of the people who later become violent. Do you think you could predict dangerousness under these conditions? One problem you will not anticipate is what is known as the "base rate" problem, which can be illustrated with the information above. Assume that the base rate for violence among the patients in question is 10% and that your test correctly classifies 76% of truly violent patients as violent (known as "true positives") and 76% of truly nonviolent patients as nonviolent (known as "true negatives")--i.e., your test has an accuracy of 76%. The corollary is that the test incorrectly

classifies as nonviolent 24% of truly violent patients (false negatives) and as violent 24% of truly nonviolent patients (false positives). Assuming a base rate of dangerousness of 10%, then 100 out of every thousand patients will be truly violent and 900 will be truly nonviolent. Thus, we can calculate the table below. This table is calculated by assuming 76% accuracy of the prediction, which means that the test will correctly predict as violent 76% of the 100 truly violent patients (76) and correctly predict as nonviolent 76% of the 900 truly nonviolent patients (684). Then the incorrect predictions are calculated by taking 24% of the 100 truly violent (24) and of the 900 truly nonviolent (216) patients. If you add the numbers in the columns you can see that the truly violent patients total to 100 and the truly nonviolent to 900, as assumed in the calculations.

	Truly Violent	Truly Nonviolent
Predicted Violent	76	216
Predicted Nonviolent	24	684

What is interesting about this table is that even though the test is 76% accurate, a large majority (216) of those predicted to be violent (76 + 216 = 292) will actually be nonviolent: 216 out of 292 or 74% are actually nonviolent. That is, if you are to detain all those predicted to be violent, three out of four of those detained will actually be nonviolent. The problem arises from the fact that the 76% correct prediction rate is operating on a much smaller number (100 in this example) than the 24% error rate (900 in this example). That is, 76% of 100 is a much smaller number than 24% of 900. This problem of an excessive number of false positives arises any time there is a low base rate for the phenomenon being predicted and it becomes proportionately worse as the base rate decreases. The consequence for the clinician is to be torn between the pressure to detain anyone who might be violent and the humanitarian and civil liberties concern over inappropriately detaining the larger number of nonviolent patients. What would you do in this situation?

2. Question 3 in this section for Chapter 2 asked you to think about the concepts of free will versus determinism as they arise in discussions of abnormal behavior. Can you see the same issue arising in some aspects of the insanity defense? For example, in invoking the "irresistible impulse" rule it is argued that in some cases persons "had lost the power to choose between right and wrong" and "were compelled beyond their will to commit the act" (p. 688). Does this imply that "free will" applies to the actions of most of us? If so, do you think that view of

human behavior is compatible with the deterministic framework usually adopted in psychology?

◊ CHAPTER 18 QUIZ

Circle the best of the four answers provided and check them according to answers provided at the back of this study guide. Be sure you understand why each answer is correct.

1. Over the years most efforts toward mental health have been largely geared toward helping people only after they have already developed serious problems. The alternative to this is: (pp. 667, 668)
   a. crisis intervention.
   c. primary prevention.
   b. *in vivo* treatment.
   d. retrospective.

2. All of the following groups are at high risk for mental disorders *except*: (p. 669)
   a. elderly people living alone.
   c. recently divorced people.
   b. married people between 25 and 35.
   d. the physically disabled.

3. According to Kessler and Albee, everything aimed at improving the human condition, at making life more fulfilling and meaningful, may be considered part of _____ prevention of mental or emotional disturbance. (p. 669)
   a. primary
   c. tertiary
   b. secondary
   d. fourth level

4. Biological measures for primary prevention of mental disorders includes all of the following except: (pp. 669-670)
   a. drug treatment of hyperactive children.
   b. family planning.
   c. genetic counseling.
   d. *in utero* treatment of genetic defects.

5. All of the following are sociocultural efforts toward primary prevention of mental disorders except: (p. 671)
   a. economic planning.
   c. public education.
   b. penal systems.
   d. social security.

6. Allen Jones is a middle-aged factory worker, husband, and father of five children. He has never previously been involved in psychotherapy until his home is destroyed in a tornado. While he attempts to find housing for his family, he discovers that his wife wants a divorce. He immediately becomes quite depressed and is unable to follow through on his house-seeking. Allen Jones is a prime candidate for: (p. 674)
   a. day hospitalization.
   b. crisis intervention.
   c. psychoanalysis.
   d. milieu therapy.

7. The purpose of consultation work by community mental health professionals is: (p. 676)
   a. crisis intervention.
   b. to reach individuals in need of help who would otherwise never be identified by any community agency.
   c. tertiary prevention.
   d. to reach a larger group of persons in need by working with intermediary agents.

8. Milieu therapy is: (p. 678)
   a. the temporary substitution of one treatment mode by another until adequate resources can be acquired to provide the treatment of choice.
   b. a general term for any form of preventive treatment.
   c. the establishment of a hospital environment itself as a therapeutic community.
   d. the integration of any two distinct forms of treatment.

9. Typically, the first step in committing an individual to a mental hospital involuntarily is: (p. 682)
   a. appointing a physician and a psychologist to examine the client.
   b. filing a petition for a commitment hearing.
   c. holding a commitment hearing.
   d. notifying the police.

10. One dilemma in attempting to rehabilitate previously violent psychiatric patients is that the mental health workers must exhibit some degree of _____. (p. 684)
   a. patience
   b. stability
   c. professionalism
   d. trust

11. Klassen and O'Connor (1988) state that they were able to identify ___ percent of people who later became violent. (pp. 685-686)
   a. 76
   b. 26
   c. 50
   d. 10

12. A clear implication of the Tarasoff decision is that a therapist must: (pp. 686-687)
    a. inform the police when a client has made global threats.
    b. warn a person whom his or her client has specifically threatened to harm.
    c. warn anyone whom he or she believes might be in danger from a client.
    d. warn the authorities when a client threatens suicide.

13. Studies have confirmed that individuals acquitted of crimes by reason of insanity typically spend _____ time in psychiatric hospitals as (than) individuals convicted of crimes spend in prison. (p. 688)
    a. less
    b. about the same amount of
    c. about the same amount or more
    d. much more

14. Under which of the following precedents did the law hold that individuals might not be responsible for their acts, even though they knew what they were doing was wrong, if they had lost the power to choose between right and wrong? (p. 688)
    a. the M'Naughten Rule (1843)
    b. the irresistible impulse (1887)
    c. the Durham Rule (1954)
    d. federal Insanity Defense Reform Act (1984)

15. In the 1960s and 1970s, state governments favored deinstitutionalization because it could: (p. 690)
    a. better meet the needs of mental patients.
    b. lower hospital population to manageable numbers.
    c. reduce state funding.
    d. rid society of an unwelcome evil.

ANSWER KEY FOR CHAPTER QUIZZES

◊ CHAPTER 1

1. c. is "away from the normal"
2. a. deviant from social expectations
3. b. adaptivity of the behavior in furthering individual and group well-being
4. b. reliable
5. d. specifies the exact behaviors that must be observed
6. c. the person's present condition
7. d. Axis IV
8. a. disorders secondary to gross destruction and malfunctioning of brain tissue
9. b. acute
10. b. Axis II
11. b. hypotheses
12. a. People high on x will usually be high on y
13. a. analogue
14. c. prospective
15. d. configural

◊ CHAPTER 2

1. b. the Edwin Smith papyrus
2. d. There are basically four types of body fluids
3. b. the influence on thinking and/or behavior of "natural appetites" and the desire to eliminate pain and attain pleasure
4. a. the anatomy of the central nervous system
5. b. death of Galen in 200 A.D.
6. d. Avicenna
7. d. Yin and Yang
8. c. King James I of England
9. b. *Malleus Maleficarum*
10. a. demons, etc. did not cause mental disorders
11. b. St. Mary of Bethlehem mental hospital
12. b. intimidate patients
13. a. The Geel Shrine, Belgium

14. d. in a humanitarian fashion
15. c. Benjamin Rush
16. d. the result of severe psychological stress
17. c. general loss of faith among the general population
18. c. neurasthenia
19. a. inhuman treatment accorded the mentally ill
20. d. infecting the sufferer with malaria
21. b. hysteria
22. c. catharsis
23. a. subjective experience
24. d. whether the outcome (reinforcer) is dependent on the animal's behavior

◊ CHAPTER 3

---

1. d. contributory cause
2. c. receptor site
3. a. re-uptake
4. a. the proband
5. c. primary reaction tendencies
6. b. id
7. b. neurotic anxiety
8. d. separation-individuation
9. b. operant conditioning
10. c. differential reinforcement
11. d. its overconcern with symptoms
12. c. our capacity for full functioning as human beings
13. c. "not me"
14. a. accommodation
15. d. basic trust
16. b. detachment
17. c. permissive-indulgent
18. a. parents' income
19. a. cultural relativism
20. b. correlational in nature
21. c. developing a unified point of view

CHAPTER 4

1. d. eustress
2. b. frustration
3. b. approach-avoidance conflict
4. d. they measure reactions to specific environmental events
5. c. mourning
6. a. protect the self from damage and disorganization
7. b. less available for coping with others
8. c. elevated levels of urinary norepinephrine
9. a. emotional arousal, increased tension, and greater alertness
10. c. 12 months
11. a. One-fourth were abandoned by husbands with no support for their children
12. b. shock phase
13. c. were exposed to abusive violence in combat
14. d. the conditions of battle that tax a soldier's stamina
15. b. frequent nightmares
16. d. There might be other adjustment problems involved
17. b. is exceedingly difficult

◊ **CHAPTER 5**

1. d. phobias
2. b. reduction in anxiety
3. c. immunization
4. c. toy rabbits
5. d. brevity, intensity
6. b. tricyclic antidepressant
7. a. mimic the physiological cues that normally precede a panic attack
8. c. anxious apprehension
9. b. GABA
10. a. compulsion
11. a. sexual content
12. d. avoidant and dependent
13. b. exposure treatment, response prevention
14. c. they take several weeks before they have any beneficial effects

CHAPTER 6

1. c. 21%
2. b. denial and rejection of the dead person
3. d. cyclothymic disorder
4. a. at least one episode of mania
5. d. deflated self-esteem
6. c. a depletion of norepinephrine and/or serotonin
7. d. response contingent positive reinforcement is not available
8. b. there is no control over aversive events
9. a. eleventh
10. d. acetylcholine depletion
11. b. the disorder is bipolar in nature
12. d. all of the above are equally effective
13. d. 60
14. d. recovery
15. a. 40, 30

◊ CHAPTER 7

1. a. somatization disorder
2. c. "I deserve your attention and concern"
3. b. ability to talk only in a whisper
4. c. conversion disorder
5. a. a conscious plan to use illness as an escape
6. a. escaping from their personal identity
7. c. generalized
8. d. dissociative identity disorder
9. b. traumatic childhood abuse
10. d. memory is a constructive act

CHAPTER 8

1. d. psychogenic physical disorders
2. d. etiology
3. a. repressed anger
4. b. the placebo effect
5. c. humoral and cellular
6. a. bacterial infection
7. b. aerobic exercise
8. c. there is direct neural control of immunological agents
9. a. angina pectoris
10. d. decelerated speech and motor activity
11. a. blue collar men
12. b. 5
13. c. 15
14. d. 85, 90
15. c. migraine headaches
16. a. the corticovisceral control mechanism
17. c. preventing pathogenic life-style behaviors

◊ CHAPTER 9

1. d. maladaptive ways of perceiving, thinking, and relating
2. a. 3
3. b. II
4. d. clinicians often do not receive sufficient training in the diagnosis of personality disorders
5. b. schizotypal
6. a. avoidant
7. a. passive-aggressive
8. c. only *prospective* studies have been possible so far
9. c. borderline
10. c. higher for males than for females
11. a. deficient aversive emotional arousal
12. d. reactivity of the behavioral inhibition system
13. b. emotional family disturbance before the parent left
14. d. ineffective discipline and supervision
15. d. in controlled situations

CHAPTER 10

1. b. psychoactive substance dependence
2. c. 12
3. a. 0.1
4. a. alcohol amnestic disorder
5. d. personal maladjustment
6. c. is associated with the common use of alcohol as a means of coping with stress
7. d. aversive conditioning
8. c. less effective than all others
9. d. 54
10. c. small, apparently irrelevant decisions
11. c. endorphins
12. a. antisocial
13. d. stimulant
14. b. LSD
15. c. decrease in size, but not number, when an adult loses weight
16. a. being born to an alcoholic parent

◊ CHAPTER 11

1. d. transvestism
2. c. an adolescent male who is shy and feels inadequate in relations with women
3. a. are young adult males
4. a. exhibitionism
5. a. homosexuality
6. b. 7, 4
7. d. the manner in which child abuse "experts" elicited children's testimony
8. d. 44, 2.5
9. c. two to one
10. a. do not consider themselves victimized
11. b. of lower intelligence
12. a. dysfunction
13. a. one-fourth
14. b. organic
15. c. the relationships between individuals

CHAPTER 12

1. a. one
2. d. older in females than males
3. c. process
4. d. cognitive slippage
5. d. increased diagnostic reliability
6. b. catatonic
7. d. schizophreniform disorder
8. c. higher concordance rates for identical twins
9. d. 100
10. a. high-risk studies
11. d. Dopamine-stimulating drugs cause hallucinations
12. b. decrement in the brain mass
13. c. cognitive slippage
14. a. schizophrenogenic mother
15. b. 25 percent

◊ CHAPTER 13

1. a. mental retardation
2. b. circumscribed
3. d. brain
4. c. loss of function
5. c. III
6. d. delirium.
7. c. 40
8. a. prevention
9. c. 6
10. a. simple deterioration
11. b. Down syndrome
12. b. continuing recurrence of small strokes
13. c. events immediately preceding the injury
14. b. dementia
15. b. intelligence
16. d. Mild
17. c. 25

18. a. fertilized egg
19. c. normal environmental stimulation
20. b. teachers' attitudes
21. b. specific
22. c. laterality

◊ CHAPTER 14

1. c. 17, 22
2. d. requires more symptoms to make a diagnosis
3. a. presenting symptoms
4. d. aggression
5. d. higher in anxiety
6. d. both medication and behavior modification were effective, but the former was better
7. b. lower intelligence
8. b. 15
9. a. antisocial
10. b. in association with one or two other persons
11. c. peer pressures to engage in delinquent acts
12. a. becoming overly dependent on others
13. d. have experiences that reduce their fears and insecurity
14. c. Antidepressants may precipitate mania in some children with latent bipolar disorder
15. b. NREM sleep
16. d. most cases are found in the upper classes
17. d. a cold and unresponsive mother
18. a. haloperidol
19. b. children are dependent on those around them

CHAPTER 15

1. b. interpersonal skills
2. a. PET scan
3. a. Halstead-Reitan
4. d. employs "operational" assessment
5. d. Hamilton Rating Scale for Depression
6. a. intelligence and personality
7. b. WAIS-R
8. c. projective and objective
9. c. assess the way a patient perceives ambiguous stimuli
10. a. MMPI
11. c. construct a validity scale
12. b. "mentalistic"
13. c. the computer integrates the descriptions it picks up
14. b. MMPI
15. d. working hypotheses

◊ CHAPTER 16

1. b. epileptics rarely developed schizophrenia
2. c. unilateral ECT
3. a. it is ineffective
4. b. maintenance doses of antidepressant medication
5. c. the advent of the major antipsychotic drugs
6. d. pain
7. d. psychotropic
8. d. reduce the intensity of delusions and hallucinations
9. a. Haldol
10. a. blocking dopamine receptors
11. d. increase the concentration of serotonin and norepinephrine at synaptic sites
12. b. imipramine (Tofranil)
13. c. bipolar mood disorders
14. b. memory impairment
15. b. had not administered drug therapy

CHAPTER 17

1. c. short-term, directive, crisis-oriented treatment
2. d. those described in terms of the so-called YAVIS pattern
3. b. clinical psychologist
4. a. motivation
5. b. Type B
6. c. transference
7. b. current ego functioning
8. c. extinguishing the conditioned avoidance of anxiety-arousing stimuli
9. c. placing the client in anxiety-producing life situations
10. c. punishment
11. a. Biofeedback is a more elaborate means of teaching relaxation
12. d. they engage in selective perception and overgeneralization
13. b. carrying out empirical research on psychotherapy
14. c. is about the same
15. c. 50

◊ **CHAPTER 18**

1. c. primary prevention
2. b. married people between 25 and 35
3. a. primary
4. a. drug treatment of hyperactive children
5. b. penal systems
6. b. crisis intervention
7. d. to reach a larger group of persons in need by working with intermediary agents
8. c. the establishment of a hospital environment itself as a therapeutic community.
9. b. filing a petition for a commitment hearing
10. d. trust
11. a. 76
12. b. warn a person whom his or her client has specifically threatened to harm
13. a. less
14. b. the irresistible impulse (1887)
15. c. reduce state funding